From a Trickle to a Torrent

From a Trickle
to a Torrent

*Education, Migration, and Social Change
in a Himalayan Valley of Nepal*

Geoff Childs
Namgyal Choedup

UNIVERSITY OF CALIFORNIA PRESS

University of California Press, one of the most
distinguished university presses in the United States,
enriches lives around the world by advancing
scholarship in the humanities, social sciences, and
natural sciences. Its activities are supported by the
UC Press Foundation and by philanthropic
contributions from individuals and institutions.
For more information, visit www.ucpress.edu.

University of California Press
Oakland, California

Library of Congress Cataloging-in-Publication Data

Names: Childs, Geoff H., 1963- author. | Choedup,
    Namgyal, author.
Title: From a trickle to a torrent : education, migration,
    and social change in a Himalayan valley of Nepal /
    Geoff Childs and Namgyal Choedup.
Description: Oakland, California : University of
    California Press, [2019] | Includes bibliographical
    references and index. |
Identifiers: LCCN 2018017682 (print) | LCCN 2018027762
    (ebook) | ISBN 9780520971219 (ebook) |
    ISBN 9780520299511 (cloth : alk. paper) |
    ISBN 9780520299528 (pbk. : alk. paper)
Subjects: LCSH: Education—Social aspects—Nepal—
    Nubri. | Social change—Nepal—Nubri. | Educational
    mobility—Nepal—Nubri.
Classification: LCC LC191.8.N35 (ebook) |
    LCC LC191.8.N35 C55 2019 (print) |
    DDC 306.43095496—dc23
LC record available at https://lccn.loc.gov/2018017682

28 27 26 25 24 23 22 21 20 19
10 9 8 7 6 5 4 3 2 1

We dedicate this book to the young people
of Nubri.
Apply your education with wisdom and
compassion, for the future of an extraordinary
society will soon be in your hands.

Contents

Illustrations

MAP

List of Tables

Acknowledgments

We sincerely thank all the people in Nubri who have facilitated our research through friendship, hospitality, and generosity in sharing information about their society. We are especially grateful to the following individuals. In Rö the late Tashi Dorje and Yönten Gyamtso, whom everyone misses dearly. Also Lama Gyamtso and Tsogyal, Lama Karma and Tsering Lhamo, Purbu Tsewang (a.k.a. Bir Bahadur) and Laxmi, Karma Chödron and the late Chöying Dorje, Sonam Tenzin and Tsering Chödron, Dawa Norbu, and Tsewang Sangmo. In Lö Khenpo Tashi Tsering, Tsogyal and Tobgye, Tsewang Döndrup, Hritar Lhamo, Tashi Chödron, and Lhakpa Hritar. In Namlha Lama Jigme, Rigzen and Lhakpa Buti. In Tsak Pema Döndrup and Pema Diki, Tsering Diki and Pasang Damdrul, Dawa Tenzin, and Nyima Gyalpo. In Kok Kunchok Dolma and Nyima Tsering. In Bi Pema Diki, Nyima Samdrup, Tenzin, Raja, and Sonam Dolma. In Trok Amji Dorje and Tsewang Buti, Tempey Gyaltsen and Lamnye Buti, Tsering Wangdu and Karsang Dolma, Norbu Samdrup and Nyima Diki, Ngawang Namgyal and Sonam Chönzom, Dorje Gyaltsen and Karma, Mani Sangmo, Changchub Dolma, Guru Tsewang, Tsewang Rigzen, and Rigzen Namgyal. Tulku Karma of Serang deserves special thanks for always being supportive of our research. In Kathmandu Ula Jigme and Khenpo Gyaltsen were especially helpful in establishing contacts with monastic communities, while Pema Norbu was indispensable when it came to arranging interviews with educational migrants. In addition, we would like to acknowledge the researchers who participated in the collection of survey data during early phases of the research. Thank you, Tsewang Palden (Trok), Nyima Sangmo (Namrung), Tsechu Dolma (Trok), Tsering Buti (Chökhang), and Ang Tsering (Lar) for such diligent work under challenging circumstances.

We also thank Sienna Craig and an anonymous reviewer for providing a professional level of constructive criticism that exemplifies the peer review process. Their insightful feedback and thoughtful suggestions led to substantial revisions and improvements. Our colleagues at Washington University in Saint Louis also deserve recognition, including Oguz Alyanak, Carolyn Barnes, and Guillermo Martin-Saiz for fruitful seminar discussions about migration theory, Michael Frachetti for helping generate the map, and T. R. Kidder for heading a collegial department with a supportive atmosphere. E. A. Quinn merits special appreciation for advancing our research via collaboration on the project Milk with Altitude, and Cynthia Beall via collaboration on the project Genes and Fertility. It is a privilege to work across subdisciplines with such outstanding colleagues. Others who provided helpful feedback at various stages of the project include Teri Allendorf, Kenneth Bauer, Rune Bennike, Sarah Besky, Mark Donohue, Paja Faudree, Kristine Hildebrandt, David Holmberg, Jessaca Leinaweaver, Kathryn March, Nadine Plachta, Pratyoush Onta, Pasang Yangjee Sherpa, Sara Shneiderman, Deepak Thapa, and Mark Turin. We also thank K. P. Kafle and Keshav Bhetwal for logistical support and for their selfless dedication to helping people in Nubri via Nepal SEEDS. Reed Malcolm, Benjy Mailings, and the entire University of California Press staff deserve praise for shepherding this book into publication, and Holly Bridges for exceptional copyediting.

I (Geoff) would like to thank Lily for the forbearance and support that allows me to conduct research in Nubri on a regular basis. Without Lily and the love of our daughters, Lienne and Pema, life would be empty. I also thank my mother and father, Peggy and Neil Childs, for opening our home to foreign exchange students like Mario Teguh and Gontran Guermonprez. Neither I nor my brother Curtis would have become actors on a transnational stage if our parents had not nudged us into cross-cultural encounters. Neil Childs once again played the patriarchal editor role by reading an early draft of the manuscript. As always, I am grateful to my late *ajo* (elder brother), Tashi Döndrup, who took me under his wing during initial fieldwork in Nubri. Without his selfless efforts to keep me warm and fed, and his biting humor to keep me grounded, I would never have lasted a month in Nubri let alone two decades and counting. An especially hearty thank-you goes to Jhang-chuk Sangmo, Nyima Sangmo, and Tinley Tsering—fellow sojourners on the research odyssey. Jhangchuk and Nyima keep me safe and sane when unforeseen glitches arise, while Tinley's cricket exploits as the second-best batsman in village grudge matches are legendary.

I (Namgyal) would like to thank Dadon for patience and understanding that allows me to conduct research in Nepal and India. I also thank my mother and late father, Tsewang Bhuti and Amdo Serso, for instilling in me the value of education and a quest for knowledge although they, like many parents in Nubri, never had any formal education. I am ever grateful to the unconditional support of my mother-in-law and father-in-law, Pema Choezin and Tashi Namgyal, and the love of my sons, Namkha and Loden, for inspiring me to pursue my academic endeavors.

CHAPTER I

Predicaments, Presumptions, and Procedures

AN EMPTY NEST

Tsering Lhamo labored up the steep incline leading to her village.[1] A taut sling pressing against her forehead bore the weight of a sack filled with grain she had just roasted and ground into flour at a water mill down by the river. Her slow, methodical steps contrasted with strenuous breathing and rivulets of sweat running down her cheeks. The hint of a smile crossed Tsering Lhamo's face when she encountered us on the trail. We helped steady her load as she slipped the sling over her head, lowered the sack onto a rock, and exhaled loudly in relief. Friction marks across her forehead bore witness to the arduous labor that embodies her daily subsistence. As we would learn, such a mark epitomizes the contrast parents foresee between their lives and the potential lives their children can achieve through education, a disparity captured by the oft-recited expression "Better a pen in hand than a rope across the forehead."

"Are you well, elder sister?" we asked. "I'm fine," she murmured without much conviction. Tsering Lhamo was widowed at a relatively young age. Now she lives alone in the village because years ago she sent her only daughter to a boarding school and her only son to a monastery in Kathmandu, the nation's capital that takes days to reach on precarious footpaths. Neither of her children envisions returning to the village, yet Tsering Lhamo never complains about the substantial workload she now shoulders. Her suffering is a direct result of the decision she made to create pathways for her children toward more comfortable and less physically demanding lives.

Tsering Lhamo is both an anomaly and a harbinger in her village. Her status as an elderly person who lives alone is not unprecedented. Some couples have no children; others endure the tragedy of witnessing all their children die before reaching maturity. Some men and women, born into poverty, remain single their entire lives because they lack the requisite assets or social status to marry. Tsering Lhamo's case is unusual today because she is a mother, yet neither of her children lives nearby. Most people her age live with, or near, adult sons or daughters who can be counted on for support. Given today's outmigration trend, it is reasonable to predict that more parents will end up like her.

We later met Tsering Lhamo's son, Dzamling Dorje, who is a monk living in a large, well-endowed monastery in Kathmandu. Slight of frame and sporting a wispy beard, he bears a striking resemblance to Nubri's lamas of yore whose images are carved on stones marking auspicious sites along mountain trails. In fact, some of those images are his ancestors, for he comes from a lineage of lamas that first migrated to Nubri five generations ago. Unlike his father, who resided in the village as a *ngagpa* (householder lama), Dzamling Dorje took a vow of celibacy and now lives in a community of monks pursuing the study of Buddhism at its highest level.[2] It was not his choice to become a monk, for he was sent to the monastery by his mother right after his father died. Dzamling Dorje explained to us,

> It was very difficult in the beginning. I came down here a few months after my father passed away and I was sad about the loss of my father. The journey from the village in those days was very difficult because the trail was very bad so it took ten to twelve days. Then there was the problem of language since I spoke only Nubri dialect. My mother returned to the village a few days after I became a monk. I had to part with my mother not long after I lost my father, and I was in a totally new place. I had a very hard time. It was very hard for about a year, so I could not focus too much on my education. But as I became used to the new environment, it became less difficult. Eventually the thought of returning home was not that strong, but I missed my mother very much.

Dzamling Dorje adjusted to his new environment and now thrives as a teacher of younger students. When we visited him, he invited us inside and offered us tea with the grace and refinement of a man who devotes his life to learning. His spartan room contained a mattress on the floor flanked by a low table supporting rosary beads, an open scripture book, and his personal tea cup covered by a silver lid to keep flies at bay. We removed our shoes and sat on the mattress as he placed a small, square carpet on the ground, where he then sat cross-legged. After exchanging small talk, we began the interview with our usual questions regarding his pathway to religion. Eventually we came to the matter of household succession and asked if he was concerned about his mother being alone in the village. Dzamling Dorje replied,

> Yes, I am definitely concerned about this. On the one hand, I am a monk and have my own monastic obligations, while on the other hand I am the only son of my mother. Therefore, it is like one person having to fulfill two different responsibilities in life. It is a difficult situation. I can't stay in the village because my place is in the monastery and my responsibility is to teach the younger monks. Living in the monastery, I am reminded often about my filial duties to my mother. I try to help her in whatever way I can. It becomes especially problematic when she gets sick. For instance, one time my mother suddenly fell ill. It was a serious health situation requiring medical rescue by helicopter. She ended up staying at the hospital for one month, and only returned to the village after resting in Kathmandu for another three months. It was very difficult under such circumstances. She is alone in the village and must take care of the large landholding that my late father left behind. She complains sometimes about the difficulties she is facing. But I can't be of much help since I am a monk.
>
> My mother sometimes asks me to visit her in the village and says it is okay if I don't want to come back for good. So, I try to visit her in the village whenever I find time. When I do visit, my mother does not mention marriage to me. But most of the elders raise this issue because, in our village tradition, the continuation of the lineage is highly stressed. Since I belong to a lama's lineage, if I don't marry, our lineage will come to an end. Although I have a sister, we only count paternal descent when it comes to the continuation of the lineage. That is why people in the village are highly concerned. I have taken a religious vow of celibacy and would very much like to continue this religious life. So, there is a clash of interest between religious and worldly life.

Dzamling Dorje's reluctance to take on the leadership of his household, the customary duty of an eldest son, has left his mother to preside over an empty nest. Tsering Lhamo does not press the matter; like other parents in Nubri she is inured to the hardships of life in an alpine environment and is determined that her children not face a similar fate. Taking advantage of new opportunities to attain religious and secular education, parents nowadays send most of their children out of the valley. By making sacrifices to ensure better futures for their offspring, they increase the precariousness of their own lives, drastically reducing the household labor force and unleashing the prospect of fending for themselves in old age. Meanwhile, young migrants are confronted with a dilemma. On the one hand, educational migration is a conduit for upward mobility. On the other hand, moving away at a young age can sever the roots of a cultural identity that is embedded within Nubri's distinctive landscape and society.

The outmigration of youths for educational purposes started as a trickle in the 1980s, slowly gained momentum in the 1990s, and has since evolved into a full-scale torrent. This study documents a complex and evolving situation involving transnational flows of philanthropic capital, demographic disparities, and household-based migration decisions that have highly uncertain outcomes. It builds upon previous research by one of the coauthors (GC) at a time, the mid-1990s, when the migration phenomenon was just showing signs of gaining traction. A product of that research, *Tibetan Diary*, centered on the life course of individuals who spent the majority of their existence in Nubri; hence the subtitle *From Birth to Death and Beyond in a Himalayan Valley of Nepal*. Since then, migration for education has become a normative step in the life course and a defining feature of Nubri society. Borrowing Knight and Traphagan's terminology (2003:13), the village has transformed from a *lifecourse* space where individuals are born, mature, and die, to a *lifephase* space where they spend only a portion of their lives.

Our purpose is not to lament a disappearing way of life or engage in a commentary on how indigenous cultures suffer under the relentless encroachment of capitalism, neoliberalism, or other manifestations of the world system. Rather, we aim to explore—through the eyes of Nubri residents themselves—the relationship between a changing landscape of educational possibilities, the emergence of a family management strategy that relies on outmigration, and the social and cultural ramifications of educational migration. The questions we seek to answer are the following: What motivates parents to send most of their children to faraway institutions for education? How do parents adapt their family management strategies in response to the new opportunities? How do social networks facilitate the movement of children from the village to specific destinations? In what ways do migration and education influence marital norms and the process of household succession? How does the quest for social and economic mobility simultaneously connect and detach young people from the social fabric of their natal villages? What are the social, cultural, economic, and demographic consequences of a migration pattern that depletes a valley of its younger generation? In brief, what is happening, why is it happening, and what is at stake? Although this book centers on the process of rural to urban migration, our perspective is firmly rooted in the village. We acknowledge that a turn toward problem-oriented research has led anthropologists away from village-based studies, yet agree with Herzfeld that "the role of the village has never been fully displaced from the discipline," and that "the village itself was also never the conceptual as well as geographic isolate that so many anthropologists, too burdened to read back into the older literature, now imagine it to have been" (2015:338). As Sara Shneiderman argues, the village remains an important point of orientation even for those who move away. Therefore, it is more productive to view the village as "a flexible set of social relations . . . rather than as a fixed point on a map" (2015b:319). Throughout this book we demonstrate how the village continues to shape the lives of educational migrants despite dwindling prospects that they will return as full-time residents.

THE ENDURING YET EPHEMERAL VILLAGE

Nubri, a Buddhist enclave populated by roughly thirty-five hundred individuals in the upper stretch of the Buri Gandakhi River in Gorkha District, Nepal, is composed of villages ranging in elevation from 6,900 to 12,500 feet.[3] The lower section of the valley, called Kutang, is inhabited by descendants of people who migrated from neighboring areas and formed a unique society that bears many accoutrements of Tibetan culture such as the clothing style, written language, and form of Buddhism. What sets residents of Kutang apart is their distinct dialect, called *kukay*, or "language of Kutang," which some playfully suggest means "stolen language" because of lexical borrowings from several neighboring vernaculars.[4]

Across the river from Kutang lies Trok (elev. 7,500 ft.), the first Tibetan-speaking village in Nubri and a major focus of this book. Trok is situated on a gently sloping tableland that is parceled into verdant fields of barley, maize, and potatoes. Houses are clustered into distinct neighborhoods surrounded by small groves of apple trees. Above Trok rises a cliff split by zigzagging ravines that look like they were cleaved by hand. In fact, Trok's residents believe that a previous settlement had been buried under debris that a demoness scratched down from this rock face.

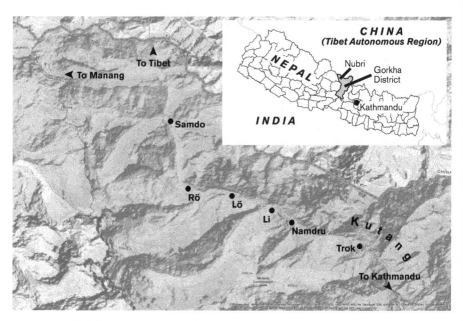

MAP I. Nubri.

Moving up valley from Trok, one ascends through a narrow gorge and enters an environment where species of pine, birch, and rhododendron populate the lush forests. High summits dominate the landscape, most of which tower to 20,000 feet and above. At Rö, a large village in the shadow of Gang Pungyen (Mount Manaslu), the valley widens into a flat plain and takes a sharp turn to the north. Samdo, the highest village in the valley, lies just above tree line. Beyond Samdo the high passes cross into Tibet to the north and Manang District to the west.

To an outsider, a cursory glimpse of village life in Nubri can spawn visions of a bucolic past. Tourists on the lookout for "unspoiled" destinations are increasingly setting their sights on Nubri. In line with utopian conceptions of Tibetan Buddhist societies (Lopez 1998; Dodin and Räther 2001; Brauen 2013), trekking agencies depict Nubri as a place that has somehow eluded all vestiges of external intrusions. For example one agency proclaims, "Hidden behind Manaslu are some of the unexplored and unknown Tibetan villages that have seen little change since medieval times," while another promises, "This fascinating trek [through Nubri] explores areas and the way of life unchanged for decades and maybe, even centuries."[5] These and other advertisements lure visitors with the prospect that a trek through the valley offers vicarious glimpses of "primitive villages" filled with "primitive inhabitants" who maintain "primitive Tibetan influenced culture and tradition." Visiting Nubri is an opportunity to venture back in time to a place where "all traces of modern civilization fade" in "villages where the harmonious agricultural life has remained unchanged for hundreds of years."[6]

Granted, tourism agencies disseminate romantic images of destinations as a means to pry money from potential clients. Such imaginative descriptions play upon people's desire to witness the unpretentious lifestyle of a bygone era. What the depictions mask, however, is the adaptable nature of a society that has been in continuous flux for generations. One hundred sixty years ago the people of Nubri came to terms with a border realignment that shifted their political allegiance from Tibet, headed by a Buddhist cleric, to the Kingdom of Nepal, ruled by members of a Hindu warrior caste. Since then they have adjusted to several major political shake-ups, all the while coping with their subordinate status as Buddhist highlanders in a predominantly Hindu nation. For more than a century their subsistence has been highly dependent on farming potatoes and maize, two New World crops which entailed major adaptations in agriculture techniques, not to mention cultural perceptions of what constitutes a proper diet. The residents of Nubri saw their position as middlemen in the lucrative trans-Himalayan trade network erode with China's assertion of power over Tibet in the 1950s, but then found equally profitable markets for their abundant timber in the 1980s and medicinal herbs at the turn of this century. Their religious affiliations have vacillated between, and combined elements of, several major Buddhist sects. Their religious institutions based on temples headed by married lamas are conceding power and influence to newly consecrated celibate monasteries. In the meantime, Nubri's residents are now centered in the cross-hairs of evangelical Christian missionaries' sights as they target Nepal's highlanders for conversion (Coburn 2017).

Social, economic, and cultural practices in Nubri have never been stagnant, a point that is obvious to the valley's residents who are versed in the Buddhist philosophy that every material object and immaterial phenomenon is characterized by impermanence (*mitagpa nyid*); the only inevitability is change itself. Today's driver of social transformation is a quest for education—both secular and religious—that motivates parents to send their children outside of the valley. Unlike other drivers of social change such as political makeovers or the adoption of new crops, educational migration has resulted in the geographic dispersion of Nubri's population, simultaneously opening new opportunities while reshaping village life, family management strategies, and intergenerational relations.

MANAGING THE FAMILY THROUGH MIGRATION

The [reproductive history] surveys thus far had been typical: eight born, five died; ten born, three died; five born, one died. They did not prepare Tashi and me for the last survey of the day. We entered Karma's home, which seemed poorer than most. She is in her early 60s, dignified yet disheveled. After completing the first part of the survey we noted that, unlike most households with residents her age, Karma and her husband do not co-reside with a married son. Rather, they live with a 42-year-old unmarried daughter. She was the first born, as we established when we began the reproductive history survey. Karma then listed eleven subsequent births, four sons and seven daughters. She clearly recalled the birth year of each, and the fate of each. With the exception of her third born, who died at age 23, all the others passed away in infancy or childhood. At the end of the interview Karma lamented, "I gave birth to twelve children. All but one of them died, but even she cannot help us much. She is *lenba* [deaf and mute]. We are very unfortunate. We have no children to help us in old age." Tashi and I left feeling depressed. We hardly spoke the rest of the day. (GC field notes, February 1997)

In the spring of 1997 Tashi Döndrup and I (GC) conducted the first demographic study of Nubri, which revealed high infant and childhood mortality. We rarely encountered a woman who had not lost at least one child to a premature death. Our research also documented a high level of fertility, and no evidence that Nubri residents rely on herbal concoctions or coitus interruptus to avert pregnancy, emmenagogues and abortifacients to thwart gestation and parturition, or infanticide, abandonment, and "aggressive neglect" to cull unwanted children.[7] People seemed more concerned with keeping children alive than preventing them from being born, perhaps because cases like Karma's were a stark reminder that high mortality can jeopardize the future of every family. The absence of family planning methods and motivations, coupled with precarious survival odds, resulted in parents having from zero to ten surviving children.

For children who did reach maturity a combination of social customs and demographic outcomes circumscribed parents' options in deciding who stayed home and who went elsewhere. Girls would generally leave through marriage to other households. It was also common to ask a local lama to ordain one daughter as a nun. She would keep her hair cropped short and don red clothing to indicate her status as a religious practitioner, but usually resided at home to help raise younger siblings and eventually assist her parents in old age. A laywoman who remained at home was usually either somehow incapacitated, like the child of Karma, or the lone surviving child capable of running a household, in which case parents would arrange for her husband to join the household. Generally, when they retired, parents preferred that a male take over the household, a duty that conventionally fell to the eldest son. Younger sons could form an independent household if they inherited sufficient land or join their elder brother in a polyandrous union (the marital practice whereby one woman has more than one husband). It was uncommon for parents to send a child to a distant monastery; the majority of male religious practitioners married and lived in the village. In fact, most people born in Nubri remained in close proximity to their natal homes and kin.

The same cannot be said today due to the high rate of educational migration, a process that disperses children across Nepal and India. To understand what is happening, and why, we use the lens of anthropological demography because it provides a robust toolkit for analyzing the magnitude, motivations, and impacts of educational migration (Greenhalgh 1995; Kertzer and Fricke 1997). Following Greenhalgh's call to "situate fertility," we treat outmigration as a complex phenomenon that must account for historical, political, economic, and cultural factors that influence how people adapt when presented with new constraints and opportunities. Caroline Bledsoe, a practitioner of the interdisciplinary approach, notes the importance of highlighting "people's active efforts to achieve demographic outcomes by restructuring household compositions and influencing children's obligations, rather than acting strictly within the biological bounds or cultural norms that seem to be imposed upon them" (1990:97–98). In line with Bledsoe's suggestion, our analysis centers on family management strategies, the idea that parents make decisions that affect the size and gender composition of the household. Sometimes decisions are calculated with long-term objectives in mind, other times they are spontaneous responses to immediate circumstances and short-term needs. In either case the decisions are made in order to fulfill social and economic objectives that include balancing a household's resources and population, marriage, income diversification, inheritance, household succession, and other matters pertaining to cultural reproduction and the domestic economy. We do not posit a uniform and predictable strategy for all families in Nubri because different decisions emerge in relation to a range of variables such as child survivorship, socioeconomic status, household tragedies, happenstance, and idiosyncratic preferences. Furthermore, exogenous factors at the national and international levels continually reshape the social, economic, and political landscapes within which parents make decisions that affect their children's futures. The family management strategy is neither static nor predetermined by social and cultural norms. To the contrary, it is dynamic and responsive to emerging opportunities.

As Greenhalgh (1995) and Skinner (1997) point out, people can manipulate their household's composition by regulating fertility (birth control), influencing survivorship (child control), and sending children out or bringing others in (child transfer). Regarding child transfer, very little scholarly attention has been focused on the role that migration can play in a family management strategy. Perhaps this is because adults are the primary focus of migration studies for well-founded reasons: they constitute the majority of migrants and are typically the ones who decide whether to move or stay put. Dobson notes that children tend to show up in the migration literature as something akin to "luggage," tagging along with parents as they move from one place to another (2009:356). When children are the focus, research tends to center on exploitative practices associated with human trafficking and child labor (Kielland and Sanogo 2002; de Lange 2007), issues migrant children face in schooling (Adams and Kirova 2006), or migrant children as transnational actors who negotiate complex ethnic and gender identities (Parreñas 2005).

Nubri's contemporary pattern of sending children for education certainly resembles a form of internal (within-country) migration.[8] Children move from a village to a city, thereby joining a global rural-to-urban migration stream driven by asymmetrical development that leaves people in villages with limited opportunities. Their movement resembles "temporary, nonseasonal" migration that is usually undertaken by young, unmarried individuals who leave a place of origin to gain skills or education (Gonzalez 1961). More specifically, Nubri's educational migration phenomenon resembles fosterage and other means of circulating children (Goody 1982; Bledsoe 1994; Leinaweaver 2008) because it involves moving young people with an eye toward providing them with better opportunities than their parents can provide (Isiugo-Abanihe 1985).

Beyond typology, Nubri's educational migration phenomenon does not fit easily with some of the main theoretical perspectives on migration. For one, when viewed through the economist's lens, migration is driven by rational decision makers seeking employment. In the case of Nubri, jobs may be a distant prospect, but the movers are children and the immediate goal is education. Second, most theoretical perspectives assume that migrants exercise varying degrees of agency (Brettell 2003), yet many of Nubri's child migrants are not even consulted about a potential move. But unlike the forced removal of indigenous children from their families so they could be educated and "civilized" (Trennert 1988; Adams 1995; van Krieken 1999), nobody is coercively separating Nubri's children from their families. Rather, parents are willingly transferring children from the familiar village society to urban dormitories packed with strangers. Finally, the literature connecting school and migration centers mainly on the effect education has on people's propensity to move after they graduate from a local institution (Baláz et al. 2004; Corbett 2007; Choy 2010; Dustmann and Glitz 2011). In the case of Nubri we are dealing not with youths who are moving after acquiring education, but with children whose parents send them outside the valley so they can become educated.

Some migration theories are helpful for analyzing Nubri's educational migration phenomenon. Specifically, we use migration network theory to understand the social basis for the geographical patterning of movements. The theory starts with the premise that migrants rely on kinship, friendship, and place of origin to form ties with other migrants and maintain relationships with nonmigrants back home (Fawcett 1989; Massey 1990; Massey et al. 1993; Brettell 2000:106–13; Castles, de Haas, and Miller 2014:39–41). The connection between people in migration destinations and sending communities is a form of social capital that facilitates movement by reducing costs and risks. Case studies show how networks create nonrandom streams of migration that result in the growth of ethnic clusters in destination communities (Grey and Woodrick 2002; Brettell 2003).

Migration network theory is helpful for analyzing Nubri's migration trend in several ways. For one, it encourages historical inquiry to unveil how social relationships between people in migration sending and destination areas evolved in the first place. In Nubri's case, a longitudinal perspective is essential for understanding how religious networks, developed decades if not centuries ago, influence the preference for today's parents to enroll their children in specific schools and monasteries. Furthermore, migration network theory allows us to examine the ways in which earlier migrants reduce costs and risks for subsequent migrants. For example in chapter 7 we explore how monks, once established in Kathmandu, play a key role in facilitating the admission of younger relatives into urban institutions.

To probe the momentum and magnitude of outmigration we employ the concept of cumulative causation, a process whereby "each act of migration alters the social context within which subsequent migration decisions are made" (Massey et al. 1993:451). "Contextual feedback" mechanisms associated with migrant ideologies and behaviors help increase the intensity of migration. For example, remittances to migrants' households alter the socioeconomic balance in a sending community by creating a sense of relative poverty among nonmigrants (de Haas 2010). Through cumulative causation migration becomes "deeply ingrained into the repertoire of people's behavior, and values associated with migration become part of the community's values" (Massey et al. 1998:47). A "culture of migration" arises when migration becomes a normative expectation (Massey et al. 1993) that is not just economically motivated but also becomes closely associated with social status (Kandel and Massey 2002; Cohen 2004; Horváth 2008; de Haas 2010:1608). Today the majority of Nubri's youths are sent outside of their natal villages for education, compelling evidence that a culture of migration has become a reality.

From a methodological standpoint, the New Economics of Labor Migration (NELM) takes the household, rather than the individual, as the decision-making unit of analysis (Stark and Bloom 1985; Taylor 1999; Cohen and Sirkeci 2011; cf. Abreu 2012). Proponents of NELM argue that migration decisions are made jointly by people who move and others who stay put. Migration is therefore part of an overall household strategy to diversify the allocation of resources, including the labor force both short- and long-term. The household collectively shares the costs and risks of migration, as well as the benefits (Massey et al. 1993). We use NELM as a starting point for investigating how educational migration can be understood as a calculated strategy. Parents in Nubri are firmly committed to forging pathways so their children can have better lives while at the same time are hoping for subsequent returns through remittances and other forms of support. By ignoring the term *labor* in NELM's title, we acknowledge that migration decisions are based on perceived future advantages from educating one's children, not on the immediate prospect of employment.

STUDYING LONGITUDINAL CHANGE

As practitioners of anthropological demography, we are well versed in the advantages of merging quantitative demographic description with qualitative social analysis. In this study we integrate disciplinary approaches to facilitate "greater contextualization of the brute demographic events" (Kertzer and Fricke 1997:24). By using population statistics as a starting

point and then summoning ethnographic perspectives to explore rationales and meanings, our explanatory mechanism strives to achieve a
"thicker demography" (Fricke 1997) that navigates between statistical
inference and people's own testimonies. We concur with Laura Ahearn
that a multimethod research approach can yield "a multifaceted account
of social change that acknowledges complexities, contradictions, and
indeterminacies" (2001:245). We also concur with Christoph von Fürer-
Haimendorf that any meaningful understanding of long-term change can
only emerge through longitudinal research. In a 1983 interview by anthropologist Alan Mcfarlane, Fürer-Haimendorf reflects on the quandary a
novice fieldworker encounters when intending to study long-term processes. He argues that the inexperienced fieldworker

> wants to study the change. The change from what? Because he hasn't seen
> what there was twenty years ago. If you really want to study social change,
> you must allow a certain period to elapse so that you can see the stages of
> change. Now, I think that it is very revealing to go back to the same society,
> see a different generation, possibly the same people, and see how are they
> when they are thirty years older or forty years older? Because we don't
> remain the same, and so naturally Apatanis or Nagas don't remain the same
> either.[9]

Our own credentials for studying change in Nubri extend over the
course of two decades. I (GC) began PhD fieldwork in Nubri from 1995
to 1997. As a novice ethnographer, I resided in the home of Tashi Döndrup, an elderly bachelor who was my host, confidant, and key cultural
interlocutor. By living with Tashi, learning the local vernacular, and
gaining rapport with Nubri's residents, I managed to conduct ethnographic research and gather socioeconomic and demographic data as
well as reproductive histories of all women aged fifteen and older in six
villages.[10] The qualitative observations and interviews combined with
the quantitative surveys from this initial fieldwork provide an empirical
baseline for assessing subsequent changes.

After research stints in India, Kathmandu, and China's Tibet Autonomous Region, I returned to Nubri for a reconnaissance trip in 2010
and was struck by the paucity of school-aged children, which led to our
investigation of education and migration. The two of us traveled to
Nubri in 2011 to interview parents about their family management
strategies and economic conditions.[11] During that trip we conducted
participant observation and completed in-depth interviews with forty-
three parents in two villages. Our purposive sample included parents
who had sent at least one child to a school or a religious institution, as

well as the rare parents who had retained all of their children in the village. We selected single parents and married couples; some poor, others relatively wealthy. We used a semistructured interview schedule with core questions centering on rationales for sending children out of the village, networks people rely on to place children in specific schools or religious institutions, and strategies for ensuring household succession. We also photographed administrative documents and interviewed local leaders about village governance and history.

In 2012 Sienna Craig and I (GC) were co–principal investigators on a project led by biological anthropologist Cynthia Beall.[12] This multisited project investigating the connection between genetic adaptation to high altitude and reproductive outcomes involved the collection of household surveys and reproductive histories of all women aged forty and above in three Nubri villages—Samdo, Rö, and Lö. In 2013 I returned on another project, led by biological anthropologist E. A. Quinn, to investigate associations between adaptation to a high-altitude environment, mother's milk, and infant growth.[13] The project's demographic component allowed us to fill in blanks from the 2012 research by conducting reproductive history surveys with women under age forty in Samdo, Rö, and Lö, as well as household surveys and reproductive histories in two more villages, Li and Trok. We now had longitudinal data covering 1997 to 2013, allowing us to quantify the direction, magnitude, age, and gender components of demographic changes (Childs et al. 2014).

What we lacked, however, was the perspectives of the young migrants. In 2014, we returned to conduct interviews with migrants living in Kathmandu.[14] We used a stratified purposeful sampling strategy to interview twenty-two people who had been sent to boarding schools, passed tenth grade, and are still living in the city, sixteen monks living in four different monasteries, and eight nuns in two nunneries. We also interviewed six older people who were some of the first to move to the city from Nubri. Our semistructured interview schedule was designed to elicit personal histories of migration and to probe migrants' relationships with natal villages and family members, including experiences of visiting the village, career aspirations, thoughts about marriage, and plans for future migration. During subsequent visits to Nubri we completed the picture by interviewing former monks who had returned to lay life, and individuals who had completed secular education and now work in the valley.

The product of numerous research trips to Nubri is a robust data set that includes quantitative data from demographic surveys and reproductive histories, and qualitative data from participant observation and in-depth interviews. The quantitative data helps track what is happening in demographic trends. Specifically, the reproductive history survey measures how many children are born, how many survive, and to what extent women are using birth control. The household survey records details on all individuals, including age, sex, education, and where they currently reside. Longitudinal analysis allows us to chart a decline in infant mortality, a rise in contraceptive usage, the first hints of a fertility transition, as well as the timing, direction, and magnitude of educational migration. Documenting these trends provides an empirical basis for using ethnographic research to address why they are happening. By examining the intentions and motivations that underlie people's family management strategies, we can better understand the demographic processes.

THE HOUSEHOLD AS A UNIT OF ANALYSIS

As mentioned above, we adopt the household as a unit of analysis for migration decision making. In ethnographic research this choice can cause confusion and therefore merits an explanation. A unit of analysis is understood in the social sciences as the "who or what" of a study (Long 2004). By focusing on the household, we do not imply that an inanimate entity is determining who goes where. Nor are we suggesting that decisions are made in a democratic manner with equal input from all household members or by a patriarchal dictator who acts with altruistic intentions. Feminist scholars have demonstrated that both scenarios are implausible; gender-based differentials affect who holds more negotiating power in decision making within the household (e.g., Folbre 1986; England 1993), and women play a larger role than previously given credit for in household economic choices (e.g., Clark 1989; Lockwood 1989). Power dynamics among household members no doubt shape decision making, but normative views on who wields power should not be taken as a reliable predictor of how decisions are made, let alone the basis for modeling decision making.

To illustrate the interplay between ideology and agency, we start by recognizing that the Nubri household ethic is similar to the Tibetan corporate family model described by Goldstein (1971); individuals are expected to pursue opportunities that benefit the welfare of their co-resident kin in lieu of personal ambitions. The household head, usually an older male, holds considerable power. As the representative of the household in communal affairs, he is seen by the outside world as the dominant decision maker. From a normative standpoint the household in Nubri is a collection of individuals who are prodded by the patriarch to collaborate for the sake of common prosperity. Good judgment coupled with selfless cooperation can help a harmonious household thrive, while bad choices and individualistic actions can lead to disgruntlement and poverty. This suggests that altruism is a guiding principle, at least for the economically successful household. Yet we still need to grapple with a question Wilk raised: "Do the members of a household act in their own self-interest, or are they behaving in an altruistic (or dominated) way, acting to further the interest of the group at the expense of their own?" (1989:25).

Chibnik criticizes the continuing tendency for scholars to orient household decision-making models around an altruistic head who other members align with out of self-interest. He asks a pertinent rhetorical question, "Does it not make more sense that most households consist of a number of people whose economic motives are a combination of altruism and self-interest?" (2011:137). We agree, and use Chibnik's statement as a launching point to the approach we take in this study. We acknowledge that the corporate household—as an ideology—has a durable influence on how parents and children envision their long-term social and economic relationships. Yet we also realize that power is permeable; just because the patriarch represents the household in village councils does not mean he makes all decisions behind closed doors. A household is a social grouping in which multiple actors can influence decisions to varying degrees based on age, gender, willingness to take risks, and other attributes. We also appreciate that individuals are idiosyncratic, which makes households—as collections of individuals—even more so. Some people may fall in line with a patriarch's decisions, while others pursue actions that do not necessarily support the corporate household ethos. Normative values provide an orientation for behavior, and perhaps some social pressure to follow conventions, but are not always a reliable predictor of actual decisions and actions.

In chapters 5–7 we present cases in which parents dictate migration decisions, especially when the migrant is too young to make a fuss or even comprehend what is happening. In some instances a husband and wife concur on a course of action, in others they disagree and one ends up overruling the other. We also present cases in which children who were not slated for school or a religious vocation pester their parents into sending them away or, in extreme cases, run away to accomplish their aims. To further complicate matters, elder siblings often pave migration pathways for younger siblings by encouraging parents to send their brothers or sisters to the city. Claiming that one parent or the other wields all the migration decision-making authority in the household can be correct in some cases but totally inaccurate in others. Furthermore, people make migration choices in an environment of uncertainty, which is especially true in the case of educational migration. Parents may hope for or anticipate a certain outcome but must wait more than a decade to see how everything plays out. Therefore, suggesting that they make migration decisions with an altruistic eye toward benefiting the household is problematic because such decisions are based on an array of short- and long-term objectives that are buttressed by a mix of social, cultural, and economic rationales. We will revisit the issue of altruism versus self-interest in chapter 5.

Adopting the household as a unit of analysis does not come at the expense of more fine-grained analysis, for we have followed Bernard's advice to collect data on the "lowest level unit of analysis possible" (2011:40), in this case the individual. In this study the household and the individual are complementary rather than exclusionary units of analysis. For example, each data entry sheet of our demographic survey covers a single household. We sought to interview the household head, recognizing that he or she is the person with the most detailed knowledge about the household. Although we asked some household-related questions about landholdings and herd sizes, most of our questions generated data on individuals, for example each person's marital status, educational attainment, and current whereabouts. Our in-depth interviewing strategy then centered on individuals in relation to the household. Specifically, we asked parents their reasons for sending a particular child to a certain institution, the social networks they drew upon to gain admission, and their hopes or plans for how that child will make future contributions to the well-being of other household members. We then asked young migrants to reflect on their own migration experiences and future aspirations, and how they envision their role (or lack thereof) in the future of their natal households. In both the quantitative and qualitative dimensions of the research, we can disaggregate our data to analyze an individual migrant's experience or aggregate it to assemble a complex picture of how household composition and intergenerational dynamics unfold over time. Scaling upward also allows us to assess the magnitude and direction of the migration stream, and to contrast demographic trends in Nubri with Tibetan exiles living in Nepal and India—a variance that turns out to be crucial for understanding where Nubri fits into the supply-and-demand chain of institutional recruitment.

As a meso-level unit of analysis the household is a link between macro-level processes and the individual life courses of migrants. Focusing on the household allows us to see how it operates over time as a seemingly cohesive yet continually fragmenting unit, while never losing sight of educational migrants who may live elsewhere but are still considered members of the domestic unit. The focus also allows us to analyze socioeconomic and cultural practices that bind households together into communities (chapter 3), and how transnational processes that drive educational migration threaten the viability of communities by depleting households of key members (chapter 10). However, not everyone agrees on what actually constitutes a household, or how it should be defined. In chapter 3 we detail precisely how the household is classified by the people of Nubri, and revisit the household concept from the perspectives of anthropology and demography. The purpose is to stress the advantages of adopting an emic definition of household instead of a standardized classification favored by demographers.

In the following chapters we consider educational migration to be an endogenous response to exogenous forces. Sending children to distant institutions has evolved into a key component of a family management strategy that is driven by the prospect of social and economic rewards but that entails risk, uncertainty, and unforeseen consequences. The book is organized as follows. Chapter 2 situates Nubri historically as a place that gradually became part of the broader Tibetan Buddhist cultural world through the migration of lamas and establishment of temples. Social networks that developed over time and are based on religious affiliation set the stage for the direction of today's migration. In chapter 3 we discuss Nubri households in the context of a local administrative system that binds people to the village through taxes and communal obligations, but also encourages men to learn liturgical skills that give them seasonal mobility and connects them to the larger Buddhist community in Nepal. Chapter 4 details the resurrection of Tibetan institutions in exiles and documents demographic changes in Nubri by analyzing the interrelated trends of fertility, mortality, and migration. We argue that population trends are key to understanding why Nubri became a recruiting ground for Tibetan schools and monasteries. Chapters 5, 6, 7, and 8—the ethnographic core of the study—examine the role educational migration plays in parents' family management strategies, the social networks that facilitate rural to urban migration, as well as migrants' perspectives on the relocation experience, connections with family, and future aspirations.

Chapter 9 centers on the ways educational migration is impacting intergenerational relations via marriage and household succession, while chapter 10 explores a range of demographic and social changes that are occurring in the wake of outmigration. Through the approach of anthropological demography, our objective is to employ quantitative and qualitative data in a mutually reinforcing manner to investigate the causes and consequences of a migration pattern that is rapidly transforming every aspect of Nubri society.

CHAPTER 2

Moving In before Moving Out

A PERIPHERAL REGION OF DARKNESS

He then went to a place of different language. After staying a month in Nelchorpug [Meditation Cave], he preached the dharma to many who were like nonhumans and thus did not have the mental comportment to be tamed as followers of the dharma. They were no better than bovines. Realizing the awareness of cyclical existence, he composed a song by offering respect to the great teacher and translator Marpa, the dispeller of the darkness of ignorance, on the plight of inhabitants of this darkness-filled peripheral region where no sunshine of the holy dharma has fallen. Although these people have attained human birth, they were mentally preoccupied only with the basic instincts of eating and drinking; no one could be found pursuing the dharma. The song on awareness of worldly suffering goes:

Listen, you who behave like nonhuman ghosts.
Due to your past karma, you have attained this ugly life.
If you commit further sins, you will surely go to the lower realms of hell.
You have attained a human life but have the mental comportment of
  bovines.
I feel a deep awareness on seeing such plight.
A great compassion arose within me,
But there is nothing I can do to help.
When I achieve the state of bodhisattva,
May they all be my disciples!
To those living in this meditation cave,
I beseech all, including the local spirits,
To strive toward the righteous path of dharma!

After composing the song, he traveled further in this region of a different language in search of disciples to teach the dharma. However, it appeared that people ran away on seeing the great teacher. Through a deep meditative absorption of great compassion for the people of Ku[tang?] and Tibet, he developed a karmic connection to this region. After offering an earnest meditative supplication, he departed to lower Tsum. (Milarepa 1985:130–31)[1]

In the above passage the great yogin Milarepa (1040–1123) describes his encounter with the people of Nubri. A key term is *takob* (peripheral region), which Tibetans use to describe a land that is uninhabited by the fourfold retinue of Buddhist practitioners (monks, nuns, male and female lay devotees) but that borders areas where Buddhism is firmly established.[2] Milarepa depicts Nubri as a place of dense gloom where Buddhist teachings have never penetrated and characterizes its residents as akin to hapless bovines who exist merely to eat and drink. Implied in the song is that they will one day become his disciples.

Because the narratives of Milarepa's travels were compiled from various written and oral accounts centuries after his death, we follow Quintman's advice to "move beyond the rote mining of Tibetan biography for historical data" (2014:175). Rather than reading this passage as a reliable description of Nubri's early inhabitants, we cite it as an example of how Tibetans draw a distinction between places where Buddhism flourishes and peripheral areas where the religion is absent or practiced in a diminished form. We use Milarepa's depiction to foreshadow Nubri's gradual incorporation into the Tibetan cultural orb, a historical perspective that is crucial for understanding the nature of today's out-migration phenomenon.

This chapter starts by describing how Nubri came to be a Buddhist society governed by various Tibetan polities, a process that included not only military interventions but also the inmigration of clerics from prominent religious lineages. By adopting Buddhism, Nubri's residents came to view themselves at the center rather than the periphery of the Tibetan world. We then describe how Nubri became incorporated into the Kingdom of Nepal during the mid-nineteenth century, an event that realigned political allegiance without changing the cultural orientation toward Tibet. We argue that the kingdom's policy of indirect rule allowed Nubri residents to retain many of their legal and administrative traditions, which helped them maintain a distinctly Tibetan identity. The chapter foreshadows that, by becoming citizens of Nepal, opportunities for secular and religious education eventually opened—but not through the efforts of the national government. The chance to send children away for education, as we discuss in chapter 4, arose when Tibetan exiles established institutions of learning. The historical perspective presented in this chapter allows us to explore how today's educational migration phenomenon is predicated on a Tibetan Buddhist cultural orientation, citizenship in the nation of Nepal, and political processes that led to the resurrection of Tibetan institutions in Nepal and India that people from Nubri can access with relative ease.

EXCAVATING THE ETHNIC STRATA

Today Nubri is linguistically divided between the upper part of the valley where Tibetan is spoken and the lower part of the valley, called Kutang, where residents speak Kukey ("the language of Kutang") which is lexically similar to Ghale (presumably through borrowing) but has a grammar unlike any other language in the area.[3] Village names provide indirect evidence that today's Tibetan-speaking settlements in the upper stretches of Nubri may have been inhabited, or at least frequented, by people from Kutang. Tibetan place names commonly consist of two, three, or four syllables, for example Kyidrong (*sKyid grong;* Village of Happiness), Nakartse (*sNa dkar rtse;* White Nose Peak), and Dragkar Taso (*Brag dkar rta so;* White Cliff Horse Tooth). However, throughout Nubri most village names consist of a single syllable that does not make much sense when spelled in Tibetan. During several conversations with residents of Nubri we wrote out place names in Tibetan and discussed possible interpretations. Many agreed that the place names have no discernable meaning in Tibetan, and therefore must have a Kukey origin. For example, the village known to most outsiders as Samagaun (*gaun* is the Nepali word for "village") is called Rö by locals. Lobpön Gyurme, who is renowned for his religious and historical knowledge, concedes, "It appears to be a very old word. People pronounce it differently, but nobody seems to know its exact meaning." Of the two variant spellings, *ros* is not found in Tibetan lexicons, while *rod* means "pride" or "haughtiness." Other monosyllabic village names include Lö (spelled blod) which is the imperative form of the verb "to chew," Li (spelled klis) which has no known meaning in Tibetan, and Trok *(phrog)* which means to "rob" or "cheat," but according to some locals, the village got its name because the original inhabitants were boastful men who liked to show off *(krog krog).* Only one monosyllabic name in the Tibetan-speaking part of the valley seems to have a clear meaning: Sho (spelled zhol) commonly denotes a house or village that is situated below something more substantial. Sho is located just below the larger village of Lö.[4]

Most village names in Kutang are also monosyllabic (e.g., Kwak, Krak, Gap, Tsak, Bi, Deng), perhaps evidence that Kutang's ancestors supplied the place names for upper Nubri. A somewhat analogous situation is found in the Baragaon region of lower Mustang, where village names such as Te, Kog, and Tshug are common. Ramble proposes that the original form of the old toponym Serib is Se. Residues of Seke ("the Se language"), found, for example, in rituals to propitiate territorial gods, suggest that the entire region was once populated by people who were ethnically and linguistically distinct from Tibetans (2008:37–39). Like Serib, the peculiar monosyllabic village names in upper Nubri hint that the original inhabitants were not Tibetan speakers and that Tibetans were relative latecomers to the valley. If this is true, then early Tibetan visitors encountered people who were linguistically and culturally different, which may explain why they perceived Nubri to be a peripheral region.

Tibetans did eventually settle and dominate the upper part of the valley. Today's linguistic divide shows up in an account by the "treasure revealer" *(tertön)* Rigzen Gödemchen (see Ehrhard 1997), who reportedly traveled to Nubri in 1389 (Rigzen Tsewang Norbu 1990:119). A description attributed to him states, "Tibetan is spoken in the upper part [of the valley]. In the lower part [of the valley], there are many dissimilar languages" (Kyimolung Lamyig 1983:2a).[5] Unfortunately, the dating of this text is uncertain. More concrete evidence comes from the biography of Pema Döndrup from Kutang (1668–1744) who makes it clear that he was not fluent in the Tibetan language when embarking on a pilgrimage to Tibet (Childs 2004:78–79). Furthermore, Rigzen Tsewang Norbu visited Nubri in 1729 and referred to a disciple from Kutang as hailing from Mon, a term that generally designates a non-Tibetan border area. In contrast, he referred to disciples from upper Nubri as being from Ngari, or Western Tibet (Rigzen Tsewang Norbu 1977). At the very least Rigzen Tsewang Norbu acknowledged a cultural distinction (and presumably a linguistic one as well) between people inhabiting the upper and lower segments of the valley.

THE CENTER COMES TO THE PERIPHERY

In the eleventh century the rulers of Gungtang, a kingdom founded by descendants of Tibet's medieval emperors (Petech 1980, 1994; Vitali

1996), incorporated upper Nubri into their political domain. According to Rigzen Tsewang Norbu, "In the middle of Gungtang is lofty and rugged Nubri. The mountain to the right resembles a king seated on a throne. The mountain to the left resembles a queen pregnant with child. . . . During his reign, Lhachogde [late eleventh CE] extended his realm beyond its extent of former times. In Nubri, the rugged mountainous area in the center [of his realm] which resembles a great highland wrapped in a silk curtain, he built a royal residence" (Rigzen Tsewang Norbu 1990:92–93).[6]

The Gungtang ruler Bumdegon further secured the area around 1280 by building a series of outposts. Rigzen Tsewang Norbu's history states, "In order to suppress the peripheral region of Nubri, he [Gungtang king Bumdegon] built the Black Cliff Fort at Rö" (1990:108).[7] Bumdegon presumably had a political agenda for building Black Cliff Fort, but at least in Rigzen Tsewang Norbu's later interpretation there was a religious dimension as well—suppressing a peripheral region (takob) involves the introduction of Buddhism. The extent to which Buddhism made inroads into the valley under Gungtang rule is unclear, but some influence is plausible given that Taiga Monastery was founded just north of Nubri around 1195 (Vitalli 1996:394, n.639). We also know that the fourteenth-century cleric Rigzen Gödemchen (1337–1409) mentions Kyimolung, which straddles Nubri and neighboring Tsum, as one of the main hidden lands where Buddhist practitioners can flee in times of political strife and moral degeneration in Tibet (Childs 1999; Solmsdorf 2013).

Political events of the seventeenth century brought Nubri closer to the Tibetan world. In 1620 the king of Tsang in central Tibet deposed the Gungtang rulers. Two decades later Oirat Mongols conquered Tsang and helped centralize political authority in Tibet under their ally, the Fifth Dalai Lama. Nubri became part of Dzonga District. The Iron Tiger Year (1830) tax assessment, based on a 1740 prototype, lists Nubri as one of the areas under Dzonga authority (Tsultrim et al. 1989:333).[8] Key elements of the household registration system implemented by the Tibetan government at that time are still used in Nubri today (see chapter 3).

A second transformative event was the inmigration of lamas, who founded temples and married local women. Some of their gyüpa (patrilineal descent groups) have distinguished pedigrees that connect them to the broader Tibetan world. By examining the inmigration of men from three different lama lineages, we can trace how historical processes helped shape religious networks that facilitate today's outmigration trend.

The Ngadag Migration

Members of the Ngadag lineage live primarily in Rö and occupy the pinnacle of Nubri's social hierarchy. They are householder lamas *(ngagpa)* who trace descent to the medieval emperors of Tibet and have a document issued in 1668 by the Fifth Dalai Lama to support their claim (Aris 1975; Childs 2004). The term *Ngadag* is generally reserved for descendants of the Tibetan imperial line, another example being Ngadag Puntsok Namgyal, who founded the kingdom of Sikkim (see Mullard 2011).

Tashi Dorje (1918–2017) wrote a brief history of his lineage based on oral and written sources. He notes that his branch of the Ngadag lineage lived in Shari, located in Tsang Yeru (the Right Horn of Tsang) along the Kyenkar River in Central Tibet (Tashi Dorje 2010:11). Chögyal Jampa Tenzin, who probably lived in the early seventeenth century, had two sons. One of them became the lama of Tradumtse, a "border taming" temple located north of Nubri. The younger son, Tashi Namgyal, "went to Rö, where his lineage remains unbroken."

> Tashi Dorje writes, "In the Fire Monkey and Bird years there will be turmoil in Tibet. Three commanders will converge on Dzonga. They will beat three great drums of war. Those who belong to the lineage of the royal descendants—go to the holy places of Kyimolung, Kutang, and Tsum! On the basis of this prophecy Ngadag Tashi Namgyal, the youngest son of Chogyal Jampa Tenzin, gradually proceeded from Shari to the joyous place of Rö in Nubri" (Tashi Dorje 2010:12).[9]

Ngadag Tashi Namgyal probably migrated to Nubri in the 1640s. We base this assessment on the number of generations that have elapsed since Ngadag Tashi Namgyal's lifetime, which suggests that he was born around 1620 (Childs 2001a). We also base it on parallels with the well-documented migration of Ngadag Puntsok Rigzen, who fled to Sikkim in 1642, also seeking a hidden land (see Mullard 2011 and Gentry 2014:484–89), and the Tibetan historian Rigzen Tsewang Norbu's claim that members of the Ngadag descent lineage "dispersed to Sikkim, Nubri, Droshö, and elsewhere" after the overthrow of the Gungtang rulers in 1642 (1974:16b). We know for certain that in 1688 a Ngadag lineage member was present in Nubri. That is the year Pema Döndrup from Kutang mentions in his biography meeting the Ngadag lama of Rö (1979:11a).

Tashi Dorje's account goes on to describe how Ngadag Tashi Namgyal entered Nubri, married, and established a permanent residence. He writes,

> After traveling aimlessly on the road for about half a day, he [Ngadag Tashi Namgyal] came to a place called Drubtob Phug [Yogin Cave]. After he saw this majestic rock shelter that would please any hermit, he decided to stay

overnight. That night, the local deity Dorje Drakey of the sacred mountain Pungyen [Mount Manaslu] of Nubri appeared in his dream and said, "It is propitious if you don't leave this place. If you travel from this place, there will be obstacles. If you stay in this sacred place, it will benefit sentient beings. Your future disciples reside in this place." After learning this prophecy, he felt better about staying in Nubri. Either because of the good omen to remain in the place or because he performed a geomancy ritual that resulted in the miraculous appearances of three auspicious springs at the back of Black Rock Fort of Rö,[10] an ancient yogin appeared and said, "If you belong to the Ngadag lineage stay here; it will be auspicious and greatly beneficial for the sentient beings. I will stay here a while and wander in the hidden valley of Kyimolung and other scared places." Not long after, the yogin left.

Consequently, Ngadag Tashi Namgyal dedicated his life to religious practice. However, a time came when he could not forsake his deep compassion for the Tibetan disciples. With a mindset toward ensuring a religious lineage through a son succeeding in the position of his father *[patsab bu]*, and through spiritual descent *[chötsab dung]*, he set forth to the place called Trok in the lower part of the valley. Dzongpön [district commissioner] Yeshe's daughter, Nekya Putrin, was staying in retreat. She bore the mark of a dakini and had a previous karmic connection with Tashi Namgyal. He went to her in secret. He married and took her to Rö, accompanied by appearance of numerous miraculous occurrences that everyone observed. Afterward, Dzongpön Yeshe with his followers approached Rö. Having learned the life story of Ngadag Tashi Namgyal, they all became his disciples and requested his spiritual protection for eternity. Soon after, the people led by Dzongpön Yeshe built a lama residence *[labrang]* called Gakyi Khangsar at Balsa Nyathang. (Tashi Dorje 2010:12–15)[11]

By settling in Nubri, Tashi Namgyal helped install Buddhism as the dominant religion of the valley, and by marrying Nekya Putrin he started a family to ensure the continuity of his lineage. Henceforth, the position of head lama in Rö has passed from father to son in an unbroken line of succession.[12]

The migration of Tashi Namgyal to Nubri represents a seminal moment in Nubri's religious history. Tashi Namgyal and his successors have a pedigree that elevates them to the summit of Nubri's stratified socioeconomic system and gives them lofty credentials in the broader Tibetan world by virtue of a genealogical link to the medieval emperors. The Ngadag legacy is on display today not only in the temples they founded in Nubri, but also in the connections they forged with prominent Buddhist masters who have had a major influence on today's outmigration, a topic we revisit in chapters 4–6.

Kyungkar, the White Garuda Lineage

Many people in Nubri are members of the Kyungpo Rabsang Karpo lineage (Kyungkar for short), which Aris translates as the "Exceedingly

Good White Garuda." Legend states that a *kyung* (Skt: *garuda*, a large mythical bird) descended from the heavens and alighted on a mountain in Tibet where it laid four different colored eggs (white, black, yellow, and green). Four youths hatched from the eggs and subsequently formed their own clans (Aris 1979:54–55; Smith 2001:333–34). References to imperial ministers bearing the Kyung name (Beckwith 1987; Sörensen 1994) and ancient inscriptions mentioning Kyung that date to the Tibetan Imperial period (ca. 650–850 CE) attest to the prominence and antiquity of the lineage.[13] Milarepa is one of its more famous members.

In the mid-1700s the people of Kutang invited Chökyi Gyaltsen, the youngest son of Kyungkar Namkha Dorje, who resided in neighboring Tsum, to be their head lama. He took up residence in Gyayul (a.k.a. Krak), a village in Kutang.[14] He and his successors fathered an unbroken lineage of sons until the last one, Chökyi Nyima (1953–2006), took a vow of celibacy. They are credited with founding and maintaining Serang Monastery, which to this day is one of the most important cultural institutions in the valley. Kyungkar lamas also spread to other villages by establishing collateral lineages.[15] For example, Norbu Samdrup of Trok tells us that Sherab Sangpo, who was probably born in the 1820s, had seven sons. The people of Trok invited one of the sons, Sherab Gyaltsen, to reside in their village. His hand- and footprints are impressed on a rock in the village marking the place of his initial arrival. Trok's residents built him a temple above the village in the retreat center called Oong, gave him some land, and agreed to provide two days of labor annually per household as corvée service *(wulag)*. The line of descent from Sherab Gyaltsen to Norbu Samdrup remains unbroken.

The presence of Kyungkar lineage members is another important link between Nubri and the broader Tibetan world. Since the time of Chökyi Nyima's untimely death, Serang Monastery has been administered by Chogtrul Karma Migyur Dorje (a.k.a. Tulku Karma) from Bhutan. Chökyi Nyima's reincarnation, also born in Bhutan, underwent an enthronement ceremony at Serang in June 2017. He is currently being groomed as the monastery's future abbot.

Kyika Ratö, a Lineage from Barpak

Lama Jigme is the incumbent of Namlha Gomba, a secluded temple and meditation retreat above Namdru that was founded by his ancestor, Sonam Wangyal. Lama Jigme told us that his lineage descends from Kyika Ratö ("Dog's Mouth, Goat's Forehead"), a mysterious figure whose purported progenies are found throughout the Himalayan region. Kyika Ratö is so named because his mother, Margyan, a consort to the Tibetan emperor Trisong Detsen, conceived a child after copulating with a dog and a goat. In one version of the legend, Kyika Ratö was exiled to the southern borderlands, where he became the king of the hidden land Khenpajong (Aris 1979: 63–82). A text describing the founding of Namlha Gomba in Nubri also mentions the banishment of Kyika Ratö, although in this case he is referred to as Margyan's son Ngangri Tsenpo and he ends up in Barpak, a large Ghale settlement several days' walk south of Nubri.[16] Lama Jigme relates the story of how his ancestor ended up in Trok.

It is said that three sons were born to Trisong Detsen. One of them had seven sons. Among them, Kyika Ratö had very abnormal facial features [a dog's mouth and a goat's horn as his name implies]. Because of this, the parents found it hard to show him to other people so they hid him inside.

One day when Kyika Ratö had grown older, he went to the terrace of the palace. A guard saw him and told others that he saw a strange-looking person on the top of the king's palace and that the person should be caught. People were called to catch the son. It was easy to catch him since he was the king's son and living inside the palace. Some people said Kyika Ratö's facial features were a bad omen so he should be killed, while others said he should not be killed since he is the king's son. They decided to dispose of the king's son, so they sealed him into a coracle and threw him into a river. But instead of floating downstream, the coracle went upstream. People were amazed by this, and Kyika Ratö was taken out of the coracle. People then said it is either a very good or very bad omen. They deliberated over what should be done. In the end they decided that Kyika Ratö should be sent into exile.

After the decision was made to send Kyika Ratö into exile, Guru Rinpoche is said to have prophesized, "a time will come when the unwanted becomes wanted." He suggested that Kyika Ratö should go to a place in Nepal where rice fields nestle amid snowy mountains. Following the prophecy of Guru Rinpoche, he went to Barpak and through karma [ley] met his consort there. They had many descendants. Some moved to Nubri while others moved to Nyeshang [Manang] and Bhutan. Our gyüpa has many members in Bhutan. You know Tulku Karma at Serang? He says that we are from the same gyüpa.

Among our gyüpa members, the one who moved to Nubri gained fame for one of his accomplishments. As he attempted to travel from Barpak to Nubri, he encountered a big river called Chulogang. It is between Bangshing and Nyak. The river was very big, so it may have been the middle of summer then. There was no bridge. Being stuck at this place, he began to meditate. In the night he offered prayers to seek guidance. If religion was to be spread to the land of Nubri, he should be able to cross the river the next day. If religion

FIGURE 1. Sonam Wangyal, founder of Namlha Monastery.
Unknown artist, photo by Geoff Childs.

was not to be spread to Nubri, then he would remain. After the prayers, he slept at that place for one night. The next morning, when he awoke, a rock had been placed across the river allowing access to the other side. It is said that the rock bridge can still be seen today. So he was able to cross into Nubri and gained disciples from all over the valley, and from Nyeshang and Tsum as well.

Lama Jigme's great-grandfather, Sonam Wangyal, traveled to Tibet several times to receive religious teachings and transmissions from renowed masters such as Śākya Śrī.[17] He also founded Namlha Monastery above the village of Namdru and purchased important sets of religious texts. Notably, Sonam Wangyal brought home an entire set of the Kanjur, 108 volumes comprising the spoken words of the Buddha, and established a fund so that villagers in Trok could perform the recitation of these texts during the third month of every year. They still conduct the ritual to this day.

COMPLETING THE BUDDHIST TRANSFORMATION

The inmigration of lamas representing prestigious lineages helped bring Nubri closer to the Tibetan world. However, in the eighteenth century the transformation from peripheral region to Buddhist stronghold was still incomplete. In 1730, Pema Wangdu (1697–?), a lama who was born in Kutang and received teachings from Rigzen Tsewang Norbu in 1729, lamented, "All practices [in Kutang] are heterodox. People kill all the wild animals in the mountains and slay by knife the sheep and goats in the valley. Even the white-direction protecting deities turned to the power of black life-cutting. Everyone—male, female, young, and old—changed to the black direction through evil thoughts. Even though this is the Hidden Valley of Happiness [beyul Kyimolung], the narrow gorge resembles a peripheral region of ignorance" (Pema Wangdu 1979:408–9).[18]

Pema Wangdu then sought to purify Buddhist practices by convincing people to abandon the custom of animal sacrifice. His actions were paralleled by shagya, or "sealing decrees," issued by lamas to prohibit hunting and other human activities in areas of sacred significance (Huber 2004a, 2004b). For example, in Trok there is a strand of trees lining the only stream that runs through the village. The rivulet is not only a crucial source of water, but also the residence of a local protector deity. A sealing decree, written "by our ancestors" as one lama told us, states that people can neither cut any of these trees nor shed the blood of any living beings within the grove. When we probed him regarding the importance of protecting forests and wildlife, he explained,

> Forests are the ornaments of monasteries and the abode of wild animals. If forests are cleared, they will be turned into meadows thereby making it easy for humans to harm the animals. There are many wild animals around here, like musk deer, mountain sheep, snow leopards, bears, and others. In addition, there are many birds with nests, including peacocks and others that live

FIGURE 2. Pema Wangdu, initiator of an 18th-century animal sacrifice ban. Unknown artist, photo by Geoff Childs.

in the snow, forests, meadows, and cliffs. All these animals cannot be hunted for two main reasons. First, we do not practice animal sacrifices to the deities. Second, we have prohibitions against taking the lives of wild animals in the mountains and valleys. This is primarily because we are a Buddhist society; hunting violates the principle of killing. You know about taking refuge in the three precious gems of Buddha, Dharma, and Sangha. If you take refuge in Buddha, you are not supposed to take life. If you take refuge in Dharma, then you must avoid causing harm to animals. If you take refuge in the Sangha, then you must avoid animal sacrifice and causing harm to animals. This is the crux of Buddhist practice.

Maintaining the forest is important for the well-being of people. For example, water is abundant and the flow unceasing if you have forest. Also, if forest is maintained, the well-being of people is enhanced through clean air, thus ensuring longer life and less disease. Furthermore, the wild animals are said to be under the protection of the nonhuman spirits who dwell in the natural surroundings. We cannot afford to offend them. If we take the lives of wild animals, it will lead to epidemics in the region and social disharmony. If we cut down the forest, it will lead not only to the deterioration of the land but to the loss of many wild animals that reside in the forests. It is easy to clear the forests, but we would lose all these animals, which are precious. This would mean that the fortune *[yang]* of the land would be lost. Thus, it has been practiced from the past not to cut down the forests or harm the wild animals. This is the main logic behind the prohibitions.

The lama's interpretation is clearly rooted in Buddhist concepts of nonviolence and the interdependence of all beings. In this philosophy, harming the environment and wild animals is not only considered innately sinful, but has the additional consequences of harming people's health and disrupting social harmony.[19] The issuing of sealing decrees and animal sacrifice prohibitions are part of the gradual movement of Nubri society closer to the center of the Tibetan Buddhist cultural realm. The Buddhist transformation is also evident in a locally produced document that provides an emic perspective on how the people of Trok village position themselves in the moral geography of Tibet and Buddhism. In the nineteenth century Trok's residents built a temple to honor a protective deity that inhabits a lake, Khaltso, high above the village. In the untitled manuscript commemorating the temple founding, the opening passage reads,

> In Jambudvipa the southern of the cosmos's four continents,
> The snow land of Tibet is the center where righteous dharma flourishes,
> At its foothills is the place called Nubri Kutang,
> Where many accomplished spiritual practitioners thrive,
> And a place called Auspicious Trok, where everyone desires to reside.
> There, all the elders duly practice the way of the ten virtues,
> And all the youths are well mannered,
> The medicinal mother lake provides all of nature's bounties,
> Young maidens bloom like flowers and are adept in music and dance,
> Children revel in joyous play like little demigods,
> To be born in such a place is the accumulation of many karmic deeds.[20]

The passage locates Trok in a nested spatial relationship that starts with Jambudvipa, the southern of the four continents in Buddhist cosmology, then the Tibetan Plateau, where Buddhism thrives, and finally Nubri and Kutang at the edge of the plateau. With this passage, the people of Trok characterize themselves as virtuous practitioners of Buddhism and mark themselves as belonging to the Tibetan cultural world.

The successive migrations of lamas from prestigious lineages helped establish not just Buddhist teachings and practices in Nubri, but also a cultural alignment with Tibet. The religious links resulted in two-way traffic between Nubri and the Tibetan Plateau. Yogins and treasure discoverers came to Nubri seeking disciples and meditation retreats, while practitioners from Nubri ventured to the seats of learning in Tibet to receive instructions and initiations. By the nineteenth century (if not earlier) the people of Nubri viewed their homeland as part of the greater Tibetan cultural world, not as a peripheral region of darkness.

CONQUEST AND INDIRECT RULE

In the 1720s a new power rose to the south of Nubri as the rulers of Gorkha commenced a series of conquests. In 1768 the Gorkha king Prithvi Narayan Shah captured Kathmandu, thereby establishing the Kingdom of Nepal. His successors then pushed the borders of Nepal toward Sikkim in the east and the Sutlej River in the west (Stiller 1975; Pradhan 1991). During a war with Tibet from 1788 to 1792 Nepal's territorial control may have encompassed Nubri for a brief period when Dzonga was occupied and sacked (Stiller 1975:192–214; Shakabpa 1984:158–69). However, a joint Manchu-Tibetan expedition pushed Nepal's army back to Kathmandu in 1792 and reestablished the former border.

Nubri eventually became part of Nepal when, in 1855, Jang Bahadur Shah captured large swaths of Tibet, including Dzonga (Rose 1971:108–16; Shakabpa 1984:181–82; Sever 1993:88–91). After a peace accord with Tibet in 1856, Jang Bahadur relinquished control over most of the occupied territories, but not his long-standing defense objective to secure territory up to the high Himalayan passes (Sever 1993:89). Since 1856 Nubri has been part of Nepal.

A geneaological legacy of the political realignment is still evident. When asked to name their gyüpa (patrilineal descent group), members of several families in Nubri respond "Thakuri." To hear this answer from people dressed in Tibetan clothing and speaking a Tibetan dialect seems surprising, because Thakuri consider themselves descendants of Rajput warriors who fled Muslim invasions in India to hill regions of Nepal in the twelfth century.[21] How, then, did Thakuris end up in Nubri?

After incorporating Nubri into the Kingdom of Nepal, the royal court dispatched a *subba* (an officer representing the king) to the valley to collect taxes and arbitrate disputes on behalf of the new overlords (see Stiller 1975:65–66). In this case the subba was a Thakuri named Beka Ram, and his appointment was in line with policies that facilitated the absorption of far-flung populations during the expansion of Gorkha's domains. Stiller describes the Gorkha pattern of rule in the following terms: "Decentralization was a major part of the Gorkhali structure of government. It allowed a high degree of flexibility; it allowed local authorities to tamper with their rule to the needs of time and place; and it allowed local people, who had always found their government close-by, to identify more easily with the conquering Gorkhalis than would have been the case if the government were conceived in terms of a more distant seat of authority" (1975:264–65).[22]

The rationale behind sending a man of Thakuri origin to govern Nubri is probably rooted in his ability to navigate cultural boundaries. In western Nepal Thakuris have long lived in close proximity to and exerted some authority over their Tibetan neighbors (Fürer-Haimendorf 1975:276–77). Fürer-Haimendorf notes that linguistic and cultural familiarity with Tibetans and the landscapes they occupied was invaluable for Gorkha forces during westward conquests. Leaders granted the right to collect taxes and custom duties to some Thakuris who spied for and fought beside the Gorkha army (1975:277–78).

According to Amji Dorje, a son of the last subba, his ancestors once lived southeast of Nubri in Dhading. During the Gorkha expansion one or more members of the family were dispatched to Khunu, the local name for Kinnaur in the upper stretch of India's Sutlej River. Henceforth, the family became known as Khunu Thakuri. For a brief period, from 1805 to 1815, Khunu fell under Gorkha control but was quickly lost to British India. Nobody knows how long Nubri's Thakuri ancestors stayed in Khunu. However, Amji Dorje recalls, "There is this Khunu lama, a very high lama, who was in Kathmandu. We went to seek his blessing, but he is so well known and respected that it was not easy to meet him. When some lamas informed him that there is a Khunu Thakuri family living in Nubri, he told them that his family moved into our house in Khunu after we left."

The lama in question is most probably Khunu Lama Tenzin Gyaltsen, a Buddhist master who was born in Sunam village, Kinnaur in late 1894 or early 1895 and died in 1977. Khunu Lama was in Kathmandu in the mid-1970s, which is the time when the meeting described above took place.[23]

From the evidence, we surmise that, perhaps around 1805, Nubri's Thakuri ancestors were sent to Khunu in an administrative capacity. The Kingdom of Nepal lost control over Khunu in 1815, so it is unclear how long or in what position they remained, but certainly the connection was enduring enough for the family to still refer to themselves as Khunu Thakuri. What is certain is that Beka Ram was deployed to Nubri after the valley was incorporated into the Kingdom of Nepal in 1856. He arrived during the reign of Jang Bahadur, the prime minister of Nepal from 1850 to 1877. The oldest administrative documents in the subba archive still preserved in Trok date to the 1860s.

Beka Ram established his headquarters in the village of Namdru. A cluster of houses still stands there today, including the subba's residence, storehouses, and a courthouse with attached jail. The buildings are arranged around a rectangular courtyard that is accessible only through two gated entrances. Nearby, Namdru's residents point to a large boulder upon which they claim the subba and his retinue conducted Hindu rituals. From Namdru, Beka Ram ruled over "five clusters of hamlets" (Tib: *yultso nga*; Nep: *pancha gaon*): upper Nubri (from Namdru to the Tibetan border), lower Nubri (from Namdru to the confluence of the Nubri and Tsum valleys), Jagat (the area just south of the confluence), lower Tsum (from Lhokpa to the hill leading to Chökhang), and upper Tsum (from Chökhang to the Tibetan border).

The size of Beka Ram's entourage is unknown. His descendants believe that he came with three others, but that he was unmarried and subsequently took a local wife. Technically speaking, commensal relationships between high-ranking Thakuris and Nubri's residents are problematic because the latter are considered *bhotey* (Tibetan) and therefore receive the lowly classification of "enslaveable alcohol drinkers" *(māsinyā matwāli)* in Nepal's legal code.[24] As specified in the 1836 Muluki Ain, a Thakuri man can accept water but not food from a Tibetan woman unless it is neutralized with oil or butter. More problematic, sexual intercourse with a Tibetan woman incurs a legal penalty (Höfer 1979:22, 41–42). Regardless of such barriers, and perhaps a reflection of long-standing familiarity with Tibetans through co-residence in Khunu, the Thakuris quickly assimilated to Nubri society. After Beka Ram's son Sala Ram, all subsequent successors have Tibetan names (e.g., Tsangpa, Tsering Yungdrung, and Tsewang Norbu). Today one cannot easily distinguish Thakuris from other Nubri residents because they wear local clothing, speak the local vernacular, and practice Buddhism. The only relic of their Hindu past is a reluctance to consume beef.[25]

CONTINUITY AMID POLITICAL CHANGE

Today, as in the past, Nubri operates under a three-dimensioned legal system consisting of the golden yoke of *gyaltrim* (royal or national law), the iron ring of *yultrim* (village law), and the silken knot of *chötrim* (religious law).[26] The latter two apply locally and can be adjusted according to circumstances, for, as one leader explained, an iron ring is malleable and a silken knot can be tightened or loosened. In chapter 3 we discuss how yultrim and chötrim operate in conjunction to regulate religious life. Here, we deal with the convergence of yultrim and gyaltrim to show how Beka Ram and his successors respected local traditions while overseeing legal matters.

Gyaltrim is imposed by the polity under which Nubri falls at any point in time. Since 1856 the people of Nubri, via the subba, demonstrated their loyalty to the Kingdom of Nepal by paying taxes. In the meantime, the subbas conducted many legal proceedings using preexisting yultrim principles, as evidenced by an archive preserved by the descendants of Nubri's last subba. Documents written in Nepali script pertain mainly to tax and tribute. Documents written in Tibetan script, by contrast, include scores of obligation contracts *(gengya)* that deal with village-level legal issues. For example, one gengya is a petition by a migrant from Tibet, named Gowa Sonam, to become a taxpaying subject of Nubri.[27] Written in cursive script on a single sheet of paper and bearing the seals of several individuals, including Gowa Sonam, it reads,

> 7th day of the 9th month of the Wood Ox Year [1865].[28] In the presence of the precious magistrate, leader of the two systems [secular and religious],[29] we, whose names and seals are affixed below, voluntarily accept this obligation contract without any changes. Basis of the legal act: We, Nubri Khampas, formerly tax payers under Dzonga [District in Tibet], have moved permanently here. Consequently, we seek the protection of the leaders and followers of Nubri with the request that we are all accepted as taxpayers of Nubri. If the leaders and commoners do not accept us as legal subjects, we face the risk of belonging nowhere and receiving no protection. From this day onward, we make the request that all of us be treated equally like other subjects *[miser]* [of Nubri]. We make the earnest plea that we will not engage in any behavior whatsoever unbecoming of a subject. In the case of even a bit of unbecoming behavior against the above written agreement, the concerned authorities can take any befitting actions and we will fully obey with whatever is decided. With sincere motivation, we swear that there will be no new claims, denials, disagreements over any order, disputes, or rebellion. In the case of going against the above written agreement, five gold coins will be offered as a fine to the concerned authority. [This document is] affixed with the seals of Gowa Sonam, Dadul, Tsering Dawa, Pasang Tsering, Dorje, Dawa Tsering, Sinon,

Karma, Tsetan, Namkha, Khampa Kunchok, Dadul, Lhakpa Tsering, Sithar, Lobsang, and Segog.[30]

Because the petition was made in 1865 we can assume that Gowa Sonam and his entourage migrated to Nubri around that time. Members of his lineage are now dispersed throughout the valley, own land, and are full members of their communities, so it is clear that the subba accepted the request and formalized Gowa Sonam's status as a legal subject. What remains unknown is the precise place from where Gowa Sonam migrated, and why. We know he was formerly a subject of Dzonga, the district Nubri belonged to until 1856. To ascertain his reason for fleeing, we visited Ngawang, a knowledgeable descendant of Gowa Sonam. While his wife Sonam Chödron served us tea, Ngawang explained, "We come from Tibet. Our gyüpa is named after a person, Sonam. In Tibet they called him a gowa [headman], whereas here we would call him a pönpo [lord]. Our gyüpa is considered high status in Nubri. Our ancestors challenged the government in Tibet, which is why we were chased out." Sonam Chödron retorted, "You guys aren't smart, that's why you were chased from Tibet!" She nearly spilled tea on the floor as she broke out in laughter. Ngawang continued, "The fight with the government happened because of water. We irrigate by rotation, but our people are stubborn. When it was someone else's turn to irrigate, we took their water; that is the root cause of the fight with the government. In any event our ancestor Sonam first settled in Lö. His descendants spread out from there."

The obligation contract shows that Gowa Sonam and his entourage underwent a formal legal procedure to become subjects of Nubri. The format of this document is not a local innovation, but is based on a Tibetan template that is still used to this day. The opening line includes a reference to a magistrate who represents the merging of religious and secular rule, a distinctly Tibetan convention. Consistent with the flexible policies Nepal's rulers permitted under indirect rule in far-flung parts of the kingdom, the subba did not impose an alien legal system. Rather, he allowed the existing and familiar system to continue.

To further illustrate continuity between past and present practices, we compared a recent land sale document with a transaction from 1929 when the subba was in charge of Nubri. The older document reads as follows.[31]

The 3rd day of the 9th month of the Earth Snake year [1929]. In the presence of the precious magistrate, leader of the two systems [secular and religious],

we, whose names and seals are affixed below, voluntarily accept this obligation contract without any changes. Basis of the legal act: Rigzin Wangdak of
Lö sold a plot of his land measuring 4 dey [a unit of measurement] near Trok
Perang to Sonam Tsering of Namdru. The price of the land has been fully
paid. To the above agreed-upon matter, the undersigned parties swear that
there will be no denials, coming up with new claims, or shifting from right
to left [shifting responsibility]. In the case of even an iota of such useless talk
of new claims by anyone, it is fully agreed that three gold coins will be
offered as penalty to the honorable magistrate. Affixed with the seals of peti-
tioner Rigzin Wangdak, guarantor Miser Dorje Gyaltsen, mediators Gowa
Kunsang Dorje and Tsering Dorje, witnesses Kargyu Tenzin of Lö and Sonam
Phunstok of Namdru and the document's drafter Ngawang of Rö.[32]

When we asked a village leader to explain how a land transaction
works today, he said that it is administered by three men, a *gowa* (headman) and two *miser*.[33] He explained that the buying and selling parties
each offer a bottle of arak (locally distilled beverage), a *khata* (ceremo-
nial scarf), and a small fee to the gowa, who then calls the miser to a
meeting. Together they compose the obligation contract. Just like the
earlier document, a recent land transaction record begins with the standard inscription and introduction protocol, and then records the name
of the plot of land, the names of the buyer and seller, and the agreed
price.[34] The two parties as well as two witnesses sign the document and
give a small payment of cash and alcohol to the village leader, who
affixes his seal. According to the leader, "Henceforth, until the snow
melts from the mountains and the water dries in the lakes, nothing can
be said about that land. Once the document is signed, it is final and
there is no need for a Nepali government land deed or any other legal
document. No one can question this written contract even if a smart or
wise son later believes that his dumb father was duped into signing it.
We continue the practice of making written contracts for every land
deal because, in the village, we still abide by yultrim."

To this day, local leaders consider yultrim to have higher authority
than national law in deciding internal village matters. Like other highland communities in Nepal (Steinmann 1991; Ramble 2008), geographic remoteness helped Nubri's leaders maintain a distinct manner
of settling legal matters even after coming under Nepal's jurisdiction.

CONTEMPORARY CONVULSIONS

Indirect rule via the subba remained intact for a century but then
changed with the inception of Nepal's Panchayat system in the early

FIGURE 3. Nubri's last subba Tsewang Norbu (left) and his son Amji Dorje (right). Photo to left by unknown. Photo to right by Geoff Childs.

1960s after a brief flirtation with parliamentary democracy (Burghart 1994). The new system changed the way that villagers interacted politically with the district and national governments. Nubri was divided into four *panchayats*, administrative units in which people could elect their own representatives. At first Beka Ram's descendent Tsewang Norbu held the leadership position in his panchayat, but not for long. Tsewang Norbu's son, who displays a portrait of his father near the family altar, explained,

> During my father's time, we were a respected family because my father was the headman. He was known as Lord [pönpo] Tsewang Norbu. Later, the panchayat system came into existence. My father was very good in litigation and very good with words. He could speak his way through anything. But he didn't know the Nepali language. The ability to speak Nepali was essential since panchayat representatives occasionally need to go to Gorkha [the district capital]. He couldn't keep hold of the leadership position. He let it go and took to drinking. His drinking habit stuck with him—he got drunk day and night. The culture of drinking that we have in our community got the better of him. My father died young.

Ironically, a man of Thakuri descent was so assimilated into Nubri society that he was ill-prepared to adapt to Nepal's new political realities.

The Panchayat system lasted roughly three decades and came to a dramatic close with the onset of the 1990 democracy movement that ushered in a multiparty system and curtailed the power of Nepal's king. Local-level administrative divisions were rebranded Village Development Committees (VDC; *gāun bikās samite* in Nepali), a reflection of Nepal's national discourse centering on development *(bikās)*. The multiparty system permitted locals to elect a chairman and second-in-command to act as liaisons between the VDC and the district-level government. The first election in Nubri was held in 1995, and relatively young men who had traveled widely and spoke Nepali won at most ballots. After a prolonged period of instability during a bloody "People's War" launched by Maoists, Nepal's legislators ratified a new constitution in 2015 and once again opened the door for local elections in 2017.

In summary, the 1856 border realignment that brought Nubri into the domain of the Kingdom of Nepal did not have an immediate affect on Nubri residents' cultural orientation. The valley remained difficult to access from the south, and indirect rule through the subba not only limited contact with central authorities but was also flexible enough to permit continuity with past administrative norms. Religious practitioners continued to travel to Tibet for teachings, and Tibetans like Gowa Sonam continued to migrate into Nubri. However, another momentous, pivotal shift occurred in 1959 with an upheaval in Tibet, including a wholesale assault on religious institutions, which resulted in the exodus of Tibetan lamas and thousands of laypeople. Nubri's cultural and political orientations henceforth converged as many of the exiles settled in Kathmandu, resurrected monasteries, and built a secular school system. We will explore the nexus of connections between Nubri and Tibetan exile institutions and the associated opportunities for education in chapter 4. Next, we examime village administrative practices to show how households and their members are bound together in a community, and how these practices are related to the outmigration phenomenon.

CHAPTER 3

Embedding the Household in the Village

RITUALS OF PROTECTION

Dargye ascended to his father's former position as *kyimdag* (head of household) after his recent marriage. Henceforth, until he passes the status to a son who has yet to be born, he will shoulder the burden of leading a *drongchen* (large household). On this crisp morning he performs a vital function for the first time. Dargye is attired in a wide-brimmed hat wrapped with a white scarf and a black woolen garment cinched at the waist by a simple woven belt. While circumambulating a small pile of burning juniper branches in his courtyard, he chants a prayer and tosses grain offerings into the air. By performing the *lhabsang* (smoke purification) ceremony he invites a protector deity to descend the cord of smoke to his home.[1] Dargye then climbs a ladder to his roof-top. He grasps a slender pine sapling with all its branches removed except a scraggly cluster at the top, to which he has tied a white flag imprinted with the image of the *lungta* (wind horse). After inserting the flagpole into a hole in the roof, Dargye steps back and recites from a text the following verses:[2]

> Kye! Kye! By planting the flagpole in the earth, may wealth cover our land and house.
> By planting the flagpole in the snow, may our people's faces become white as snow.
> By planting the flagpole in the water, may our descent lineage become long like the river.

By planting the flagpole in the fire, may our fortune burn bright like the flame.
By planting the flagpole in the wind, may our reputation spread like the wind.
By planting the flagpole in the rocks, may our life force become as firm as a rock.
By planting the flagpole in the meadow, may our people and our wealth multiply like the grass in the meadow.
To the eight classes of deities and spirits, and to the assembly of spirits of the earth,
By not committing even a single injurious act, and by setting our minds to spiritual deeds,
May our life, fortune, wealth, fame, authority, possessions, and power rise like the waxing moon.
May there be auspicious good fortune everywhere. Ki! Ki! Glory to the gods![3]

After completing the chant, Dargye climbs down to the courtyard. He has fulfilled a worldly householder's most basic duty: to entreat the assistance of spiritual forces so they can ensure health, wealth, and well-being for his family. A wide grin testifies to his elation at assuming the leadership position of his household, while the shallow crevices on his youthful forehead are a harbinger of the incessant worries and burdens his new status entails. As kyimdag, he is responsible for managing the inner workings of the household by delegating daily chores, deploying assets, and influencing who stays and who moves out of the household—something that is especially relevant in today's context of educational migration. He has also entered a contract with his village's administration that entails debt, annual interest payments, and an array of duties connected with the ritual cycle. With elevated status comes enormous responsibility. Some men thrive and improve their family's standard of living. Others buckle under the pressure and endure chronic poverty.

This chapter focuses on Trok, a village renowned for its thriving cultural life and—like all villages in the valley—a high rate of outmigration among youths. The purpose is to describe how Nubri residents use economic and cultural practices to forge a community out of individual households. We begin by justifying our preference for using an emic definition of the household rather than the demographers' standardized version. Simply put, the latter cannot be reconciled with realities on the ground. Afterward, we detail how *yultrim* (village law) and *chötrim* (religious law) work together through a loan and repayment system to generate funds for communal rites that are designed to benefit all community members. The chapter concludes by linking men's village-refined religious skills with their seasonal migration. Moving to Kathmandu during the winter in order to parlay liturgical skills into income allows men to forge long-distant ties with Nepal's broader Buddhist community. This chapter begins to explore rural-urban links via Buddhist social networks that facilitate educational migration, and foreshadows household succession conundrums that inevitably arise when young people are no longer raised and enculturated within their natal villages.

THE HOUSEHOLD IN DEMOGRAPHY, ANTHROPOLOGY, AND NUBRI

The household continues to be an important unit of analysis in anthropology, yet it is not always carefully defined (Chibnik 2011:134). Here we avoid that pitfall by delineating the household in local terms and describing how households are bound together through economic endeavors that support cultural activities. We use Trok as a case study because its administrative and religious systems remain robust and therefore can illustrate principles that are common throughout Nubri. The purpose is to present an emic perspective on the household that is critical for understanding the dynamics of migration decision-making and the dilemmas educational migration engenders for the long-term continuity of households and communities.

Every household *(drongba)* in Trok is classified according to its composition and assets. The most economically productive households typically consist of a married couple, their children, and perhaps a member or two of the senior generation. Categorized as *drongchen* (large household), they constitute the bedrock of the community whose members provide the bulk of capital and labor to support rituals and other communal endeavors.

The drongchen is led by a *kyimdak* (household head) who acts as the household's representative in most economic, political, and legal matters within the village. Kyimdag succession ideally passes from father to eldest son, but can pass to a younger son when circumstances warrant. Partible inheritance means that parents must devise an orderly transfer of property that avoids dividing an estate to the point that sons are left with insufficient resources. One option is to make a son a monk and thereby reduce the possibility that he will marry and lay claim to household property. Another option is fraternal polyandry, a marital practice common in many Tibetan societies whereby brothers take a common wife (Goldstein 1976; Schuler 1987; Levine 1988). Fraternal polyandry reduces partitioning by keeping sons together in one household under the leadership of the elder brother who acts as kyimdag.

An orderly kyimdag succession generally starts with a son's patrilocal marriage, which signals that the time to form separate households is near. The father (or mother if she is a widow) bequeaths most assets to a married son and passes the kyimdag responsibility. Henceforth the son occupies the drongchen and his aging parents can either continue living with him or live independently, in which case they are reclassified as *porang morang* (single man and single woman). Porang morang households still contribute to village social and economic affairs, but at a reduced level. Although classified separately for taxation purposes, the drongchen and porang morang share resources and labor. For example, a son usually helps his aging parents till their fields while they babysit his children. The only other household classification is *pochö* (male religious practitioner), a name that implies a dwelling consisting of a solitary person.[4]

At the village level, households are tracked and taxed under the authority of yultrim (local law). Every three years leaders conduct a *lebngö* (household review) to record the number of residents, land holdings, and cattle in each household. They also note changes since the last review, including additions through births and marriage, subtractions through death and household fission, and the creation of new households. The resulting *zhibzhung* (main or detailed register, also called *mayig* or the "mother document") is the basis for determining each household's annual tax payment to the village coffer.

Village leaders in Trok allowed us to photograph a register titled "Male Earth Tiger Year [2010] Household Review, the Mother Document."[5] The document first lists all the drongchen households by division within the village.[6] The name of each household head is entered followed by his landholding (recorded in *dey*, the common Tibetan unit of land measurement), the number of household members, female cattle, and horses.[7] Household membership is determined on a de jure basis and therefore includes people who may not actually live in the village, such as daughters and sons in boarding schools or monasteries. Subsequent pages of the 2010 mother document record the same information for porang morang and pochö households. Table 1 summarizes data recorded in the document.

The household register is the basis for an annual tax calculated on the basis of members and female cattle.[8] The tax remains the same until the next review is conducted in three years regardless of changes in

TABLE 1. SUMMARY OF TROK'S HOUSEHOLDS BY CLASSIFICATION

Classification (n)	People (range)	Land Units (range)	Female Cattle (range)
Drongchen (39)	6.3 (3–12)	60.4 (10–135)	5.1 (1–14)
Porang Morang (18)	3.7 (1–9)	33.4 (6–93)	2.6 (1–6)
Pochö (9)*	1.7 (1–9)	8.0 (0–17)	1.2 (0–5)
Total (64)	5.0 (1–12)	45.9 (0–135)	3.8 (0–14)

*All but one pochö household had a single member. The anomalous household had nine members but did not possess any land or cattle.

assets or household composition. Although the sum for each household is nominal—usually a few rupees and a small amount of grain—it is symbolically meaningful because payment signals village membership, which comes with the right to access common resources (mainly forests and pastures) and to participate in rituals.

The household registration system has been in place for a while as verified by a manuscript from the village of Gyayul that was likely drafted prior to 1950.[9] In the "Document Containing a Proper Tax Assessment of Gyayul"[10] each household has a separate entry that first identifies the household head, states the number of houses he owns, and then enumerates residents and landholdings before concluding with the tax assessment. For example, "Rigzin Wangdu. One house, five people, forty-six units of land. Eight coins, six measures of grain."[11]

Gyayul's assessment equation includes household members, but unlike Trok it uses land units rather than bovines. Gyayul's old register enumerates 42 households populated by 174 residents who paid 130 measures of grain and 238 coins to the village treasury.

In May 2016 we were granted permission to photograph Gyayul's most recent register, which had been completed two weeks before our arrival. The document is kept in a box made of woven bamboo and sealed with white scarves. As a condition for opening it, we made a formal petition to village leaders by presenting them with a standard fee of two bottles of arak. They opened the container and removed the most recent register, which lay on top of all previous versions. The format is precisely the same as the pre-1950 document.

Table 2 reveals that, although the number of households has remained constant, Gyayul's population and average household size has risen. However, the number of full-time residents is probably about the same considering that most youths now live in educational institutions outside of the village. Demographic trends help explain why the amount

TABLE 2. COMPARISON OF THE TWO HOUSEHOLD REGISTERS, GYAYUL PRE-1950 AND 2016

	Households	People	HH Size	Land (dey)	Land/ HH	Tax (coins)	Tax (grain)
Old (pre-1950)	44	174	4.0	1,444	32.8	238	131
New (2016)	44	248	5.6	1,215	27.6	265	163

of coin and grain tax have risen by 11 percent and 24 percent respectively (a reflection of the de jure population increase) while units of land under cultivation have declined by 16 percent (a reflection of the diminishing labor force).

The household registration system is based on a Tibetan template and is undoubtedly a residue from before 1856 when Nubri was under a Tibetan administration.[12] Similarities include the fact that the household register is referred to by the same term (*zhibzhung*, land settlement), is compiled every third year, and is the basis for determining a household's tax obligations. A difference is that the system is now localized and exists independent from higher levels of political authority. A system that was implemented in Nubri by a Tibetan administration to extract state revenue has evolved into one that is used to fund village-level endeavors.

Nubri's enduring registration system is a compelling reason to avoid standardized definitions of the household. To wit, demographic research requires rigid, consistent definitions of variables to facilitate statistical analysis and comparisons across space and time. The United Nations Population Division (UNPD), which sets the standard for much of the world's demographic research, defines a multiperson household as "a group of two or more persons living together who make common provision for food or other essentials for living. The persons in the group may pool their incomes and have a common budget to a greater or lesser extent; they may be related or unrelated persons or a combination of persons both related and unrelated."

A household can consist of more than one family or it can be composed entirely of nonrelatives. The main elements of the definition are common residence and economic cooperation. As for family, the UNPD defines it as "those members of the household who are related, to a specified degree, through blood, adoption or marriage."[13] The main difference is that family members, but not household members, must be related. Household and family describe the exact same social unit when all those who share a residence are related. In other cases the family can be a subset of the household only if some people living under the same roof are related through birth, marriage, or adoption.

We concur with anthropologists who question the utility of applying a universal definition of the household in ethnographic research (Hammel 1984; Wilk 1989; Fricke 1994; Sanjek 1996; Chibnik 2011).[14] If we tried to adopt the demographers' definition, our analysis would suffer because it is incongruent with the way that people in Nubri categorize and think about domestic units. Children living in monasteries, boarding schools, or elsewhere away from home do not co-reside with their parents or "make common provision for food or other essentials for living." Thus they would not belong to the same household (or family, for that matter) as their parents. However, parents consider educational migrants to be members of their household who, albeit currently absent, may one day return to inherit property and perpetuate the family or remain away yet contribute financially through remittances. Village administrators also count educational migrants as members of their parents' households until customary processes relieve them of that status.[15] We therefore follow Wilk and Miller's lead of being more open to and realistic about household membership flexibility (1997). According to Wilk and Miller's categories, a typical household in Nubri consists of full-time residents (those who sleep there regularly and contribute labor and income to the domestic fund) and absent members (those who live elsewhere but retain the right to return). By using emic concepts we diminish the ability to engage in comparative analysis in order to avoid applying a template that is at odds with the actual situation.

BINDING HOUSEHOLDS THROUGH RELIGIOUS COOPERATION

Individual households are amalgamated into a community through a system in which yultrim and chötrim work in tandem to generate revenue that supports an annual cycle of fifteen Buddhist rites held in Trok's five communal temples *(gomba)*.[16] To accomplish this objective, a representative from each household is assigned to either yultrim or chötrim duties. The former manage the villages' secular affairs, including the household registration system described above, while the latter supervise religious undertakings. A household's obligations can shift between the two, as one man explained: "I represent one of the nine chötrim households. Previously I was serving yultrim, but one of the nine members of the chötrim passed away. I was nominated to fill the vacancy. It is the law of the gomba that once you are nominated for chötrim membership, you cannot back down from it. If one of the members passes away, his replacement should be arranged on that same day. Once nominated, you cannot shirk the duty; it is written in the regulations of the gomba."[17]

Trok's ritual cycle is funded through two primary means: the sharecropping of gomba lands and an obligatory loan and interest system between the gomba (lender) and each household (borrower). Gomba, which is often glossed as "monastery," refers to the collective of Trok's five communal temples. Gomba landholdings have increased over the years through bestowals by people who do not have offspring or who wish to gain merit. Most village households farm at least some of these fields on a sharecropping basis. Poorer households with less privately-owned land tend to farm more gomba fields.

Village administrators manage religious affairs with the help of a *beyig* (interest document) and *timcha* (formulation of rules) associated with each ritual. The former specifies the revenue sources through which a particular ritual is funded. The latter specifies how the funds are allocated. To illustrate how the system works, we start with a simple example. For the Fourth Day of the Sixth Month ritual, a celebration of the Buddha's first sermon, the beyig commences with a preamble praising the Buddha and then reads, "First, regarding the interest owed on [the loan of gomba] fields, 80 dey of grain must be repaid for the loan of the 10 dey Shakhang field, and 7 dey of grain must be repaid for the loan of the 6 dey Pangchug field. Regarding grain interest, drongchen households must repay 2 dey of grain for the 6 dey of grain loaned. Porang morang households must repay 1 dey of grain for the 3 dey of grain loaned. Pochö households must repay 3 phulu for the 1 dey and 3 phulu of grain loaned."[18]

Note that each gomba field has a name, a quantified area, and a specified amount of grain the sharecropper must remit each year. According to the beyig, whoever farms Shakhang field must hand over 80 dey of the harvested grain to the gomba. Any yield above 80 dey is for the household to keep, but if the yield is less than 80 dey, the household must make up the difference from other fields. The document also reveals that interest payments vary by field quality. Shakhang field is prime agricultural land close to the village, so the ratio is 8 dey of grain remitted for every dey of land planted. For the outlying Pangchug field, the ratio is 1.2 dey of grain for every dey planted. Proximity to the village is one of the main criteria for determining field quality. Closer

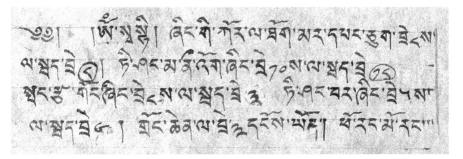

FIGURE 4. Page from a beyig (interest document).
Photo by Geoff Childs.

fields require less effort to haul loads back and forth, and are easier to defend against wayward cattle and marauding langurs and bears.

The grain interest referred to in the beyig is an annual repayment of a loan the gomba makes to each household. A household's classification, determined through the yultrim registration system, is the basis for assessing the amount of grain to be repaid each year. When a new drongchen forms, the kyimdag accepts a mandatory loan of 200 dey of grain from the gomba. The loan constitutes the principal on which the household is obliged to make an annual interest payment at a rate of one-third the initial loan. Thus, every year until its demise or dissolution the drongchen household is obligated to repay 66 and 2/3 dey of grain (roughly 80 pounds). The beyig specify how much of the annual repayment is allotted to each ritual.

A son who ascends to the kyimdag position inherits his father's debt and continues to pay the same annual interest fee. Meanwhile, his father and/or mother are reclassified as porang morang. They take a new loan of 100 dey (half that of a drongchen) that also entails an annual interest payment of one-third the principle. Pochö households, the poorest, take an initial loan of only 50 dey. Once a person turns seventy he returns the principal to the gomba and is henceforth exempt from any further duties or interest payments.[19]

The beyig allows us to calculate how much funding for the Fourth Day of the Sixth Month ritual comes from each income source. Table 3 shows that 109.5 dey (55.7 percent) is procured via household interest payments and 87 dey (44.3 percent) from the two fields.

Meanwhile, in the *timcha* (formulation of rules) document it is written, "On the fourth day of the sixth month, three ritual feasts and three measures of butter [for butter lamps] shall be offered. Eight dey of corn

TABLE 3. SOURCES OF FUNDING FOR TROK'S FOURTH DAY OF THE SIXTH
MONTH RITUAL

Source	Amount (dey)	# of HHs	Subtotal (dey)	% of Total
Drongchen	2	39	78	39.7
Porang Morang	1	18	18	9.2
Pochö	1.5	9	13.5	6.9
Loan Repayment Subtotal			109.5	55.7
Shakhang Field	80	1	80	40.7
Pangchug Field	7	1	7	3.6
Field Subtotal			87	44.3
TOTAL			196.5	100.0

are required for making *torma* offerings, and 1 dey of corn for the recitation of the hundred thousand verses.[20] Four rolls of molasses and one vessel of *chang* [fermented beverage] are also required."[21]

While the beyig specifies grain procurement, the timcha provides a general guideline for how it should be used. It is up to the chötrim and his assistants to convert some of the grain into alcohol and food for the ritual participants, and to acquire butter, molasses, and other substances required for the ceremony.

The two most elaborate rituals of the year are the annual reading of the Kanjur during the third month, and Dumje during the tenth month.[22] The Kanjur interest document begins with a brief invocation and then lists thirty-five fields with 265.5 dey of arable land from which 1,006 dey of grain interest is to be procured. The interest payments for several fields listed in the document have been circled, signaling that those are no longer cultivated. Eliminating fallow fields from the equation reduces the totals to 957 dey of interest owed on 234.5 dey of land. Drongchen, porang morang, and pochö households each owe 45, 22.5, and 12 dey of grain respectively.

The Dumje interest document lists twenty-three fields with 172 dey of arable land on which 490 dey of grain interest are owed. Those totals also drop to 449 dey of grain owed on 153 dey of land after subtracting fields that are no longer cultivated. In addition, the document specifies that 3 dey of grain are owed for using a particular pasture, 15 dey for each of the two water mills closest to the village, and 12 dey for a mill that is farther away and difficult to access.[23] Meanwhile drongchen, porang morang, and pochö households owe 2 dey, 1 dey, and 3 phulu on their loans. The total procurement for each ritual is listed in table 4.

TABLE 4. SOURCES OF FUNDING FOR TROK'S KANJUR AND DUMJE RITUALS

	Kanjur			Dumje		
Source (# of households)	dey/HH	Total	Percent	dey/HH	Total	Percent
Drongchen (n=39)	45	1,755	54.4	2	109	13.2
Porang Morang (n=18)	22.5	405	12.5	1	18	3.0
Pochö (n=9)	12	108	3.3	0.5	5	0.8
HH Subtotal		2,268	70.3	—	131	17.0
Fields/Pasture		960	29.7	—	449	75.9
Water Mills		0	0.0	—	42	7.1
Land + Mills Subtotal		960	29.7	—	491	83.0
TOTAL		3,228	100.0	—	622	100.0

Two significant points emerge from the data in table 4. First, the funding requirement for the Kanjur reading is, by far, the highest of all annual rites. This is presumably because it takes many days to complete and involves numerous participants who must be fed and served arak several times a day. Second, the proportion of funding derived from each source differs by ritual. Even though the Kanjur procurement from fields is nearly twice that for Dumje, gomba lands only account for 30 percent of the total. Most Kanjur income is derived from interest payments from households. This is because 67 percent of a household's annual loan repayment is allocated to this ritual.[24] In contrast, Dumje is funded mainly through interest on fields, a pasture, and the water mills, which together constitute 83 percent of the total procurement.

Trok's system of economic obligations and religious observances has helped forge a sense of common identity and purpose among village residents. Prior to the onset of educational migration most households had, or could anticipate reproducing, a sufficient labor force to meet communal expectations. Nowadays, the costs and duties are overstretching some households, especially the poorer ones, because educational migration is depleting their labor forces. We will return to this topic in chapter 10.

LITURGY, INCOME, AND MOBILITY

We conclude this chapter with the winter activities of men whose services are in high demand in the broader Buddhist communities of Nepal. Trok's traditional administrative system, which incentivizes religious learning, has a derivative benefit: it enables spatial mobility and the expansion of social networks that, in turn, facilitate the outmigration of youths for religious and secular education.

In former times most Nubri households subsisted primarily on farming, herding, and trade. Nowadays socioeconomic variation between villages is widening due to income disparities. Unlike residents of the highest villages in the valley who earn cash from mountaineering, trekking, and trans-Himalayan trade, people in Trok are unable to capitalize on today's most lucrative economic niches.[25] Nevertheless, the men of the village are renowned for their skills in reciting Buddhist texts and performing religious rites and therefore are well positioned to earn money by conducting services in the homes of Kathmandu's Buddhist householders. They do so by engaging in a process akin to seasonal labor migration. During the winter months, when agricultural activities are at a lull, they undertake the long trek from the village to Kathmandu, establish a temporary residence, and seek patrons. They earn income by performing Buddhist rites for members of the Tibetan exile community as well as families who migrated from other highland regions in Nepal such as Solu-Khumbu, Yolmo, Manang, and Mustang. For some men, cash received through household religious services is the only way they keep their families above subsistence level. For others, the income makes them comparatively well-off in the village. According to our relative wealth survey, households that rank at the wealthier end of the spectrum typically possess a solid asset base of agricultural land and animals, as well as an adult male who earns income by performing Buddhist rituals.[26]

Several men explained how the seasonal migration works. Norsang said,

> Money is very scarce in this village, so I go to Kathmandu to read texts in order to get food for my family. I read texts for Tamang, Tibetan, and Nyeshang [Manang] householders. I go with friends in the twelfth month [January] and stay for two months. I leave my wife in the village because it is expensive [in Kathmandu] and I must fend for myself. I stay in someone's house, a person I know. I don't have to pay rent but do pay for my own food. We don't have a main patron [jindag]. We just go from one place to another and people call for us. Sometimes we go without anything for a week, other times only a day. Each of us gets 500 rupees per day plus food. We read various religious texts. Usually we can complete a reading in a day, but sometimes it takes one and a half days.

Kunga told us,

> I go to Kathmandu to perform *shabten* [prayer ceremony to promote long life, repel negative influences, or bring good fortune] and *tsok* [religious feast

offering].[27] I have no choice but to go in order to make a living. Although most of the patrons are Tibetan, I also perform religious services for Gurungs, Sherpas, and Nyeshangpa. My friends call me when they get invited to do prayers. Some of them are disrobed monks. Others did not go to monasteries but learned the rituals at home. In our tradition one of the sons should learn religion and perform the monthly ceremonies at the village monastery. So when they come down to Kathmandu, they go to perform rituals. The big rituals involve the recitation of all the twelve great volumes of Yum scriptures.[28] It takes many days, at the end of which we conduct an offering ceremony. We also propitiate deities through incense offerings, and sometimes we do *narak* [ceremony for a deceased person].

As for the honorarium *[kuyön]*, you cannot say exactly how much people will offer. Some rich families give less while some poor families give more. These days, because of inflation, no patron will give less than 500 rupees for a day of religious service. It all depends on the patron's generosity and devotion. There is a Buddhist saying, "If a patron makes the religious practitioner happy, the wishes of the patron will be fulfilled. If the religious practitioner does not perform the ritual properly, he will earn bad karma." This saying indicates that it is very important for the religious practitioner to devote the right dedication to prayers, which includes the wishes of the patrons and the benefit of all sentient beings, but does not include a wish for anything for oneself. If he devotes proper dedication, the wishes of patrons and everyone will be fulfilled. If he thinks only about his own share of the offerings, he will incur bad karma.

Norsang and Kunga both allude to the link between liturgical skills honed in the village's ritual cycle and the ability to earn seasonal income. A by-product of men's quest for cash earnings is that they become familiar with Nepal's broader Buddhist community, including the secular and religious educational facilities where many of their children now reside. Kunga is a poor man whose meager landholdings include two plots, both of which lie at considerable distance from the village. One of them is so small and far away that he no longer considers it worthwhile to cultivate. To make ends meet he spends two months each winter in Kathmandu reading texts in the homes of Buddhist patrons. Through the knowledge he obtained about urban institutions he has successively enrolled all five of his children in boarding schools. Kunga and his wife now inhabit an empty nest.

In this chapter we have described a village administrative system that unites households through communal obligations. Agricultural production is not just a matter of subsistence. Via the monastic loan and repayment system, farming supports monthly rituals that are the focal point of village social and cultural activities. Although rigorous, costly, and time consuming, the rituals are performed with devotion and enthusiasm.

They provide an opportunity for residents to cooperate in complex ritual performances and to prepare meals together in a shared kitchen rather than individually in their own homes. Men and women alike understand that rituals afford them an occasion to temporarily suspend the toil of daily routines and dedicate themselves to higher causes. The grander rites always conclude with an empowerment ceremony *(wang)* that draws every villager to the temple during the evening and that is followed by singing and dancing that lasts until dawn.

A household's full participation in village cultural life is predicated on the kyimdag having at least a modicum of religious training. In other words, education has been highly valued in Nubri society for a long time. This is why a father ensures that his designated heir spends time at the feet of a Buddhist practitioner learning to read, write, and perform rituals. Nubri's men have earned respect in Kathmandu's Buddhist communities by polishing their liturgical skills through an intensive ritual cycle. Seasonal migration to the city connects them to the monasteries and schools in the nation's capital that cater to Buddhist highlanders. Liturgical competency is therefore a factor in today's outmigration trend because it expands parents' social networks from the village to urban spaces. But mere exposure to the city is not enough to open the doors of educational institutions to Nubri's children, because admission is contingent on opportunities created by divergent demographic trends, a topic we explore in the next chapter.

CHAPTER 4

Whither the Young People?

PORTENTS OF A BARLEY HARVEST

Golden stalks of barley sway gently in the wind. The mountain air resonates with singing and chatter as work parties composed of six to ten people move methodically through each plot of land. The advance team of women and teenage girls deftly pluck the ears of barley with bamboo sticks. Men and teenage boys follow, methodically cutting the hay with their sickles. Children run about, chided by parents for getting in the way, or commanded to stack the hay so it can be carried back to the storage sheds. On the side of the field sits a cradle; a swaddled baby coos as its mother takes a break to feed her. An elderly couple descends a pathway, snaking through the fields from a cluster of houses above. As they empty the contents of a basket containing food and drink, men and women congregate for a lunch break. Animated discussions and flirtatious exchanges punctuate the meal in the field—social interactions that break the tedium of agricultural toil. (GC's field notes, Trok Village, May 1997)

The barley stands ready for harvesting, but there are few people in the fields. A middle-aged husband and wife work alone; all their children are in Kathmandu. Two sixty-year-old women, neighbors, move slowly and silently through the field plucking ears of barley. When the field is finished, they pull sickles from their belts, stoop, and begin cutting the hay. Jigme, a middle-aged father of five, works unaccompanied in his field. When I ask why he is alone, Jigme replies, "My wife is too sick to work today, and all my kids are away." Old Dorje sits cross-legged in a nearby field. Although he can barely walk, he is still able to cut a few stalks of hay before scooching forward to cut a few more. A few toddlers scamper about, but they are too young to be of any help. The barley harvest remains an essential task in the village. But the composition of the work crew is strikingly different than before. (GC's field notes, Trok Village, May 2016)

FIGURE 5. Threshing grain at harvest time.
Photo by Geoff Childs.

Comparing the annual barley harvest two decades apart provides a glimpse into how demographic processes are propelling social and economic transformations in Nubri. A scarcity of youths in villages like Trok means that it is now rare to witness robust work teams comprising people of all age groups. Elderly folks engaging in strenuous agricultural tasks—formerly an inconceivable notion—has become commonplace due to the diminishing labor force. Figure 6 brings some clarity to the situation by disaggregating Nubri's population into those who live at home and those who live elsewhere. Among the estimated de jure population of thirty-five hundred individuals, over one thousand (about 30 percent) live elsewhere (see appendix). Of particular significance is the fact that 74 percent of males and 72 percent of females aged ten to nineteen no longer reside with their parents.

In this chapter we analyze fertility and mortality trends to show how they relate to outmigration, the main driver of demographic change in Nubri today. We first situate educational migration in a broader political economic context, namely, the resettling of Tibetan exiles in Nepal and India who established the secular and religious institutions that many Nubri children now attend. Through the ensuing demographic analysis, we argue that population factors played a key role in prompting Tibetan institutions to seek new recruits from the highlands of

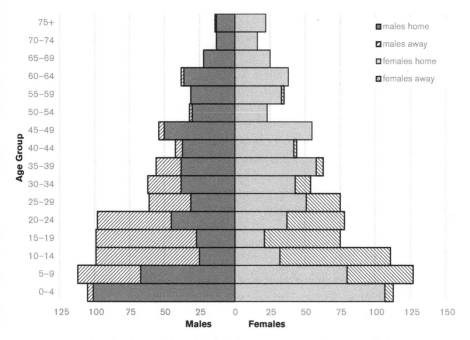

FIGURE 6. Age-Sex Composition of Nubri's Migrant and Nonmigrant Populations
Sources: Beall, Childs, and Craig 2012 Household Demographic Survey; Quinn and Childs 2013 Household Demographic Survey.

Nepal after the number of children in the exile communities dwindled. Due to the persistence of high fertility in Nubri, residents of the valley were well positioned to take advantage of the new opportunities.

TIBETAN EXILES AND THE EMERGENCE OF MIGRATION PULL FACTORS

In the early 1950s China reasserted control over Tibet. Following several tense years that included an open rebellion, Tibet's spiritual and political leader, the Dalai Lama, fled to India in 1959 with roughly 120,000 followers. China responded with policies that had a devastating cultural impact. Religious institutions were systematically defunded, depopulated, and destroyed (Avedon 1986; Goldstein 1998; Shakya 1999). Many high-ranking clerics sought exile in places where their religious traditions and lineages would not be threatened with extinction. Nepal, which shares a border with Tibet and has a long history of cultural and economic exchange, was one of their primary destinations. As refugees, they could not replicate the land tenure system that previously funded monasteries in Tibet (see Goldstein 1989:1–37). But as Klieger argues, Tibetans successfully invoked a traditional priest-patron relationship *(chöyön)* to generate economic support from foreigners (1992).

Over the next decades the Tibetan exiles, supported by the Dalai Lama and administered by the Tibetan government-in-exile, embarked on a project to create communities in India and Nepal that emphasized nationalism, the continuity of Buddhist teachings, and education (Goldstein 1978; Klieger 1992; Choedup 2015). The ambitious plan included the creation of a secular school system to provide universal education for exile children (Nowak 1984; Pema 2003; Rigzen 2003). Tibetan clerics were also remarkably successful at rebuilding monasteries. By the mid-1990s there were an estimated forty-five monasteries scattered about the Kathmandu Valley (Frechette 2004:111–12). Today there are even more.

For several decades, the secular and religious institutions served primarily Tibetan children born in exile, children whose parents smuggled them across the border from Tibet, and young people who escaped China in order to practice Buddhism beyond the state's suffocating scrutiny. Even though Nubri's residents have maintained close ties with Tibet and share religious, linguistic, and cultural affinity, they are not considered Tibetan in a political sense (i.e., from Tibetan areas located within China). This meant they were ineligible for admission to the Tibetan exiles' schools, as we discovered in 1998. Upon securing a scholarship for a boy from Nubri, we approached a school in Kathmandu and spoke with the headmaster. When he heard the boy's Tibetan name and learned that funding was in hand, he seemed enthusiastic to accept the child. But when we mentioned that the boy was from Nubri, he responded, "Nubri is in Nepal. He is not Tibetan." Admission denied—geopolitical criteria trumped ethnic affinity.

Eventually political and demographic processes constricted the supply of new recruits from Tibet and the Tibetan exile community. China increased border surveillance, and at the same time the exile communities were undergoing a rapid and sustained fertility decline from over six births per woman in the mid-1980s to less than two births per woman by 2000 (Childs et al. 2005). The supply of potential students further dwindled since the 1990s due to widespread emigration of Tibetans to Europe and North America (Choedup 2015). In the early 2000s the school that formerly denied entrance to students from the Himalayan region reversed course and opened its doors. By doing so, it followed the lead of private schools affiliated with monasteries or run by lay Tibetans that began accepting students from Nepal's highlands in the 1990s.

Monasteries faced a similar enrollment dilemma that started even earlier. In the 1970s one of the first institutions established in exile was already undergoing attrition, a situation that was reversed only with the influx of youths from Tibet once China relaxed the border (Lempert 2012:159). However, subsequent travel restriction for Tibetans in China, combined with the exiles' fertility decline and a preference to send their children to secular schools rather than monasteries, created a new recruitment problem. Today the majority of new recruits to Tibetan schools and monasteries come from the northern borderlands of Nepal, India, and Bhutan. Moran estimates that two-thirds of the monks in Kathmandu's monasteries are from Nepal's highlands (2004:61). In South India, Doeguling has the largest monastic population in exile, consisting of nine monasteries and one nunnery. Of the 5,048 monks and nuns, 2,468 (33 percent) are from the Himalayan region (Choedup 2015:99). At Sera, also in South India, only 3 percent of monks are from India (presumably from the Tibetan exile community). Of the 11 percent who are from Nepal, the majority came after 1998 (Lempert 2012:160). Monks from the Himalayan areas will soon constitute the majority in these monasteries because they comprise the bulk of the younger cohort.

Because Nubri lies within the boundaries of Nepal, the valley remains a Buddhist stronghold that now plays an important role in the pan-Tibetan cultural and religious revival. The readiness to admit students from Nepal's highlands has not gone unnoticed by parents. As one father of nine children ranging in age from two to thirty-five (from two wives) comments, "The situation was different in previous times when you couldn't find a lama and monastery willing to take your child. These days you can send your child to monasteries everywhere; the avenues have opened up." The avenues he refers to were paved by divergent demographic trends between Nubri's residents and Tibetan exiles.

THE DEMOGRAPHY OF SUPPLY AND DEMAND

In a dispassionate analysis, Livi-Bacci asserts that a society with high fertility and mortality like Nubri epitomizes demographic inefficiency: "From a demographic point of view, old regime societies were inefficient:

in order to maintain a low level of growth, a great deal of fuel (births) was needed and a huge amount of energy was wasted (deaths)" (1997:112). Since Notestein's (1953) classic formulation of demographic transition theory, modernization (i.e., industrialization, urbanization, and mass education) has occupied center stage as the driving force behind demographic change (Alter 1992:18–20). Some scholars view demographic transition as a triumph of reproductive rationality over fatalism (Tilly 1978; Cleland and Wilson 1987; Marston and Cleland 2003). However, one cannot simply attribute the persistence of high fertility and mortality in a society like Nubri to a lack of people's ability to make "rational" reproductive decisions, especially since an assemblage of social, cultural, political, and economic forces shapes fertility (Greenhalgh 1995). Nubri's marginal status in the national effort to deliver reproductive health services is evident when we consider that, for the country as a whole, the majority of Nepal's birth-control users obtain contraception through either government hospitals and health posts (79 percent in 1996, 69 percent in 2011) or private medical institutions (14 percent in 1996, 20 percent in 2011) (Pradhan et al. 1997; Ministry of Health and Population et al. 2012:99). In 1996 there were no health-care facilities whatsoever in Nubri, and in 2011 there were only a few recently established clinics run by nonprofit organizations. Not surprisingly, contraceptive usage in Nubri remains low. On average, Nubri women who used contraception started at age 31.9 after experiencing 4.9 pregnancies and having 4.0 living children. Current usage peaks at 35.6 percent of women between ages thirty-five and thirty-nine. Rates for all age groups fall well below the national average (see table 5).

Contraception raises moral dilemmas in Tibetan populations.[1] In the Tibetan Buddhist view on cyclical existence, a person's consciousness principle *(namshey)* moves from one bodily incarnation to the next by exiting the corpse shortly after death, transiting through an intermediary realm *(bardo),* and entering the womb of a new mother at the moment of conception. By interfering with the cycle of life, some feel that "using contraception may actually block a natural process of uniting a consciousness principle with its karmically-ordained mother through this 'closing of the womb door'" (Craig et al. 2016). One could argue that culture poses a barrier to Tibetan women's adoption of birth control. However, the men and women we interviewed in Nubri seem willing to circumvent such ethical considerations. For example, one middle-aged woman has experienced eight pregnancies—six live births

TABLE 5.   BIRTH CONTROL USAGE IN NUBRI AND NEPAL COMPARED

	Nubri 2012–2013		Nepal 2011
age	ever used	currently use	currently use
15–19	0.0	0.0	14.4
20–24	12.5	12.5	23.8
25–29	17.5	17.5	39.8
30–34	31.6	21.1	52.2
35–39	42.2	35.6	59.9
40–44	35.6	24.4	59.9
45–49	31.0	21.4	48.0

SOURCES: For Nubri Beall, Childs, and Craig 2012 Reproductive History Survey; Quinn and Childs 2013 Reproductive History Survey. For Nepal Ministry of Health and Population et al. 2012:95.

and two miscarriages. When we asked whether using birth control is considered unethical, she responded, "People say such things. But I have no such thoughts. In the past we could not control [reproduction] and had many children. If we did anything with birth control, people would call it sinful and look down upon us. Before there weren't any nurses here [in the health posts established in 2009]. After my sixth and before my seventh pregnancies [late 1990s] I went to Tibet and had an injection and took several birth control pills."

When we queried a middle-aged *amji* (practitioner of Tibetan medicine) about the ethics of birth control, he responded, "My wife has opted for injections every three months. As a medical practitioner, I don't know if this is wrong, but this practice is looked down upon and considered unethical from a Tibetan cultural point of view. There are medical means nowadays to avoid conceiving for up to three years. From a Tibetan perspective, such an act is a bit sinful *[digpa]*."

Despite reservations, he did not object to his wife's using birth control. Other men are less receptive, albeit spousal differences usually center on incongruent opinions about family size rather than moral dilemmas. While collecting reproductive histories, we heard several women report disagreements with their husband over how many children to bear, and they confided that they were using birth control without his knowledge. When we asked the leader of a local women's association whether spouses sometimes disagree over the use of contraception, she replied, "Yes, there are such fights. There have been a few such cases this year. We went to mediate and found that [disagreement over how many children

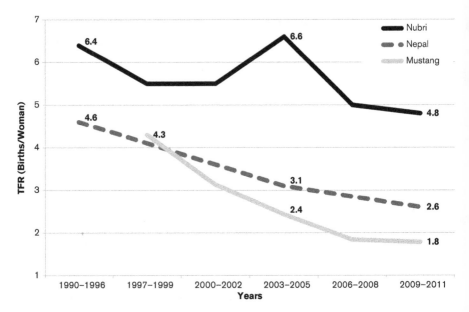

FIGURE 7. Total Fertility Rates in Nubri, Mustang, and Nepal Compared
Sources: For Nepal, Ministry of Health and Population et al. 2012:78. For Nubri and
Mustang, Craig et al. 2016.

to have] to be the cause of the fights. We counseled them not to fight. We told people that there is a big difference between the past and the present, and that we have to think carefully and plan the family. The young men in the village say that women these days are thinking only about themselves."

The gradual uptake of contraception coincides with a decline in Nubri's Total Fertility Rate (TFR) from 6.4 births per woman in 1990–96 to 4.8 in 2009–11 (figure 7).[2] Nevertheless, fertility remains considerably above the national average, which dropped from 4.6 births per woman in 1993–95 to 2.6 in 2008–10 (Ministry of Health and Population et al. 2012:78). Nubri's fertility decline also lags behind culturally similar areas of highland Nepal, such as Mustang. The earlier uptake of contraception in Mustang is related to several factors, including socioeconomic development, local availability, and seasonal patterns of rural-to-urban mobility (Craig et al. 2016).

Age-Specific Fertility Rates (ASFR) during the time frames 1997–99 and 2009–11 provide a more nuanced picture of reproductive change in Nubri (figure 8). There is almost no difference in ASFRs among women

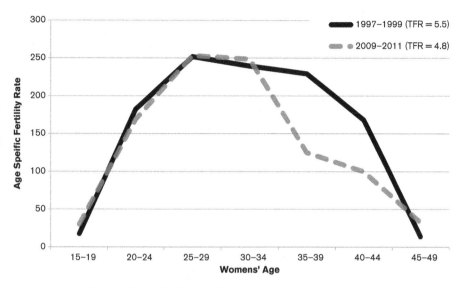

FIGURE 8. Age-specific Fertility Rates in Nubri, 1997–1999 and 2009–2011
Sources: Beall, Childs, and Craig 2012 Reproductive History Survey; Quinn and Childs
2013 Reproductive History Survey.

aged fifteen to thirty-four, yet the ASFR for women aged thirty-five to
thirty-nine dropped significantly. The decline for older but not younger
cohorts is consistent with the finding that the average birth-control user
had already experienced roughly five pregnancies and was thirty-two
years old at first usage.

The absence of health services also influenced mortality. Figure 9
shows a decline in Nubri's infant and childhood mortality over the
course of about three decades. The most significant improvements coin-
cide with some of the first interventions by a nongovernmental organization to support local Tibetan medical practitioners and organize
health and sanitation training programs.[3] In 1996 Nubri's infant mortality rate was about two and a half times higher than the national average (217 vs. 79 deaths per 1,000 live births), whereas by 2011 they were
roughly equal (41 vs. 46 deaths per 1,000 live births) (see Pradhan et al.
1997:102; Ministry of Health and Population et al. 2012). The sharp
reduction signals that a mortality transition is underway in Nubri.[4]

The mortality decline nudged Nubri into a nascent phase of demographic transition. Births outnumbering deaths generated population
growth.[5] Longitudinal data presented in table 6 shows that the de jure

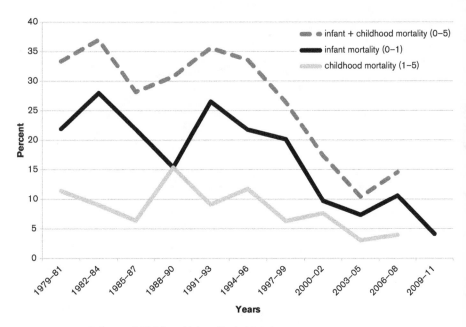

FIGURE 9. Infant and Childhood Mortality in Nubri, 1979–2011
Sources: Childs 1997 Reproductive History Survey; Beall, Childs, and Craig 2012
Reproductive History Survey; Quinn and Childs 2013 Reproductive History Survey.

TABLE 6.   POPULATION CHANGE IN NUBRI, 1997–2012

	Population	1997	2012	Change
Rö	de jure	554	604	+ 9.0%
	de facto	499	470	− 5.8%
	# living elsewhere	55	134	+ 143.6%
Lö	de jure	461	527	+ 14.3%
	de facto	395	353	− 10.6%
	# living elsewhere	66	174	+ 163.6%
Trok	de jure	295	314	+ 6.4%
	de facto	243	197	− 18.9%
	# living elsewhere	52	117	+ 125.0%
Total	de jure	1310	1445	+ 10.3%
	de facto	1137	1020	− 10.3%
	# living elsewhere	173	425	+ 145.7%

SOURCE: Childs et al. 2014.

population of the three largest villages increased by 10.3 percent between 1997 and 2012. Table 6 also shows that the de facto population of the villages declined by 10.3 percent. The fact that the population of people born in Nubri rose while the number of people actually living in the valley shrank can be accounted for only by outmigration.

Scholars often cite population growth as a causal factor for migration, which may be the case in Nubri because the population increased in an environment of chronic scarcity.[6] People persistently worry about having enough food to feed their children, so a decline in infant mortality would only exacerbate that concern. When we asked a father of five whether it would be difficult to manage his family if he kept all children at home, he responded, "Yes, it would be difficult. There would not be enough food. Having small kids at home is a hindrance to work. With many kids at home you need more food and can't do as much work. If you send some kids out, then there are fewer at home. You can arrange the work and do it more efficiently.

Another man concurred:

> The reason for this movement [of children out of the village] is not because people can afford to migrate but because of hardships. It is difficult in the village because there are no big factories that can employ people. You can only get one crop a year from farming, and that one crop you must safeguard from wild animals and inclement weather. A family needs enough food to last a year, but can get only three months of food from farming. So you need to look for opportunities that will feed everyone for the remaining nine months of the year.

The inability to balance household resources with the number of residents is certainly a powerful migration push factor. However, poverty cannot explain the direction and magnitude of outmigration for the simple reason that sending a child to a boarding school or monastery depends on the willingness of others to share the costs of rearing that child. The trend of sending children to monasteries and schools founded by Tibetan exiles, we argue, is partially driven by supply and demand issues stemming from fertility differentials (figure 10). Fertility remained high in Nubri well after it fell below replacement level in the exile communities. Throw in emigration from Tibetan settlements to North America and elsewhere and the demographic contrast is clear: Nubri (and presumably other highland communities of Nepal) was experiencing population growth while the Tibetan exile population in South Asia was in decline.

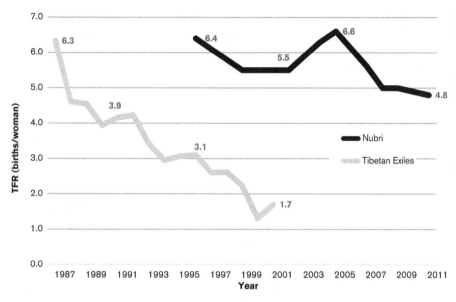

FIGURE 10. Total Fertility Rates in Nubri and Tibetan Exile Communities Compared
Sources: Tibetan Exiles, Childs et al. 2005; Nubri, Beall, Childs, and Craig 2012
Reproductive History Survey; Quinn and Childs 2013 Reproductive History Survey.

One lama recounted how monks from Nubri have helped his monastery thrive. He wrote,

> After building the monastery in Boudha [a Buddhist center in Kathmandu], it was difficult to find children who wanted to become monks. I decided to ask some people I knew about finding children who wished to be monks. They said, "Nowadays all people want to go to school and study or to do business and earn much money. It's almost impossible to find children to become monks."
>
> After hearing this, I was very depressed and disappointed but nevertheless I made a fruitful aspiration with good motivation. . . . As a result of that, Tenzin Dorje became the first monk from Nubri Village, Gorkha, Nepal. Eventually the number of monks grew and flourished and soon there were almost as many monks as in the monastery in Tibet.[7]

The lama's observation indirectly references the exiles' fertility decline as a reason he turned to a place like Nubri to keep his monastery viable. He attributes the initial recruiting woes to the Tibetan exiles' focus on education and upward economic mobility, two factors that reflect a higher parental investment in children that typically accompanies a small-family norm.[8]

TABLE 7. NUBRI'S NONMIGRANTS AND MIGRANTS BY SEX AND YEAR

	1997		2013	
	% in	% out	% in	% out
males	60.8	39.2	26.3	73.7
females	88.8	11.2	28.5	71.5
total	75.8	24.2	27.3	72.7

SOURCES: Beall, Childs, and Craig 2012 Household Demographic Survey; Quinn and Childs 2013 Household Demographic Survey.

Karma Chögyal, one of the first from Nubri to gain admission in a resurrected monastery in Kathmandu, explained the logic of recruiting monks from Nepal's highlands. He said,

> For many of these monasteries who go to collect new recruits, the continuation of their religious lineage [chögyü] is very important. And the continuity of religious lineage depends on the continuity of the monastic community. In other words, having only piles of religious scriptures does not help to continue the religious lineage because there should be a monastic community of practitioners. That is why monasteries are concerned about getting monk recruits, and it is something that will persist because many new monasteries are coming up in Nepal. The monk recruits in the past were mostly from Tibet, but this has basically stopped in recent years. This is one of the reasons [why monasteries are targeting rural Nepal for monk recruits].

Karma Chögyal refers to a time when monasteries could count on Tibetan communities to provide the requisite number of recruits. That situation no longer exists, so he frames recruitment from Nepal's highlands as essential for ensuring the survival of the teaching lineage. Schools encountered the same quandary (finding new students or facing closure) due to dwindling enrollment. As a result, new educational opportunities opened for children from indigenous Buddhist communities in Nepal. The following analysis documents the impact these developments are having on Nubri's population.

THE PATHWAYS AND MAGNITUDE OF OUTMIGRATION

The longitudinal data in table 7 quantifies the magnitude of changes since 1997. In the sixteen years that elapsed between household surveys, the percentage of boys sent outside for education increased from 39.2 to 73.7, while the percentage of girls increased from 11.2 to 71.5.

Not only did migration surge in volume, the gender discrepancy seen in 1997 (3.5 males were sent for every female) was nearly erased.

In 1997 many parents expressed reluctance to send a girl to school because they did not see a benefit in educating females. Perceptions have since changed, as one father explained,

> In our old tradition we favored sons over daughters. During my father's time a boy was much preferred. I guess that is because the work we used to do is hard labor. But at present, due to education, it doesn't matter that much. So nowadays there is not much difference between a son and daughter. If well educated, a girl can be better than a boy. It is more useful to have a well-educated daughter than an illiterate son. In the past the lack of proper education made us like cattle. We couldn't seize opportunities and couldn't exercise our rights because of being illiterate. These days I feel that education has reduced our preference for sons over daughters.

Although son preference is still evident in Nubri (for example, parents continue to name some daughters Buti which literally means "bring forth a son"), education and the potential to engage in nonagrarian livelihoods seem to be changing the gender-based valuation of children. Nevertheless, today's educational migration is by no means gender neutral. Among the migrant population aged five to nineteen, a higher percentage of boys (48.6) than girls (34.1) is sent to religious institutions, a difference attributable to long-standing gender inequities: monasteries outnumber nunneries and receive better funding, while monks have higher social status than nuns (Havnevik 1989; Schaeffer 2004; Gyatso and Havnevik 2005).

The diversity of sending destinations is impressive. Our household survey enumerated children studying in at least eighteen schools in Kathmandu and several more in India, monks living in thirteen different monasteries in Kathmandu in addition to others in Sikkim, Dharamsala, and the Tibetan settlements in the south of India, and nuns in five different institutions in and around Kathmandu plus two in India. Table 8 breaks down the percentages of migrants by where they reside. Not surprisingly, Kathmandu with its concentration of Tibetan monasteries and boarding schools is the most popular destination, accounting for 63.4 percent of the migrants. Eleven and a half percent still live in Nubri, albeit not in their natal households but in branch monasteries constructed by institutions located in India and Kathmandu that have a history of recruiting novices from the valley. Other sending destinations in Nepal include the towns of Gorkha and Pokhara, and Manang District just west of Nubri.

TABLE 8. NUBRI'S MIGRANT POPULATION (PERCENT) AGED 10–19
BY DESTINATION

Aged 10–19	Males	Females	Total
Nepal, Kathmandu	58.9	68.4	63.4
India	17.1	15.0	16.1
Nepal, Nubri	17.8	4.5	11.5
Nepal, other	6.2	9.0	7.5
Abroad	0.0	3.0	1.4
Total	100.0	100.0	100.0

SOURCES: Beall, Childs, and Craig 2012 Household Demographic Survey; Quinn and Childs 2013 Household Demographic Survey.

In summary, Nubri's educational migration phenomenon is linked to the impelled relocation of Tibetans from their homeland in the 1950s and 1960s. By resurrecting monasteries and building schools, the exiles erected an infrastructure of possibilities that eventually benefited Nepal's highlanders when divergent demographic trends emerged between the communities. The outmigration of children from Nubri started in the 1980s, gained momentum in the 1990s, and became a large-scale phenomenon in the 2000s when parents became equally willing to educate daughters as sons. Now, the majority of Nubri's youths live away from their parents as boarders in secular and religious institutions.

Nubri's educational migration phenomenon comes with costs and benefits. The goal of educating children outside of the valley risks estranging them from natal communities; young people are removed from village life at a critical juncture and enculturated in a different sociocultural milieu. To exacerbate the disconnection, education simultaneously builds the capacity of the younger generation to pursue a greater range of occupations and erects disincentives to return to a place where there is a mismatch between newly acquired skills and available jobs. While education opens opportunities for the younger generation, it leaves the older generation with a debilitated labor force, new challenges to household succession, and vulnerabilities in old age. We will explore these topics in the concluding chapter. Next, in chapters 5–8, we analyze parental strategies and social networks that facilitate the movement of children from natal communities to urban institutions.

CHAPTER 5

Becoming Monks

FAMILY OBLIGATIONS VERSUS RELIGIOUS ASPIRATIONS

Renouncing mundane activities and forsaking the secular life,
this meditator living alone without companion is so delightful.
No need for snotty, diarrhetic children is so wonderful.

—(Stearns 2000:91)

In the passage above Godrakpa Sonam Gyaltsen (1170–1249) comments on the distractions family life poses to the dedicated ascetic, a sentiment that aligns with the life story of his intellectual forefather. Śākyamuni Buddha began life as the wealthy and pampered Prince Siddhārtha. To embark upon the quest for enlightenment, he abandoned his parents, wife, and newborn child. Eventually diagnosing the root causes of human suffering, he prescribed an antidote consisting of rigorous intellectual, moral, and physical discipline. Likewise, Sonam Gyaltsen viewed separation from family as a prerequisite for pursuing the altruistic goal of enlightenment for the benefit of all sentient beings. Putting such a goal into action, however, has consequences because every individual begins life embedded in a web of kinship relationships from which it is difficult—and often impossible—to disentangle.

The tug-of-war between spiritual aspirations and family obligations is a recurrent theme in Tibetan biographical writings. Shabkar Tsogdruk Rangdrol (1781–1851) from Amdo struggled mightily to disengage from his family so he could learn from the great masters of his time (Ricard 1994). Sonam Lodro (1456–1521) from Dolpo recounts, "Although I had a great urge towards the religious life, yet because we had great worldly possessions, my old father and my other relatives said that I must continue in the world. But still I did not listen to them" (Snellgrove 1967:86). Pema Döndrup (1668–1744) from Nubri faced the prospect of returning to lay life after the death of his brother, who was the main support for the family. His parents prodded him to return from his meditation retreats, marry his widowed sister-in-law, and thus carry on his brother's productive and reproductive responsibilities. Pema Döndrup refused to comply, and his parents suffered immensely as a result (Childs 2004).

Shabkar Tsogdruk Rangdrol, Sonam Lodro, and Pema Döndrup represent a small sample of people who resisted the entreaties of family members and remained steadfast in their determination to pursue an awakening of the mind that Buddhist teachings offer. They serve as a reminder that a Buddhist practitioner can rarely sever completely from the natal household. As Mills comments, "In regard to their natal village households, monks' membership is effectively inalienable, but ideally they progressively disavow the principal activities and disciplines of that household" (2009:166).[1]

In this chapter we follow Martin Mills's lead by exploring economic and sociological connections between monks and their natal households (Mills 2000, 2003, 2009). The connections are vitally important for understanding educational migration for two reasons. First, most monks do not enter a religious institution of their own volition. As Melvyn Goldstein points out, "In Tibet, monks were almost always recruited as very young children through the agency of their parents or guardians" (Goldstein 2009:4). The same holds true for Nubri's monks today, which underscores the need to consider the household as the locus of migration decision-making. Second, even after entering a monastery, monks remain economically connected to natal households, generally through support received (Mills 2003:65–68) but also through remittances given.

In the following section we present the life stories of two men from Nubri. The first case shows how family life can be an impediment to spiritual development, whereas the second case illustrates how the travails of marriage and householding can prod a man to flee the village for the fellowship of a monastic order. The case studies not only illustrate the tension between worldly life and religious ambitions, but also set the stage for analyzing the motives and means for sending a son to a monastery, and the roles that social networks and cumulative causation play in the monastic migration stream.

BETWEEN ONTOLOGICAL REALMS

Sonam Sangpo is a middle-aged householder lama who is well regarded in the village and always occupies one of the seats of highest prestige during communal ceremonies. By virtue of being born the eldest son of a lama, he is expected to study Buddhism and be a leading figure in the annual ritual cycle while running a household replete with children, agricultural land, and a herd of bovines. On the day we visited he looked exasperated. Stoking the hearth so his wife could boil water for tea, he barked a stream of commands to his unruly children. Sonam Sangpo wants to devote more time to religious practice, yet domestic life proves to be a continuous distraction. During our interview about his family, he lamented,

> My parents didn't send us elsewhere to school or a monastery. No matter how many children we were—five, six, seven, eight—we were all kept in the house to do work. It is a fact that there was no such monastery or school in our village during that time. So we were all a bunch of idiots [kukpa] who could do only one kind of job. Therefore, I cannot claim to have a good knowledge of religion. That's why, even if I am poor, I firmly believe in giving my children the best education at all costs so they can have a better life. I am willing to endure the worst situation to realize this dream.
>
> I have hit rock bottom. As a Buddhist practitioner, I haven't undergone *shedra* training [formal monastic study center]. I studied a little bit of Buddhism the way it's taught here in this part of the world. I did some meditation and retreat, but I didn't get an opportunity for shedra training. Without shedra training, you miss something to make a good start or lay a strong foundation for the spiritual journey in Buddhism. I sent my sons to monasteries hoping they will receive good teaching. This is my only expectation. We parents have many difficulties. We have to uphold the village's law, and we are willing to bear the hardship. We want our children to be better off. I have endured the hardship. I don't want that for my children.
>
> I am disenchanted with the life of worldly suffering [jigtengi tenpa]. From my own experience, it is full of hardship and regrets. I've had enough of it. I don't know if the life of a layperson is in my children's karma, but I wouldn't want any more of it. I've had a very tough time. If I wanted to do retreat in the hills even for a month, there would be nobody here to manage the household, and everything would go to waste. This has been the story of my life. In some villages people go here and there to do business. But in our village there is no prospect of doing any business; people just tend the fields. Besides the land I received from my parents, I bought a few plots of land for the

sake of my children. I had to take out loans and have had a very hard time repaying them. There has not been a single moment of happiness in the household for years, just constant worries. Based on this, I wanted my sons to lead meaningful lives as monks for the benefit of this life and future lives. If by karma or luck they decide to marry, it is their wish. But I am fed up with the kind of life I've lived.

Sonam Sangpo sees his inability to disengage from family life as an impediment to serious religious practice. Ironically, a cultural template for removing himself from the bustle of village life dangles just beyond Sonam Sangpo's reach. People in Nubri distinguish the village, deemed the "Realm of Worldly Sufferers" *(jigtenpey yul)*, from the temple complex, referred to as the "Realm of Religious Practitioners" *(chöpey yul)*. The physical separation between realms need not be great, but the ontological distinction is significant. The perpetuation of human misery through physical labor, reproduction, and interpersonal squabbles characterizes village existence. Life in the Realm of Religious Practitioners is quiet, contemplative, and geared toward awakening the mind. By combining the obligations of household productivity and religious practice, a lama like Sonam Sangpo is caught between realms; he resides in the shadow of the Realm of Religious Practitioners while deeply embedded in the Realm of Worldly Sufferers.

Urgyen Nyima is a soft-spoken middle-aged monk who disengaged from a disorderly family life by entering a monastery in Kathmandu. We met him one day at his residence perched upon a hill overlooking the ancient Buddhist site of Swayambunath. Sitting in his tidy room, Urgyen Nyima filled our cups with black, salted tea. He then sat down on a small mat, straightened his robe, and stiffened his spine to signal that he was ready to commence the interview. With little prompting, he began to narrate the story of how he became a monk.

In Nubri there were many cases in which parents separate after children are born. The children face hardships. That's what happened to me. My mother had three children. One died at a young age. After that I was born, and then my brother was born. My father then left my mother and married another woman. There is a rule: a daughter goes with her mother while a son goes with his father. We were boys so my father kept us. I had a stepmother, but she was not my real mother. She would feed me, but she wouldn't give the love I needed.

We were very small at that time and I was just able to walk. I was on my mother's back [still being carried] when they separated. My younger brother was small then and still breastfeeding. So when he needed milk, somebody would carry him to my mother, who would nurse him. Sometimes I would take him on my back to my mother so that she could feed him, then I would bring him back. I wanted to go to meet my mother, but my father wouldn't let me. He used to beat me. Sometimes I would go without telling him, but people would inform my father. He would tell me not to go to my mother, and warned if he found out he would beat me. In addition, my mother had one sister who was really bad. She would beat me for coming to meet my mother and then send me back to my father. While I was being beaten, my mother would cry. There was no one to love us. I still remember these things. It was a very tough time. My eyes still fill with tears when I talk about it.

Slowly we grew up. My mother used to tell me and my brother to get married. The sooner we married, the earlier she could come live with us. But then she went on pilgrimage to Bodhgaya, in India, where the Dalai Lama was giving a teaching. She died under a train. My mother did not have much money and didn't know the language. I think she was lost in her own thoughts when the train was coming. She fell on the track and the train ran over her. One moment she was there, the next moment she was dead. She wanted me and my brother to get married so that she could stay with us. Her wish went unfulfilled.

I didn't marry until many years after her death. Many people were telling me to get married, as I was getting quite old. I didn't listen, because my mother was dead; she was the one who really worried about me. I even started studying religion. My maternal uncle was at Pharping [outside of Kathmandu]. I went to visit him, and he said, "You are two brothers, so it is good if one of you studies religion. The younger brother looks clever, so it is okay if he lives a worldly life. But you appear to be a bit foolish, so it is good if you study religion." But my father didn't allow me to stay there, so I returned to the village.

Eventually my father arranged a marriage for me and my brother [polyandry], and we received some of my father's land. Parents make decisions according to their own wishes. If you don't like it, there is no alternative. Children are not supposed to act upon their own wishes. My father made decisions whether we liked it or not. We were forced to accept his decisions. Marriage is not for one or two months, or one or two years. It is for a lifetime. But we were not happy or satisfied, so we separated from our wife and stayed alone for a year.

My brother wanted to remarry, but I wanted to practice religion. He brought home a woman—they had fallen in love. The two of them wished for me to stay with them. Once again everyone was encouraging me to get married. Even the girl requested this. She prostrated in front of me. Everyone was forcing me to remarry, but I said it's my life and it's my choice to lead my life as I wish. You can bind a bovine, but I am a man and can do as I wish. So I told them not to force me. I didn't want to remarry, because I had a desire to learn religion. This worldly life is full of suffering and I didn't have education. When you don't have education, you become discouraged. I always had a strong desire to study religion.

One day all the relatives from my side and her side were preparing the wedding ceremonies. When they were ready, I took a stand. I went up to the temple [located just above the village] and stayed with some monks. Many people came and said everything is ready and asked why I was at the temple. I told them, "I don't want to get married, I want to study religion." All the relatives of the bride prostrated before me and said, "We have great expectations of you, but you won't comply." They told me that I should have made my intentions clear from the beginning. Even the bride came and requested me to marry her. So I complied and stayed at home for two years.

To study religion you should come to Kathmandu. Religious education is not good in the village. Although many people said I can't study religion at such an advanced age [he was thirty at the time], I came down to Kathmandu and went straight to the monastery. I implored the Rinpoche with all my problems. An old woman asked me what had happened in the village, and whether I had created problems there. She said that I shouldn't be accepted at once because if I were a married person from the village I would bring trouble upon the monastery. I told her that I came here only after clearing all the troubles. I told her that, in a few days, my father and uncle were coming and she could ask them. In the meantime, an elderly lama was very good to me. He said it's very good that I was following religion. He said that religion is one's own choice, so who cares about the problems. In the end I was accepted and I got my robes.

Urgyen Nyima sought respite from an unsatisfactory family life, but advanced age and a lack of prior training prevented him from pursuing a full course in monastic studies. Fortunately, the upkeep of studious monks requires helping hands, so Urgyen Nyima found a role as a caretaker *(nyerpa)*. Although he regrets his limited understanding of esoteric Buddhism, Urgyen Nyima takes solace in the swap he made between homespun village clothing and the crimson robes of a monk. Were it not for the rise of Tibetan monasteries in exile, it is doubtful that this particular escape route would have been possible, especially in light of the pressures he faced to remain in a polyandrous union and work for the common welfare of his household.

The stories of Sonam Sangpo and Urgyen Nyima provide some insights into the tensions between family life and religious pursuits, and help illuminate factors that both impel men toward and prevent them from pursuing religious vocations. In the next section we further explore these themes by examining the complex array of motives and cultural rationales that lead parents to send their young sons to reside and be educated in distant monasteries.

ON THE MERITS OF MONASTIC MIGRATION

Based on interviews with elderly monks about pre-1959 Tibetan society, Goldstein generated a list of parents' reasons for sending a son to a monastery (1998:16–17). Some reasons are associated with the household's welfare, such as poverty, a tax requirement imposed on those who farm monastic estates, and a desire to minimize asset fragmentation by removing a son as a potential inheritor. Other motivations are more rooted in social and moral concerns, such as a desire to acquire status and prestige by supporting religion, or to gain merit by dedicating a son's life to religion.

Our interviews unveiled a spectrum of similar reasons why parents make their sons monks. Although some responded with stock answers such as "it is our custom as Buddhists" or that "practicing religion benefits all sentient beings," others answered in a way that reflects a moral calculus involving benefits for household members throughout the cycle of birth, death, and rebirth. For example, several reasoned that by making a son a monk, they and their child accrue blessings *(chinlab)* and good fortune *(sodey)* that can come to fruition in this lifetime or beyond. One father stated that it is good to have a monk-son who can perform funeral rituals and prayers—activities that will help him navigate the intermediate realm between death and rebirth. Other parents expressed a desire to counter the inevitable sins one commits when engaging in agro-pastoral subsistence. For example, one man stated, "We commit so much sin *[digpa]*. Because of that we need to earn merit *[gewa]*. It may or may not be helpful for us or our son in this life, but it will definitely be helpful in the next life." His wife elaborated, "We commit sins when we farm. When we plow, we kill insects. Also, by amassing wealth we develop egocentric pride *[ngagyel]*. To counter our sins we have our sons become monks."

Besides moral and metaphysical rationales, some parents framed their responses within the suffering they experience while eking out a living in Nubri's harsh environment. They see monasticism as a means to release a son from the incessant toil of village life. One man told us, "I made my sons monks because lay life is so hard. You must carry compost from the forest to the village, then from the village to the stable, then from the stable to the fields. We are always carrying loads. It is a very tough life. There are so many obligations, like obligatory communal religious service. If my sons attend a monastery they get better food, better clothes, and, if they stay there, a better life."

Potential long-term financial benefits can also motivate parents to send a son to a monastery. One mother said quite directly, "Whatever help we get from him is good. I am praying he will be of great benefit to us." Upon probing, it became clear that she was thinking about remittances.

Monks are often dispatched to Buddhist patrons' homes to perform household rituals. They typically receive a minimum donation of Rs500 per day of service. Although we have heard parents talk about financial support they receive from their monk-sons, there are moral implications tied to the acceptance of money originally donated to a religious practitioner. Karma Chögyal, a middle-aged monk who has attained the status of *khenpo* (preceptor),[2] explained the quandary as follows:

> To tell you honestly, there are many monks, not only from Nubri but also from other regions, who can provide financial assistance to their families. If we think in terms of such worldly affairs, then I should be really ashamed of myself [for not providing financial assistance to his parents]. I am a khenpo, so people might have high expectations [of material benefits] based on my position. But I am not doing anything to help [his parents] and do not plan to do anything in the future. However, I don't feel shameful because whatever a monk possesses in terms of wealth is all from donations *[kor]* offered in the names of both living and dead people. To share such wealth with your family is not something to be proud of. Doing so is like distributing unvirtuous deeds *[digpa]*. I don't see any particular merit in sharing wealth attained through donations. Thus, from a religious perspective, I don't have any regrets [for not providing financial assistance to his parents]. If viewed from a worldly perspective of competition, when compared to other monks, I have done very poorly.

Karma Chögyal's comment cuts to the heart of friction that can arise between the parents' desire to benefit monetarily by making a son a monk and the moral predicament of converting alms into remittances for a layperson. His pointed criticism acknowledges that the practice is common if not widespread.

CHILDHOOD INCLINATIONS AND MONASTIC MIGRATION

Karma Chögyal did not want to become a monk when he was a child. His father ordained him at a young age because, with two sons, he had to manage their inheritance in a pragmatic way. He sent Karma Chögyal to a monastery in Kathmandu and kept the younger at home. Reflecting on his route to monasticism, Karma Chögyal said,

> It was not my desire to become a monk. It was my parents' decision. At that time, to speak from a Buddhist perspective, I did not have the proper motivation to become a monk *[nyechungi sampa]*.[3] Further, I did not have any desire to study Buddhism. I was more interested in playing and having a good time like any other nine-year-old child. My parents had decided that I

should go down to Kathmandu and become a monk, and I came down thinking that Kathmandu would be a fun place. That was how I became a monk, and to tell you the truth, I don't recall much about the early years here at the monastery. What I do remember clearly is that I was not a serious student until I turned fifteen or sixteen. I did not have any clear idea about what it meant to be a monk and to study Buddhism. I did learn how to play religious instruments and perform rituals, but I did not know much about the meaning of dharma. Apart from developing a form of affective attachment [shatsa] to my own lamas and monastery, I did not develop any deep conviction and motivation to study and practice dharma. Since I did not know clearly what it means to be a Buddhist and what Buddhism means, back then my belief was based on plain faith rather than a more reflexive conviction toward the study of Buddhism.

When I was in my early teens, I would sometimes get angry at my parents for making me a monk. I used to think, "Why did they send me so far away to become a monk when it was not my desire at all to be a monk?" I used to have thoughts about how lay life would be more fun. However, later as I grew up and saw how the high lamas and teachers were taking great care of us, I realized that this religious path is the right one for me and that it all depends on how much effort I put into my religious practice. That is how I developed a deeper conviction [ngeshey] to pursue higher studies. Around the age of eighteen I started to have less interest in the religious rituals and rites [chöga chaglen]. I began paying more attention to the religious texts for the higher study of Buddhism.

I am no longer upset with my parents. Instead, I rejoice in having parents like them and appreciate what they have done for me. Although I was born in a poor family, I pray that I am reborn again and again in such a place and to such parents, because mere economic wealth does not mean everything in life. I am very proud to be born in Nubri because the basic temperament [shiga] and nature [rangshin] of the people are very good. I am very glad to have such wonderful parents.

With the passing of time and a deepening appreciation for Buddhist teachings, Karma Chögyal's attitude toward his parents mellowed from resentment to gratitude. He came to recognize monasticism as an opportunity to lead a contemplative life removed from the sufferings of mundane existence.

Not all boys are sent to monasteries by parental decree. Whereas it took Karma Chögyal years to appreciate his status as a monk, other boys discovered the impulse earlier in life while still living in the village. For example, Gonpo told us, "As a child, when I saw monks in my village I really got a strong desire to become a monk. In the village I always had to go with the cows and work in the fields, whereas the monks looked very carefree in their robes. I always told my father to make me a monk." Similarly, Kunchok said, "As a child I didn't know about religion, but I did have a strong desire to become a monk. I used to tell my father that I want to become a monk, and that I want to go to a monastery. It was not that I wanted to know religion in-depth; I just had a strong wish to become a monk. When I was small I saw many monks come to our village from India and Kathmandu. They were highly respected and looked very peaceful. So I got this strong wish that I too wanted to be like them."

Respect and a relatively carefree lifestyle seem to have motivated these boys to pursue a religious vocation. Others exhibited early inclinations through childhood play. For example, Hritar told us, "I always wanted to be a monk from a very young age. When I was in my village I liked to practice religion. I always used to go to temples to observe the monks praying. At home I used to pretend to be a monk by beating the lid of a pot like they do at the temple." His statement echoes the recollections of Tashi Dorje (1919–2017), who recalled, "When I was young, I wanted to be a monk. While watching our father perform rituals, my brothers, sisters, and our friends from the neighborhood got the idea to act out our own religious ceremonies. Behind our house was an overhanging rock. That was our temple! When a group of children gathered there, we would make offerings and recite prayers. All of the children took part in our game" (Childs 2004:66).

Moving further back in time, Pema Lhundrup (born in 1708) from Nubri wrote,

> When I turned three or four years old and could thus remember, I wished to practice only religion and nothing else. Other children indulged in ways of playing that included killing birds, setting snares, hunting, beating up younger children, shooting arrows, cutting grass, splitting wood, playing husband and wife, and playing lovers. In my childhood I played at building temples and other religious structures, creating grand feast offerings with many large and small sacrificial offerings, making statues, spinning prayer wheels and performing rituals, beating drums and blowing conches, playing cymbals with flat stones, playing mask dance with sacrificial offerings of animal dolls made of doughballs and throwing these offerings as ritual weapons. (Pema Lhundrup 1979:598–99)[4]

The recollections of Hritar, Tashi Dorje, and Pema Lhundrup indicate that religious inclinations, articulated through childhood amusement, can foreshadow a life devoted to religious practice. They also remind us that there is no uniform answer to the question of why parents make their sons monks, or why boys and young men choose to pursue such a life course. Parental decisions can involve any combination of idiosyncratic circumstances, ontological deliberations, pragmatic considerations, and prodding from a son. No doubt parents are following a cultural rationale (it is noble to support religion) that comes with benefits (merit and respect). However, any assumption that parents act with altruistic intentions—a common assumption in economic models of household decision-making—is complicated because different levels of altruism are in play. For one, relinquishing a son to a monastery is perceived to be beneficial for all of humanity because by doing so, parents selflessly support religion (altruism at the societal level). Parents also tell us that they are willing to relinquish a son's contribution to the household's labor force so he can lead an easier life (altruism at the household level). To complicate matters, parents rationalize the decision in ontological terms by stating that they accrue merit by making a son a monk, a spiritual benefit that helps avert misfortunes in this lifetime and unfavorable circumstances in the next. Some also mention the prospect that his future earnings can bring remittances. Such motives seem to align more with self-interest than altruism.

Examining the situation from the monk's point of view, many view monasticism as a pathway to an easier, less stressful life, a motive that seems to be propelled at least partially by self-interest. However, at the beginning of this chapter we discussed the tussle between religious aspirations and household responsibilities. Achieving enlightenment is seen to benefit all sentient beings, which of course includes members of one's household. Yet pursuing esoteric Buddhist practices at the highest level is best accomplished by removing oneself completely from the household, which can impact negatively the well-being of other household members. Altruism, when construed in the narrow sense of unselfishly advancing the household's economic interests, is at odds with the Buddhist notion of altruism that considers the interdependence of all beings. With advanced religious practice a monk may realize that disengaging from household entanglements enhances his ability to achieve spiritual insights that—from his altruistic vantage point—benefit all of humanity. He can rationalize that household members may suffer in the short term but benefit in the long term. At a more basic level, Karma Chögyal argues that even supporting one's household through remittances is morally problematic because it tarnishes the merit attached to alms. The interlacing of altruism and self-interest makes any attempt to clearly demarcate the two akin to forging a dichotomy from a continuum.

Regardless of how the resolution comes about, admission to a monastery depends on finding an institution that will accept the novice.

Next we explore the means that facilitate the movement of children from rural households to urban institutions. We focus on social networks that shape the migration pathway, and financial support that makes monasticism an option that is not entirely dependent on a family's socioeconomic standing.

RELIGIOUS NETWORKS AND MIGRATION DESTINATIONS

Two propositions from migration network theory frame the following analysis. First, migration flows are shaped by social networks that link people in sending and destination communities. Migration is not a random event, but is contingent on the social capital embedded within personal relationships. The second is that a social network reduces the costs and risks of migration. Moving to a faraway destination filled with unfamiliar people is a daunting proposition. Knowing someone at a potential destination, and counting on that person's knowledge and assistance, reduces the uncertainly of making the move.

There are numerous monasteries in exile that accept novice monks from the Himalayan highlands, but Nubri's children are not dispersed randomly among them. Rather, their placement shows a distinct pattern that is shaped by social networks based on religious affiliation. To highlight the role that these networks play in monastic admissions, consider the relationship between Tulku Urgyen Rinpoche (1920–1996; born in Nangchen, eastern Tibet), the sons of Tulku Urgyen, and members of Rö's Ngadag lineage of householder lamas. Tulku Urgyen recounts how he first heard about Nubri. On the day of his enthronement at Lachab Monastery in Tibet, his teacher Samten Gyatso expressed a premonition that disruptive times were descending on Tibet and that "evil influences will come from the east." Samten Gyatso said, "If it happens that you are forced to leave [Tibet], you must go to Nubri." When Tulku Urgyen inquired about Nubri, Samten Gyatso explained,

> Right now it belongs to the Gorkha king in Nepal and so is no longer under the Tibetan government. A descendant of King Trisong Deutsen still lives there [i.e., a member of Rö's Ngadag lineage], as well as a couple of my disciples with deep faith in the Dharma. When you leave here, you will first go to Central Tibet, but after a while there you will be unable to remain. At that time, go to Nubri. The Nubri people are humble and simple. They are not rich, but they have deep appreciation for the Buddhist teachings. The one you must contact is the descendant of the Dharma king Trisong Deutsen. (Tulku Urgyen Rinpoche 2005:177–78)

While staying at Tsurphu Monastery in the mid-1950s, Tulku Urgyen consulted Karmapa on where to go in the event he needed to escape the impending threat to religion posed by China's incursion into Tibet. Tulku Urgyen proclaimed, "My only wish is to go somewhere without a single Chinese communist," then rattled off a list of potential destinations that included Nubri. He continued, "I mentioned the connection my uncle had with some people in Nubri, explaining, 'A lama living there descends from King Trisong Deutsen and, since he's a disciple of my uncle, if we go there at least we won't starve. Please give me your advice as to the best place to go. The thought of staying here keeps me awake at night'" (Tulku Urgyen Rinpoche 2005:319).

Tulku Urgyen then recalls meeting a group of devotees from Nubri and instructing them for nineteen days. He described one of those men, Tashi Dorje, in the following terms. "He is a very stable, solid person, without a speck of deceit. His father had been a disciple of both Samten Gyatso and Karmey Khenpo. We met for the first time at Tsurphu, because Tashi Dorje's family was connected to Karmey Khenpo. The family had come to Central Tibet to find his reincarnation, who turned out to be a cousin of mine" (Tulku Urgyen Rinpoche 2005:337).

In his history of the Ngadag lineage, Tashi Dorje mentions meeting Tulku Urgyen at Tsurphu around 1955–56 and then inviting him a few years later to visit Nubri (Tashi Dorje 2010:42, 46–47). Tashi Dorje's account is verified by Karma Chögyal, whose father was also instrumental in bringing Tulku Urgyen to Nubri. He explains,

> There was a special connection to Tulku Urgyen Rinpoche from my father's time. My father had studied a little in Tibet, and he had met Tulku Urgyen for the first time at Tsurphu. Back in those days, people from Nubri used to visit Tsurphu to seek teachings from Karmapa. My father went to Tsurphu two times. During one visit he wanted to receive some empowerment and transmission on the Chokling tradition. He approached Karmapa. After receiving one empowerment teaching, Karmapa instructed my father and his group to visit Tulku Urgyen, who was undergoing retreat in a cave near Tsurphu. Tulku Urgyen was the holder of both the descent and religious lineages [dungyü and chögyü] of Chokling tradition, and he gave many religious instructions to my father and others, a total of twelve people from Nubri. That is how a special connection was established between Tulku Urgyen and Nubri's people. After the teachings, they requested Tulku Urgyen to visit Nubri. He agreed to visit in the future.

Karmapa determined through divination that Tulku Urgyen should go to Sikkim (Tulku Urgyen Rinpoche 2005:319), where he once again encountered the practitioners from Nubri who "insisted I return with them to Nubri to give the New Treasures. They refused to leave without me" (Tulku Urgyen Rinpoche 2005:332). He therefore approached Karmapa with a request to visit Nubri, and said, "They are a gentle people and their devotion is steadfast. I know the people of Nubri are of humble means, but they are persistent in their request for me to come" (Tulku Urgyen Rinpoche 2005:334–35).

Tulku Urgyen went to Nubri, where he consecrated sacred objects, gave extensive teachings, and was generously rewarded with offerings (Tulku Urgyen Rinpoche 2005:339). He also mentions a son he fathered with a woman from Nubri (Tulku Urgyen Rinpoche 2005:353). According to Karma Chögyal, "Tulku Urgyen visited Nubri and stayed for almost a year. That was how another special relationship was established. People in our region have very deep reverence for the father and son lineage of Tulku Urgyen, whose secret consort [sangyum] is someone from our Ngadag lineage. They treat us very respectfully because they have seen the sealed document bestowed by the Great Fifth Dalai Lama attesting that our lineage is related to the early Tibetan emperors."

Tulku Urgyen's first wife, from Tibet, gave birth to two sons. His "secret consort" is the only child of Tashi Dorje, a venerable member of Nubri's Ngadag lineage and the person most responsible for arranging Tulku Urgyen's visit. She also bore him two sons. All four sons were recognized as reincarnate lamas and now head prominent religious institutions in Nepal.

The social bond between Tulku Urgyen and the people of Nubri began as a master-disciple or priest-patron relationship; Tulku Urgyen bestowed religious instructions and the people of Nubri reciprocated with material support. The foundation for the relationship was laid by Tashi Dorje's father, Tinley Özer (born around 1880). Both Tinley Özer and Tashi Dorje were disciples of Tulku Urgyen's root lama, Samten Gyatso. Tulku Urgyen indicates the importance of the religious connection when he states that "since he's [Tashi Dorje] a disciple of my uncle, if we go there at least we won't starve" (Tulku Urgyen Rinpoche 2005:319). Tulku Urgyen then forged a kinship connection during his visit when he accepted the daughter of Tashi Dorje as his "secret consort."

Not surprisingly, the monasteries and nunneries founded by Tulku Urgyen Rinpoche and his sons nowadays house scores of monks and nuns from Nubri. One monk explained, "Because Tulku Urgyen regards us highly, he advised my father, who had four sons, to make at least two sons monks. Back then, for a layperson, there was not much opportunity for education. It was a life of herding yaks and carrying loads. At that time, I was only nine and not really old enough to become a monk. But my father brought me to Kathmandu with my older brother so that he could save the trouble of making another journey, which was very difficult in those days. He made us monks here."

Dzamling Dorje explained how the religious network influenced his pathway to becoming a monk. He is not only a member of a lama lineage, his father was also the reincarnation of a Ngadag ancestor. He explained, "My father, who passed away when I was nine, was a disciple of Tulku Urgyen, so they had a special connection. I knew Tulku Urgyen from childhood because I used to come down [to Kathmandu] in the winters with my father. We stayed at the monastery where Tulku Urgyen lived. My father said that it would be great if I could study under Tulku Urgyen. That is how I came to this monastery after my father passed away. Even though my father was no more, I knew that the monks would treat me well here because they knew my father."

The network created by ties with Tulku Urgyen extends beyond the upper echelons of Nubri's religious society. For example, Topgye is the son of a commoner. He explained, "I came here because we belong to the same sect and have very close relations with the lama. Tulku Urgyen Rinpoche visited our valley. He has many disciples in our village. When many lamas came to Nubri, they brought much good fortune [tashi] to our village. So we have relations with those lamas. We believe in the law of cause and effect [ley gyumdre]. So I think I ended up here due to my merit and past karma."

Some monks took a more roundabout path to a monastery run by Tulku Urgyen's sons. Mingyur, who also comes from a relatively poor family, described his experience:

> I went to three different monasteries. I had bought all my robes and was set to enter the first one that people in my village had recommended to my father. He had some connection with two monks there. But when I came there one day I saw a big monk badly beating a novice and felt very anxious and frightened. I thought I won't be able to stay there as I was also going to get the same beatings. I told my father I won't stay there and really gave him much trouble. So my father agreed and looked for other monasteries. There was one nearby, but my father did not know any monks there. When we entered, we were told that Rinpoche was not present and it's not possible to get admission without his permission. So then we went to another monastery. But the lama told us that they take only ten students a year and I was a little late. He told me to come next year. After that my father directly brought me here. Rinpoche was not present, but grandfather [a term of endearment,

in this case referring to Tashi Dorje] from my village was there. I had met grandfather when I was very young. He visited our home and my father accompanied him to a nearby pilgrimage site. I went with them and remember it even now. My father reminded him about the pilgrimage and then grandfather recognized us. He agreed to admit me and gave me my religious name.

Mingyur's admission process reminds us that pathways to monasteries can be strewn with obstacles. After rejecting the first institution, Mingyur's father tried to get him admitted to others but found their doors closed. In the end he relied on a social connection, and the memory of a past pilgrimage, to gain admission for his boy.

Monasteries and nunneries headed by Tulku Urgyen's sons now house 41 percent of Nubri's monks and 59 percent of Nubri's nuns aged five through nineteen—clear evidence that a social network rooted in religious connections, regional association, and kinship has shaped the direction of outmigration from the valley. Of course, none of this could have been accomplished without a fundamental shift in how monks and nuns are financially supported, the topic of the next section.

THE REVIVAL OF MASS MONASTICISM

Migration streams tend to gain momentum through cumulative causation (Massey 1990:4–5). As parents in Nubri saw others around them successfully enroll a child in a monastery and began to comprehend the array of social and economic benefits they could potentially realize by following suit, they become more inclined to send their own sons to institutions. In Nubri's case, cumulative causation is contingent on external factors, especially the transnational flow of capital to fund monasticism in exile and demographic trends that prompted monasteries to begin scouring the highlands of Nepal for new recruits. If parents in Nubri bore the main responsibility for supporting their children in monasteries, it is unlikely they would send so many sons to faraway destinations.

Before 1959 monasteries in Tibet "were not run as communes with monk canteens providing food for all monks" (Goldstein 2009; see also Lopez 1997:20). Monks depended on sources outside of the monastery for subsistence, generally their natal households.[5] Residents of small monasteries throughout the Himalayan region also depended on their families' support. In a Gelukpa institution in Ladakh, India, monks lived in small residences called *drashag*, or *shag* for short. A shag is typically a small house, constructed and owned by a village family as a residence for a son who becomes a monk. The monk's residence is a privately owned extension of his natal household. He depends on two sources for food: his household for regular supplies and the monastery during communal rituals (Mills 2003, 2009).

Nubri did not have a celibate monastic tradition, so the few men who were sent to monasteries in Tibet prior to 1959 required familial support and therefore came from relatively wealthy households. Today, financial assistance flowing into exile monasteries has reduced the resources parents must devote to sustaining a monk-son. Much support comes through the patronage of affluent Buddhists, especially foreign sponsors in East Asia (Taiwan, Korea), Southeast Asia (Malaysia, Singapore), Europe, and North America (Moran 2004; Zablocki 2009, 2016). In the 1990s Tibetan lamas could garner $40,000 to $60,000 from a single tour to Europe or North America. Many used that money to finance monasteries in Nepal and India (Frechette 2004:111–12). Single donations from wealthy Buddhist patrons from Asian nations could rise into the hundreds of thousands of dollars (Moran 2004:81–82). In addition, some monasteries directly solicit sponsorships for individual monks. A cursory internet search using the terms *sponsor, Tibetan,* and *monk* uncovered more than fifty donation conduits. In some cases eligible monks highlighted on a website are from Nubri.

A result of the new funding paradigm is that the financial burden of supporting a monk has shifted from the family to the institution or, more specifically, from a village household to a transnational network of patrons. Nowadays parents view the financial responsibilities tied to monasticism as a one-time expenditure rather than a lifelong commitment. When enrolling a son in a monastery, parents must supply him with clothing, bedding, and other necessities. In addition, they are expected to sponsor a tea offering for the entire monastic community *(mangja)* and distribute alms to each individual monk *(gyed)*. Parents report spending between 14,000 and 20,000 rupees (roughly $140–$200) on the initial expenses. Thereafter their costs are minimal and mostly voluntary.[6] Parents have effectively been relieved of the long-term financial obligations a son requires to pursue a full-time religious occupation. International funding for exile monasteries therefore plays a large role in facilitating outmigration from Nepal's highland communities.

Cumulative causation has led to the revival of what Goldstein terms "mass monasticism," where "size rather than quality became the objective measure of the success of monasticism (and Buddhism) in Tibet" (1998:15). The pre-1959 Tibetan government's support for religion partially accounts for the fact that monks constituted somewhere between 10 percent and 30 percent of Tibet's male population. Now roughly half of all Nubri males aged five to twenty-nine are monks, which would certainly qualify as mass monasticism and represents a novel development in a society where, until recently, celibate monks were the exception rather than the norm. Although Nubri's parents did not embrace monasticism in the past, they now adopt it with enthusiasm. Admitting a son to a monastery provides an opportunity to gain merit (a cultural rationale) and prestige (a social rationale) while simultaneously raising the hope for future remittances and ensuring the long-term viability of the household by reducing the number of inheritors (economic rationales). It is easy to see why Nubri's parents adjusted their family management strategies to include an option infused with so many culturally consonant benefits.

Yet the rise of mass monasticism in exile has some downsides. Many suspect that greed and fraud sometimes trump honorable religious motives. One monk from Nubri condemned some recently founded institutions that have dubious credentials and cannot properly educate monks. He explained his objections:

> The founder of a new monastery should be a highly respected lama. I usually tell people that there is nothing surprising about the construction of a new monastery. In the Tibetan Buddhist tradition, building the three representations of Buddha's body, speech, and mind is regarded as very meritorious. However, it is not right to build a big monastery and get some monks, then post images on the internet and make it a project to garner donations from foreign patrons. If the monastery is used only to raise money, then it is very bad, because people are being used for economic gain. I am against such activities. I also emphasize that the priority of a monastery should be education. If education is neglected, we are just exploiting people for money. I am against such people because they are not concerned about the monks' education. They are more interested in having a certain number of monks who can be photographed and made part of a project to raise money from abroad. This is something very wrong. There are cases of some monasteries in Kathmandu where the education was so bad that many monks disrobed. It is said that some of these disrobed monks later became vengeful against their former monasteries, accusing the monastery of ruining their lives.

Mass monasticism has the potential to generate mass defections because once ordained, not all monks remain monks. Some leave the monastery for personal reasons; others are expelled for violating rules.

We will return to the topic of the *dralog* (monk who returned to lay status) in chapter 8. Next, we turn to nuns who have never enjoyed the same prestige or material support as monks, but who are nonetheless transforming their lives through transnational financial support that enables outmigration.

CHAPTER 6

Becoming Nuns

THE NUN SERVES HER FAMILY

The aroma of roasting barley infuses the mountain air as we enter the courtyard of a modest dwelling. Ani Tsering (b. 1949) sits beside an open fire, stirring barley grains in a skillet until they dance about, propelled by the popping of their shells. After a few moments Ani Tsering transfers the vessel to the stones paving her courtyard and extinguishes the flame so that the unburnt ends of the sticks do not go to waste. In a sunny corner sits her eighty-year-old mother, body withered by a lifetime of childbearing and agricultural toil, the only perceptible movement coming from her lips as she recites prayers.

Ani Tsering's small house sits on the grounds of Pema Chöling, the temple complex above Rö. She is a village-based nun in Nubri who helped raise her younger siblings, then lived with her two fathers until they died, and still fulfills the role of primary caretaker for her mother. Despite being symbolically detached from the village, gender-based social norms continue to ensnare Ani Tsering in a web of worldly obligations. Here is how she describes her life:

> My parents made me a nun at a very young age. It was not my decision. We nuns are made to work for our parents all our lives. Because I am the eldest child, I had to work very hard to help raise my younger brothers and sisters. Now my sisters are all married and my brothers have started their own households. After I had done all the hard work and all of them were settling

into their own lives, I came up here to live at the monastery. At the time I was in my forties.

When I was around fifty, my parents came up here to live with me. I had to serve my parents as well as one of the lamas. At the same time I had to work to make a living for myself because my parents were not wealthy. I had to fetch water, clean the house, collect firewood for my kitchen, and I needed money to buy an iron stove and other things. So I did not get to care for my parents very well because I had to work so much.

If you are a nun, you don't receive many possessions [from parents]. A daughter who marries receives some wealth because parents lose face if they don't give her some. But since we nuns don't marry, we don't get much of anything. I have only one small plot of land that my parents gave me, but it is not enough to feed me. I am single and have to farm the land by myself. For plowing, I ask others with draft animals for help because I don't have any cattle. We do labor exchange. For one day of plowing, I have to return two days of manual labor. I understand that farming is a sinful activity but, for the sake of my stomach, I have to farm.

We nuns recite prayers for a month or two in winter starting in the twelfth month [of the Tibetan calendar, January]. In addition, the nuns and monks under my lama gather for religious offerings [tsokpa] once every month in the main temple. Food is provided during these rituals. Other than that, we receive no allowances. The aid that comes from down valley [e.g., from the government or nonprofit organizations] does not reach up here to the monastery; it all gets distributed in the village. We have to go here and there [to make a living].

There are several elderly nuns like me at Pema Chöling. We must fend for ourselves. If one of us falls sick, a nun who is a neighbor might help. Mainly it is relatives and family members from the village who come to check on and take care of us. But villagers don't treat us very well. They look down on us. Nobody invites us to their homes or offers us anything. In fact, we have to help them sometimes. I have to go and work for them when they need help, but they do not reciprocate by returning the help.

In light of the difficulties expressed by Ani Tsering, we asked whether her life is easier or more difficult than that of a laywoman. She responded,

Compared to a laywoman, I think a nun leads a more pleasant life. Having children means protecting them from illnesses, and as they grow up you have to provide for their education and welfare. You have to nurture children and conduct healing ceremonies [kurim] in times of sickness. Being a nun is easier because you need to worry only about yourself. As long as you are warm and have a full stomach, you can pray to your root lama and the three jewels and don't have to worry about anything else. You don't have to worry about children suffering from sicknesses or anything.

Nevertheless, in our region nuns are made to work like servants and are not given any education. To be a real nun, education must be given, no? I have no education and can't even speak the Nepali language.[1] When I interact with Nepali traders, the only word I know how to say is *chaina* ["do not have"]. I cannot say any other word. It makes me sad sometimes. I don't have any education, I can't speak Nepali, and I don't have any skills. The only thing I know how to do is pray to the three jewels [Buddha, his teachings, and the community of practitioners], work, and collect firewood.

Nowadays, before dawn I get up and recite prayers. Afterward, I eat breakfast then begin the day's chores. During the day I collect firewood, fetch water, cook, and clean the house. In winter, I find it very difficult to fetch water and firewood since I am old. When there is heavy snowfall, I still need fire to keep warm. So I stock up firewood and buy some essentials to prepare for winter.

That is what my life is like. I never received any education, but was made to work like a servant for all my siblings, who then went on their own ways. Eventually I ended up here where I have to fend for myself, working here and there to earn a living. That is life not only for me, but for other nuns in our region. As I get old, and see what has happened to me, I feel kind of sad. It feels like my appetite increases but I am unable to work hard. I have no one to talk to about my life conditions. You asked me to talk about my life today. Otherwise, who can I talk to? I just keep it to myself.

Ani Tsering's story is a reminder that a woman's path to religious attainment can be strewn with obstacles rooted in gender roles and ideologies (Gutschow 2004). Recognition of the gender imbalance in Tibetan Buddhism has sparked several debates—for example, whether nuns should be allowed to attain full ordination on par with their male counterparts (Tsomo 2004; Mrozik 2009; Mohr and Tsedroen 2010; Heirman 2011). These deliberations within Buddhist circles not only highlight persisting inequities, but also hint at the changing status of Tibetan nuns in a transnational religious environment. Ani Tsering represents a fading tradition of village-based nuns whose socioeconomic obligations overshadow their religious aspirations. Meanwhile, her younger counterparts live in well-endowed institutions in Kathmandu and India, where they study a range of topics from scripture to mathematics. This chapter explores the role that educational migration plays in transforming the nun's role from a servant for her parents' household to a disciple of the Buddha's teachings.

FROM SERVANT (*YOGMO*) TO DISCIPLE (*LOBMA*)

In rural Tibetan society the nun option seems tempting given the hardships that domestic obligations and childbearing impose on women. Orgyan Chokyi (1675–1729), a nun from Dolpo, had a miserable childhood. Born to a vindictive mother and a leprosy-ridden father who wanted a son, she was named Happiness Dashed (Kyilo) and habitually berated and beaten. After her father died, Orgyan Chokyi requested ordination. An elderly nun advised, "You must persevere in the Dharma, for if you were to do worldly work in Peson [her village], you would be forced into corvée labor spring, summer, winter, and fall without rest. As a corvée laborer you would carry water and work all the time. Meet the Dharma, take refuge, study: then you will not suffer" (Schaeffer 2004: 139).

Living in a nunnery could not fully protect Orgyan Chokyi from domestic duties, and she encountered continual distractions by having to serve lay patrons. During one burst of communal religious activity she lamented, "In the kitchen of mistaken conventional reality, with no leisure day or night, I was saddled with the work of [preparing] food and drink" (Schaeffer 2004:157).

The situation was similar in Nubri, where, until recently, it was common for parents to ordain an eldest daughter like Ani Tsering as a nun. An oft-expressed cultural rationale is that, by committing her to a life dedicated to religion, both parents and daughter gain merit. However, by observing the daily routines of village-based nuns, one can deduce that pragmatic motivations supersede cultural rationales. Before the outmigration phenomenon started, most nuns were retained within their households to care for younger siblings, help with farm chores, and eventually act as primary caretakers for aging parents. The life of the village-based nun does include some training and spiritual practice. For example, during the first month of the Tibetan lunar calendar lamas provide basic liturgical instructions, and each month nuns are expected to participate in community rituals. However, beyond intermittent ritual engagements and with the exception of bearing and rearing children, village-based nuns' activities do not diverge considerably from those of their lay counterparts.[2]

In recent years Tibetan lamas have increased the number and improved the quality of monastic options for women. They have done so by constructing nunneries around Kathmandu and in India supported by the transnational flow of religious patronage described in the previous chapter. Several of these institutions feature a curriculum that includes rigorous Buddhist studies in a *shedra* (formal monastic study center) alongside courses in English, mathematics, nursing, medicine, and computer skills.[3] The integrating of secular and religious education occurred in a transnational context of Buddhist modernism (see Drefyus 2003 and Lempert 2012).

Nowadays, parents' motives for ordaining a daughter resemble those for making a son a monk and sending a child to school. Specifically, many want a better life for their child, or as one woman put it, "so she won't have to scratch the earth and put a rope on her head." Another mother said, "I only wish her happiness. I have to struggle and live a hard life. I guess with good education, she will have a better chance at life." One person reasoned, "If she gets married, she will face lots of difficulties. Being a nun, she can have a happy life. Moreover, she devotes her life to a meaningful cause." The last reason reflects the Buddhist philosophy that religious practice is geared toward benefiting all sentient beings. Other parents envision benefits beyond this lifetime by framing their expectations in relation to cyclical existence. One father said, "She will have a better present life and future lives. In this life she can do prayers and light butter lamps, so it will help her avoid being reborn in the hell realm." Another extended the benefits to the family, stating, "It will benefit her in the next life. She will be happier, and it will alleviate her parents' bad karma."

In contrast to anticipated returns from monk-sons, most parents do not foresee economic benefits coming from nun-daughters; only one parent we interviewed mentioned potential remittances. A more commonly expressed sentiment reflects the enduring notion that a nun's role is to serve her family. When asked about the benefits of making a daughter a nun, a father said, "If you make your daughter a nun, she will develop compassion and be nice to her parents. She will help with religion when we die. If we get ill, she can help." Another declared, "If your daughter is a nun, she can come home to look after you in old age or you can go to her at her nunnery."

The shift away from a village-resident nun preference is illustrated by our demographic data. The majority of nuns aged thirty and above (74 percent) reside in their natal villages; in contrast, the majority below age thirty (91 percent) inhabit nunneries in Kathmandu and India. Among nuns aged ten to nineteen, only one out of forty-eight resides locally; she is the caretaker for her elderly grandfather, an important lama. As is the case with monks, the connection between Nubri and Urgyen Tulku plays a key role in shaping the religious outmigration stream: 59 percent of Nubri's nuns aged five through nineteen reside in an institution founded by the great master or one of his sons.

Of the eight nuns from Nubri we interviewed for this project, parents had designated only two of them initially to be village-resident nuns. One of them, Pasang, was ordained at a young age by a local lama. As the eldest daughter in her family, she seemed destined to follow a traditional life course. However, as she explained,

> I was a nun under [lama's name], but it was not working out for me because there was very little opportunity for religious study. Because most of the time I was sent to do work associated with worldly life, there was no opportunity for doing pure religious practice.
>
> I learned that [lama's name, based in Kathmandu] takes anyone from Nubri who wants to become a nun. I wanted very much to join his nunnery. When he visited Nubri he announced that parents could send their daughters to his new nunnery and that the quality of education is very good. And he announced that anyone willing to become a nun would be accepted. That is when I decided to come down to Kathmandu to join this nunnery because there is not much opportunity for religious education back in the village. My parents approved, and I approached my lama to inform him that I wanted to join the nunnery. He told me to be a good nun, and said I would be working all the time if I stayed here in the village.

Pasang's case illustrates how the village-based nun, who is enveloped by her family's domestic requirements, is being supplanted by the nun who resides in an institution with fellow devotees. Nubri's younger nuns now think of themselves more as disciples of the Buddha's teachings than as servants for their families.

PATHWAYS TO CELIBACY

The decision to become a nun is sometimes in the hands of the parents. For example, Diki told us, "It used to be the practice in the village to make someone a nun at a very young age if she frequently falls sick. I was very ill a few months after I was born, so my parents made me a nun by offering my hair to a lama [in the village]. I was told very early that I was a nun." In some cases girls became nuns after family tragedies. Pema first expressed a desire to become a nun after she was orphaned at age eleven; Buti and her two younger sisters were sent to nunneries in Kathmandu after their father died. Other girls seek the monastic option to evade difficult circumstances. Dolma's mother kept her at home because the family needed the labor. She recalled, "We started working in the village from a very young age. My parents wouldn't allow me to become a nun even if I told them that I wanted to become a nun. We needed every hand in the family to help make a living. Later, as I became older and saw others going down to become monks and nuns, I became interested in becoming a nun. That is how I decided to become a nun. Although my parents asked me not to become a nun, they did not stop me from going down to join the nunnery."

Reflecting on her decision to become a nun, Dolma explained, "I think the laywoman's life is hard because she has to bear many children. For many women in the village it also means never-ending work. Further, it depends on what kind of husband a woman has. Some husbands drink a lot and are always drunk. When you think about such things, you realize that a nun's life is definitely a happy one. You don't have to worry about such things at all."

Tashi became a nun to escape an unwanted marriage. At age nineteen her parents accepted engagement beer *(longchang)* from another family, signifying that she was formally pledged to their son. According to Tashi,

> The idea of becoming a nun came about when I realized how this worldly life is full of never-ending work, and it is meaningless in the end. I had no desire at all in getting tied down in this cyclic existence *[jigten khorwa]*. I had seen how my mother has suffered in her own life, and I knew that I would go through the same fate if I were to marry.[4] Since my parents had already promised my hand in marriage and the boy's parents agreed, I realized that they would marry me off at any cost without letting me know in advance of the wedding day. That is why I decided that the only option left for me was to run away.
>
> My father and I came down [to Kathmandu] on a trip, and I returned to the village carrying some loads. After staying in the village for a few days, I learned about this marriage proposal and the plan to marry me off. When I told my mother I didn't want to marry, she gave me a good beating. She admonished me a lot, but I did not have any hard feelings because she is my parent and cares about me.
>
> My mother's beating coincided with the day news reached the village from a lama informing parents that now was the time to send daughters to Kathmandu; new nun recruits would be accepted in the coming month. So I lied to my mother, saying that father asked me to come down to collect another load of goods. But she said I did not have to go and gave me a really good beating. Despite the beating, I decided to leave anyway. My mother said that if I left, she would not think of me as her daughter anymore and that I should not think of her as my mother. It made me so sad to hear these words from my mother. I thought I would never return home.
>
> After reaching Kathmandu I met my father and told him I wanted to become a nun. He didn't object and said it was fine because I was already set on becoming a nun, but worried that if I later disrobed my life would be difficult. I assured him that I would remain a nun all my life, that all these worries of our minds are impermanent, and that one cannot hold on to one's mental fears and worries. My father relented and advised me to be a good nun.

I did not return home for the next eight years. When I met my mother, she had mellowed a lot and was happy to see me again. She was proud about what I had done and acknowledged her mistake by saying that she was the one who had not thought properly. She even apologized to me for the wrongs she had done me.

These stories are not unique. Tibetan women throughout history have pleaded with their parents to become nuns and have sought refuge in nunneries after family tragedies or to escape undesired marriages. This is not to suggest that most women who become nuns do so to flee adverse domestic situations. Nevertheless, eluding the travails of village life is far easier and less risky today than in the past because young women can join well-endowed institutions that actively seek new recruits and provide room, board, and education.

GENDER AND THE PRECARIOUSNESS OF VIRTUE

Our interviews suggest that it is more common these days for a girl to ask to become a nun, or to take matters into her own hands by running away to a nunnery, than for her parents to make the choice for her. Whereas few parents expressed reluctance for their sons to become monks, many stated quite bluntly that the nun option is fraught with potentially shameful consequences. As one man explained,

> The reason I didn't send my daughters to be nuns is because I have some reservations. Being born as a girl, you have no control over your body. Others might take advantage of you. As a result, you must discontinue being a nun. Once you are nun, you have to remain one until you die. It is matter of great dishonor and shame if a nun gives up her vows and elopes with a man. You are surrendering your body, speech, and mind to your lama and the Buddha's teachings when you become a nun. So, disrobing, running away with a man, getting pregnant, and so forth bring great disappointment to one's teacher and bad karma to oneself. That's why I didn't send my daughters to be nuns.

Similarly, when we asked a mother if she planned to send her young daughters to a nunnery, she responded, "I am not going to send them to become nuns. It is source of great anxiety for both parents and children because they may bring anger and disappointment to their lama. It is also hard for them to obey all the discipline in the nunnery. If they become committed nuns, that's okay. If not, it causes the lama to become furious. I prefer them to go to school and later get married, or to find good jobs, which would be much better."

Another mother explained, "If you send a daughter to become a nun, she will take vows from the lama and have her hair cut. After that, it is a great sin if she disrobes. Bad times are upon us. Nuns are getting disrobed left and right. If I send my daughter to school, then she might become well educated. If not, at least she won't bring great sin onto herself."

The pathway for a monk to return to village life is much easier than for a nun. As Pema told us, "Monks who disrobe don't face too many difficulties. But society regards it as something very bad when a nun disrobes. Further, a monk's religious education will be of use if he disrobes. If a nun disrobes, there is no way anyone would invite her to perform *shabten* [prayer ceremony to promote long life, repel negative influences, or bring good fortune]."

The liturgical skills ex-monks learn in the monastery are useful in the village context and also can be used to generate seasonal income in Kathmandu. But as Pema pointed out, no such opportunities exist for former nuns. Furthermore, parents often encourage or even expect a son to disrobe so he can succeed his father as head of the household, as we will discuss in chapter 8. Gender shapes the prospects for return migration because sons, not daughters, inherit the majority of land and bovines that are critical for agropastoral subsistence. Social and economic variables therefore erect higher barriers for an ex-nun to surmount if she wishes a return to village life: acute shame versus mild embarrassment for renouncing vows, partiality for sons as successors, and a preference to engage male, rather than female, practitioners to perform household rituals. Some former nuns have returned to their villages, married, and started families. However, they are fewer in number compared to former monks and tend to conceal evidence that they once dressed in the red attire of the celibate nun.

DEMISE OF THE VILLAGE NUN?

In the near future nuns will no longer represent a significant component of Nubri's resident population. All the nuns we interviewed were fully aware of the traditional practice of designating a daughter to be a village-based nun, but only one anticipated caring for her parents in old age. Sangmo told us, "[My parents] are quite young at the moment. However, they say that their two nun-daughters will take care of them in old age. Although my elder brother is in the village, he has his own family to take care of. I am not able to help my parents at all right now because I am struggling with my own education. Once I complete my education, I hope to take care of my parents."

The other nuns did not envision a similar future. Pasang's parents built her a small residence at Pema Chöling, the monastery complex where Ani Tsering lives, but she made it clear that she will not return to live there as a caretaker. Rather, she prefers to continue studying and plans to undertake a long meditation retreat. Tashi, the woman who became a nun at age nineteen to escape an unwanted marriage, was adamant about not returning to her village. She emphasized, "I want to continue my religious practice and I don't have any plans to leave the nunnery. What will I do if I leave the nunnery now? I have already wasted half of my life. I don't want to waste any part of my life anymore. I only wish to get more opportunities to undertake retreat and practice."

Perhaps her reticence is related to the changing opportunity structure for female religious practitioners. We asked each of the nuns to contrast her own experience with that of a village-based nun. Diki, who actually started as a nun in the village, said,

> The nuns in the village know how to read and they might also know how to meditate. However, in terms of religious education, they are not in a position to achieve much because living in the village means that they are not able to fully avoid work associated with worldly life. They cannot devote their mind to religious practice because they have to help their parents. Getting bogged down in everyday existence in the village poses great obstacles to a pure religious path. Here at the nunnery, we do not have to worry about the affairs of worldly life. We can focus entirely on religious practice.

Buti commented, "Due to the kind grace of Rinpoche, everything is provided for us in this nunnery, including food and clothing. Nuns in the village, however, have to take care of themselves. Although they get some food and gifts whenever there is a big religious ceremony, they don't get to study much since they have to work for their daily livelihood as well as help their parents in farming and herding. We can just focus on our studies, whereas village nuns have to work for everything they need including food and clothing."

In contrast to village-based nuns, studious women residing in the contemporary nunneries are encouraged to enter an eight-year course in a shedra for higher Buddhist studies. Those who complete the course receive the title *ani lobpön* (nun spiritual master). Additionally, the nunneries create long-term roles for their residents through the expectation that they offer services in proportion to their age and education by working as administrators, disciplinarians overseeing younger members, and other duties. One nun from Nubri even holds the indispensable role of driver for her nunnery and is tasked with everything from fetching supplies to conveying ill nuns to the hospital. The nuns we interviewed place high value on their education, are proud of their achievements, and recognize that such opportunities are scarce in their natal villages.

Meanwhile, Ani Tsering continues to reside at Pema Chöling where she remains physically removed from, yet deeply embedded within, the bustle of village activity. Each year she witnesses the dwindling of her companions as the forces of aging and mortality whittle toward extinction the village-based nun tradition. Meanwhile, the shifting role of the nun from servant to disciple is forcing laypeople in their forties and fifties to contemplate a fundamental question of rural existence that we will address in the final chapter. Who will provide care for the elderly?

CHAPTER 7

Becoming Students

THE SON GOES FIRST

Khandro gave birth to eight children, but only three survived. Tsomo and Yangkyi are her daughters. Lobsang, the youngest, is her only son. The children came of age in the 1990s, when education, both secular and monastic, was becoming a common option for boys, but not yet for girls. Khamsum, their father, explained the family's situation:

> I have a hard time making a living by doing backbreaking farm work. Without education my son would end up like me, so I managed to pay for some of his tuition. Because I have only one son, I couldn't send him off to be a monk. I need someone to whom I can pass the ancestral property and the charge of the household, one who will uphold the village regulations and cultivate the land. If he were to become a monk, he wouldn't be permitted to marry. That's why I sent him to school.
>
> Tsomo is our eldest child. She went to school here in the village when she was little. However, she couldn't continue her education due to our livelihood problem. We were short of helping hands. My wife and I were the only ones who could work. Because of that I couldn't give her an education. I sent her to work in our fields.

Here Khamsum outlines a family management strategy that entails sending his only son to school while keeping his eldest daughter at home to help with agricultural chores. Eventually he planned to follow the customary route of marrying his girls off to other households once confident that his son would return as the new head of household. However, that plan quickly began to unravel. Tsomo's younger sister, Yangkyi, began pestering her father and mother so she could go to school. Yangkyi recalled,

> When I was very young I didn't know about education. My sister always used to say, "I want to go to school, I want to go to school." But I didn't say anything. One day she told me, "I am too old to go to school now, so you should go." So I told my father, "I want to go to school." But he didn't want to take me down [to Kathmandu]. Every winter he used to go down, so when he was preparing for the trip I cried and I cried. I wanted to go with him, but he didn't want to take me. My mother scolded my father and said, "Let her go. Maybe you can find a school for her." So my father took me down.

Khamsum recalled Yankyi's resolve and commented,

> Yes, Yangkyi was making a lot of fuss about going to school. Because many children were going, she wanted to go as well. Here in our village school one cannot advance to higher grades, and we were set with domestic work [because they did not send Tsomo to school]. So I took Yangkyi with me to Kathmandu. But without the means to pay fees, it was difficult to get her an education. I tried admitting her to a convent school, but the father there told me that they had no vacancy. Then I went to another school, but they turned me down saying they only admit orphans. I pleaded that although she is not an orphan, we could not afford to give her an education, and she really wants to study. Then they said, "In that case, we will accept her." They also agreed to find her a sponsor.

Yangkyi continued the story: "I stayed in that school for only one month. Because there were so many students, the new ones were shifted to another school. I cried a lot thinking that because I was admitted to one school and then ended up at another, my father wouldn't be able to find me. The teachers consoled me, saying they will show him the way from the first school."

Yangkyi completed her primary education and is now pursuing higher studies in Kathmandu. Her sister, Tsomo, however, never managed to get fully on track with her education. She said,

> Because my brother and sister were enrolled in school [in Kathmandu] there was no one left to work at home. My parents needed me. When I was sixteen, a person began teaching evening classes in my village. The teacher told me I was intelligent and should attend class six at the school in Phillim [one day's walk down valley from her village]. So the teacher made a certificate stating that I had passed class five, when in fact I had only attended up to class one or two. With the certificate in hand I informed my parents that I wanted to continue studying, and they gave me permission to attend the school in Phillim. I joined class six.

There were no tests when I was attending the evening classes in the village. So in Phillim, for almost a month, I was in big trouble because I was not used to regular school. There were two of us from our village, me and my friend. She was very tense because she was unable to learn anything. Her behavior became crazy, so she returned home.

After two months I started to understand something, so I started to study harder in the hope that I would learn more. After four months we had exams and I passed all of them. Afterward I was encouraged. I could keep up with other students who had studied continuously. But as the year drew to a close and we neared the final exam, the Maoists came.[1] They told all the students to attend their program or else we wouldn't be allowed to sit for the exam. We had no choice because we didn't want to miss our final exam. I didn't want to stay for another year in class six. Some ran away from school, but most of us attended the program.

The Maoists walked us down valley for two days to a village where they were holding the program. They gave us some rice and lentils and put us up in villagers' houses. During the day they tried to show their program, but it was raining and the wind was blowing everything around. After several days we were allowed to go back to the school to take our exams.

After the exam was over, I returned to my village for a two-month holiday. My parents had been very worried. Some parents even went to the school only to find it empty. When the holiday finished and I was ready to return to school, my mother stopped me. My father had no objections to my returning, but my mother was worried that the Maoists would take me. I told her not to worry. If the Maoists tried to take me, I wouldn't go with them but would come back home. But my mother didn't listen at all.

Khamsum explained,

I was in Kathmandu at that time. I heard the news that my daughter was in the group that had been taken by the Maoists to a meeting, but I was pretty sure they wouldn't harm the children. Nevertheless, it was around the time when tensions were building between the army and the Maoists. War was looming and there was great danger to life. If you were associated with the Maoists, the army would shoot you dead. They wouldn't hesitate to kill you if you had anything to do with the Maoists. So my wife, fearing for our daughter's life, refused to allow Tsomo to return to school. Tsomo insisted on studying up to tenth class, but since that incident we did not allow her to continue. She returned to help us with the agricultural work.

Tsomo completed her tale of disrupted education:

About one month after school had resumed, the teachers sent letters home requesting that students return even though it was late. Once again, my father had no objection, but my mother did. A teacher passed through the village. He was returning to the school, so I told him that I would go along. But when I had packed all my bags and was ready to go, my father warned that if something went wrong, the doors of my home would be closed to me forever. So I gave up. After that my mother became very ill. I still held out hope of returning to school if she recovered, but she remained very sick for two or three months. I was still getting letters from my teachers asking that I return to school. I couldn't because my mother was very sick and my father was away from the village attending a religious ceremony. I was left alone at home with my mother.

We begin the chapter with a case that illustrates some of the challenges and dilemmas that arose during the initial years of educational migration. The 1990s was a time when new opportunities were emerging and parents were adjusting their family management strategies in response. Education for girls was still a low priority, so Tsomo and Yangkyi had to cajole their parents into allowing them the opportunity to learn. Yangkyi overcame her parents' reluctance, which enabled her to enter a school in Kathmandu. Tsomo, by contrast, was the elder daughter, whose labor was sorely needed on the farm. Her ambition to study was continually thwarted by familial obligations and the dangers stemming from Nepal's civil war. Meanwhile, their younger brother's education continued more or less uninterrupted until he completed tenth grade. This family exemplifies how a range of variables, from gender and birth parity to political instability, can lead to different educational outcomes.

In this chapter we address the questions of why and how parents are sending children outside of Nubri for school. The following sections recount the obstacles local education has faced over the past decades, explore parents' thoughts on the benefits of secular education, analyze educational migration within a framework of migration network theory, and extend the cumulative causation argument by linking monastic migration with the sending of children to secular schools. We conclude by speculating on the potential for educational migration to enhance rather than reduce socioeconomic disparities in Nubri.

EDUCATING NUBRI CHILDREN: A FITFUL START

The reason Khamsum and Khandro sent their children away from the village for education was that government services in Nubri were nearly nonexistent in the 1990s. Ramshackle schools lacked basic necessities such as textbooks and teachers, prompting a local joke that the structures could be more gainfully used as animal pens. High caste Hindu teachers from the lowlands would show up—irregularly and unannounced—open the school for a few days, herd any children who happened to straggle by, and then attempt to instruct them in a language (Nepali) that the students did not understand. Teachers often griped about "backward" villagers and dreadful accommodations, while parents quibbled about the teachers' haughtiness and lack of commitment to stay for more than a few weeks at a stretch. Teachers who did stay for an extended period had limited access to their accustomed foods, forcing them to rely on unfamiliar (and, to them, unpalatable) local staples. Tsetan, who is now in his thirties, recalled how one teacher used to extort food from his students by refusing them entry if they showed up without a "gift." Commanded by his teacher to bring an egg one day, Tsetan became despondent when he found that his hen had not produced the required entrance fee. In desperation he clutched the bird and attempted to squeeze out an egg. The hen died. Rather than show up empty-handed, he skipped school that day.

Getting an education in the early 1990s was extremely challenging. We found this out from Mingyur, a middle-aged man who described his experience:

> My father sent me to the village school when I was thirteen [1990], but we didn't get much time to study. My father said education is not going to work out because there are lots of children at home, so I should take the cattle to pasture, collect wood, and do other chores. The Nepali teacher told me that I wouldn't be able to study very well here, so he asked me to come along with him. I made a ruse to go down valley to get corn, but I actually ran away from home and stayed in my teacher's village for a while.[2] I sent a message to inform my parents, telling them that I am sorry for wanting to study but not to worry.
>
> At that time I faced lots of problem. I had no money and there were no classes on Friday and Saturday so I had to work in the teacher's home. I stayed there for nine months, and then got into a school in Gorkha where I stayed for three and a half years. My father found me and said it is worthless for me to attend school. I told him that I want to study here, and that I was not coming home. My father said, "No. We have many small children at home and we are short of labor." During those days life was very hard. I used to carry rice from the lowlands to the village three times a year during winter [each round-trip took two weeks].
>
> Then my mother died. She was young, only thirty-nine. There were four children at home and my father was facing problems, so I came back. I am the eldest child. I really wanted to study but I had no money.

The lack of local opportunities forced parents and aspiring students like Mingyur to seek education outside of Nubri. As outlined in chapter 4, the growth of Tibetan exile institutions and the emergence of differential demographic trends created new opportunities for Nepal's Buddhist highlanders. Parents, often at the urging of their children, began to contemplate the potential benefits of secular education.

As the phenomenon of sending children out for education was gaining momentum, the state of local schools began to improve, but not rapidly enough to stem the tide of outmigration. Purbu Tsewang, a man from Rö, had been sent by his parents to an aunt's home in neighboring Manang. By completing primary school at the top of his class, he was awarded a scholarship to attend college in Kathmandu, where he majored in education. In the late 1990s he returned to Rö and assumed leadership of the local school. Together with a newly constituted school board and Lama Jigme, the village's young and progressive head lama, they created a boarding school that housed over one hundred students in its heyday. However, enrollment fluctuated erratically, especially when representatives of monasteries came through the valley seeking recruits.

Rö's boarding school inspired others to follow suit. Nowadays, with the help of foreign donations, several schools are operating in Nubri at a level that seemed unachievable a mere decade ago. Yet all of them face the same problem: how to compete with the well-endowed schools in Kathmandu. Recruiting teachers is a major problem because most educated individuals prefer to stay in the city. Keeping a school running at high altitude during the frigid winter months is also a daunting challenge. Children who pass fifth grade (the highest level offered locally) sometimes must repeat a grade if they get an opportunity to study further in Kathmandu. Karma Chögyal, a monk living in Kathmandu, often visits his natal village in Nubri and takes time to observe the local school. His analysis of the situation mirrors many of the concerns that parents have expressed over the years. He said,

> We are deeply aware of the problems created by taking children away from the village [to attend schools or monasteries elsewhere]. This might be misunderstood as undoing very good works, something similar to the Tibetan saying "wiping away your footprints with your hands."[3] I would argue that it is not really that. It is true that many people have worked so hard to build such a great school up there in the village. Despite having such a great building and huge investments, it is a great waste of everything if the future of these children in the school is played with. Just because there is a school in the village, one cannot tell the parents that they can't send their children to outside schools, because the time spent by children in school is very precious and whatever happens during this time cannot be turned back. If the school up there is really creating an environment whereby everything is done to ensure that the future of children is benefited, then I would fully agree with the point that taking children away from the village school is absolutely wrong. If the village school is doing a great job, then sending children away to outside schools is really a case of wiping away your footprints with your hands. If the school is not doing a great job, it is like rubbing a dried bone in

front of a dog's nose [i.e., an enticement that lacks sustenance].[4] We should make sure that all these investments [in the school] bear good results and achieve what they are intended to do. Otherwise, it is like sprinkling water upon something without really quenching the thirst.

Karma Chögyal's assessment is a reminder of how difficult it is to run a school in rural Nepal. Keeping steady enrollments is challenging because parents are more than willing to seek outside options for their children if they believe the local school is substandard. Frank discussions such as these can be demoralizing for people like Purbu Tsewang, but they have also motivated him to continue striving toward the goal of keeping children in the village by providing a viable educational opportunity. The fact that several schools are still running—and continue improving—is proof that those efforts are bearing fruit.

In contrast to the simple process of enrolling a child in a local school, parents who seek opportunities outside Nubri must navigate the complex admissions terrain in Kathmandu, find sponsorships or somehow arrange school fees, and trek down valley several times a year to ensure their children have places to stay during holidays. Many are willing to take on these challenges because of the value they now confer on education.

VALUING EDUCATION

In a fundraising video by an organization that seeks to educate children from Nubri, an American man comments on the common problem of absentee teachers in villages and then states, "In the villages they don't value education because no one's there to teach them the value of education or how that's going to help them change their world for the better."[5]

The man's claim is erroneous on many levels. First, how could a people who do not value education devise a multifaceted village administrative system (see chapter 3) that is contingent on maintaining detailed *written* records? Second, he presumes that people in Nubri are incapable of appreciating education without the guiding light of foreigners. By doing so he reproduces the ethnocentric bias that attending a secular school is the only valid indicator of "education." But in Nubri religious learning has a long history. Lama Gyamtso, one of Nubri's most venerated clerics, reflected on his own experience to explain the significance of a Buddhist education and its spiritual as well as practical applications:

> Tibetan studies have been taught here in our society for a very long time across many generations. From my own experience, I have seen that it is very relevant for earning a living as well as developing skills like speaking,

reading, and writing. There are many things you can achieve by studying Buddhism. Just as one can study higher and higher to become a teacher in a school, in Buddhism you can pursue studies that are more advanced. For instance, one starts by learning the basic alphabet, and then progresses to debate, higher practices, and initiations. One can go further and receive oral transmissions, then do meditation.

In life you will come across both happiness and suffering. When you are trained in Buddhism you are trained to deal with these emotions. Just as fire will have heat and water will have moisture, emotions will have their own properties. Thus, Buddhist training will help one face life and deal with happiness and sufferings.

Education has long been a core feature of Nubri society. For centuries Nubri's men (and to a much lesser extent women) have been undertaking religious training ranging from long-term meditation sojourns to short-term instructions. During the first month of the lunar calendar many spent several weeks in retreat *(tsam)* at a monastery complex near their village. By residing with elderly lamas, young men learned to read, write, and improve their liturgical skills. Some studied under medical practitioners *(amji)* who taught them how to diagnose and treat a variety of ailments. Others studied under astrologers *(tsipa)* and learned how to interpret complex charts and compose natal horoscopes.

Nowadays if the people of Nubri do not value education, then why are they sending the majority of their children to distant schools and monasteries? Even a person like Lama Gyamtso, who never had the opportunity to study at a secular school, said,

> Although I am an elderly person who now stays away from society, I believe that school education is very important. School education will help you earn a living since you are taught the ways of life. Since schools were established I have seen how important [secular] education is. Without water you cannot have food. Similarly, education is something very essential. I am an old person who received only one type of education and never received school education. But it is not because I don't appreciate school education. Back then, we had no idea of what school education is. Today, school education is very important and something everyone must have.

Similarly, when we asked the middle-aged monk Karma Chögyal about the value of secular education, he responded,

> Modern secular education is great. This is the twenty-first century, when education is key. That is something His Holiness [the Dalai Lama] always stresses. I think people are realizing the importance of education as the number of children being sent to schools is increasing. This is a very good development, and it helps the future of these young children and in turn our own

community. I always tell our people that the real inheritance we can bequeath to our children is education. The inheritances of a few beads of coral, nuggets of gold, or the dilapidated traditional house are not that worthwhile. In fact, a drunkard son might fritter away all these things in a few days. However, if you have education, you don't have to worry about losing it or its value decreasing.

I tell people not to buy coral or turquoise with the money they earn because there is the danger of losing these things. I tell parents instead to invest it in their children's education. If you have four children, you must set aside some capital to invest in their future. It is immoral for parents to just go on producing children like animals and not care for their future. Some people use this common saying: if dogs can find food to eat, why should humans worry about making a living? This is immoral; this is not taking responsibility. Once you produce children, you should take responsibility for their future. So it is a good thing now that people are sending their children to schools. I think it is great if we can send our children to schools run by Tibetans because they will receive both traditional Tibetan education as well as modern secular education.

If one asks people in Nubri how they view education, one simply cannot conclude that they "don't value education." Our interviews revealed two related themes that illustrate how personal experiences frame the way parents express the importance of schooling their children. Parents are acutely aware of the limitations their own lack of education creates in a rapidly changing society, and they view education as an escape route from the drudgery of village life. For example, when we asked a forty-three-year-old mother of six whether education for her children is important, she replied emphatically,

> It is very important because we, the parents, did not receive any education and had to work hard all our lives to make a living. We can speak neither English nor Nepali. We speak only our own language. Because our children learn English, Nepali, and many other things, they don't have to carry loads on their backs [to make a living]. If they do well in their education, they can use their hands to write to make a living instead of carrying loads on their backs.
>
> Due to my lack of education, I neither know how to ask for food nor how to find a toilet [when traveling outside of Nubri]. When buying clothing or food, I don't know how to count and say [numbers] in Nepali. I feel like a deaf-mute *[lenba]* who must use hand signals. Because of what we went through, we want our children to have better lives.

A twenty-seven-year-old mother of three concurred:

> I did not receive any education. Our parents were poor and could not afford to send us to faraway schools. There used to be a government school in the village, and the teachers from the outside would come and stay for a short

time and then leave. So we ended up spending our young lives fetching water and collecting wood. [Without education] you face difficulties when you go outside [of Nubri] because you cannot speak [Nepali] or write letters or even write your name. Although you know what you think or want, you cannot communicate it to others.

Because we did not receive any education when we were young, our lives turned out like this. We know how life is when you do not have education. We don't want our children to go through life like we did. We want better lives for our children. That is why we are giving our children education.

A fifty-year-old mother of eight expressed a similar sentiment:

If our children want to be equal or hold their heads high, then education is important. Here we just put a rope on our head [to carry a load] and scratch the earth [farm] to make a living. If our children have education, whether they stay here or go outside they can lead a less difficult life. When we went to Kathmandu, we found out that we are like deaf-mutes *[lenba]*. We decided to send our kids for education so they wouldn't have to scratch the earth and put a rope on their head, so they can have easier lives.

Many mothers and fathers alike now see education for daughters as a superior alternative to marriage within the village. When we asked whether it is better to retain a daughter in the village and send her as a bride to another household or send her to school at an early age, almost everyone chose the latter option. One father said quite bluntly, "I had no education because my parents didn't know about it. Look at my own suffering! I want the best for my kids. Sending my daughter as a bride is useless. She will only be working for others. But if she gets education she can go places, she might find a good job with a salary."

Similarly, a thirty-nine-year-old mother reflected on her own lack of education and sufferings as a bride:

The current reality is that we are stupid *[kukpa]*. We know our lives are hard. If children know English, Nepali, and accounting, they can lead better lives than their parents. If we send a daughter as a bride, she will have to work hard. Without working hard you can't even eat. I came [to this household as a bride] at age nineteen. I suffered a lot. I gave birth to many children. I had eight kids, but only three survived. Now I am not healthy, I have many illnesses. I can't do hard work, I can only do chores at home. I have back pains and am unable to eat much. I must rest often while working. If my daughter gets an education she can take better care of herself and children. Look at us, we don't know how to take care of ourselves or raise kids. I underwent many hardships. I don't want my daughter to suffer like that.

Despite consistently and commonly expressing recognition of their own limited prospects and a desire for their children not to suffer a

FIGURE 11. Children and parents, 1990s. All of them later migrated for education.
Photos by Geoff Childs.

similar fate, parents often struggle to secure schooling for their kids. The next section explores the pivotal role connections (and lack thereof) play in school admissions.

THE EFFICACY OF STRONG AND WEAK TIES

In a pair of influential articles, Granovetter distinguishes between weak and strong ties to theorize the way social networks affect the propensity to migrate (1973, 1982). He qualifies the strength of an interpersonal tie according to several variables, including time spent together, emotional bonding and affection, and the degree to which people engage in acts of reciprocity (Granovetter 1973:1361). Strong ties characterize relationships with close kin and friends; weak ties involve more distant interactions and less intimacy. Regarding migration, Granovetter argues, "Weak ties provide people with access to information and resources beyond those available in their own social circle; but strong ties have greater motivation to be of assistance and are typically more easily available" (1982:209). Weak ties are especially important because they provide information and resources that lie outside the domain of one's network of strong ties, yet they are also variable. A poor person's weak ties are more likely to be beneficial with someone of higher than lower socioeconomic status (1982:209; see also Lin, Ensel, and Vaughn 1981).

Granovetter research, and that of those who followed suit, focuses mainly on labor migration. Here we argue that parents must rely on a combination of strong and weak ties to get their children into schools. The strong tie is often a monk who has a kinship relationship that obligates him to help a family member, while the weak tie is a *jindag* (sponsor) who provides the financial support for a child's education that parents cannot afford. School administrators who connect children and their families with potential patrons—generally foreigners of relatively high socioeconomic status—typically arrange the sponsorship. The student-sponsor relationship can be considered a weak tie because it often involves limited contact between two people who may never have met before, mainly through sporadic correspondence and the occasional visit mediated by school administrators. Even after years of support, most parents we interviewed know virtually nothing about their child's sponsor.

The jindag, as a weak tie, facilitates migration by granting financial support. Meanwhile, admission into a school often depends on a strong tie. Many students enter a school with the help of an administrator, plucked from the ranks of an associated monastery, who has a kinship relationship with the child and her parents. This may seem counterintuitive because, in an environment of mass monasticism, one may expect monks to steer young people toward religious institutions rather than secular schools. Bear in mind, however, that monks in Kathmandu are not sequestered from society. To the contrary, most are immersed in the modernity of urban life and are continuously exposed to the broader world through travel, social media, and links with the international Buddhist community. In addition, the difference between religious and secular education in Tibetan monasteries has never been clear-cut. Many monasteries now offer courses in English, mathematics, and other subjects alongside Buddhist studies (Dreyfus 2003; Bangsbo 2004; Lempert 2012).

As discussed in chapter 5, parents began sending some of their sons to monasteries in the 1980s. Although outmigration was a mere trickle at that time, monks established a foothold in Kathmandu and subsequently acted as a conduit for further migration. By the 1990s a monastery-school nexus formed when some abbots opened secular educational facilities that cater to Himalayan communities. Many administrators of these schools are monks whose positions rotate every few years. There seems to be a correlation between an administrator's place of origin and children who are admitted under his tenure. For example, one recent graduate reported, "I have an uncle in that school, my mother's brother. He enrolled me and my cousins. He was a monk in the associated monastery, so he knew the school very well. He was working as an administrative assistant at the school when we were admitted."

Other young people informed us that they got into a school through similar connections. One woman recalled, "At the time of my admission my *agu* [father's brother] was the principal of the school, so he had a good connection with the school's director. He helped my father get a spot for me." Another graduate explained, "My agu is in Kathmandu. He turned [responsibility for] my studies over to his son, who is a monk [at the monastery that oversees a school]. He talked to the director and I got a sponsorship." A girl of similar age said, "I have an *ashang* [mother's brother] who is a monk in the monastery, so he knew the school very well. He even worked as the director's assistant when I was new in the school. He enrolled me and my cousins."

The importance of strong ties is further highlighted when considering the cases of parents who lacked good connections. Some said that they contacted schools directly and literally begged administrators to accept their child. The strategy sometimes worked, but other times ended in failure and humiliation. We heard many poorer people grumble that better-off parents have an easier time finding admission and sponsors for their children. This raises a question: Does a reliance on social networks for moving children from the village to urban-based schools enhance existing socioeconomic disparities in the village?

REPRODUCING INEQUALITY?

In chapter 4 we presented evidence that population growth and economic scarcity can be an incentive for parents to manage household sizes by sending children to religious and secular institutions. It would therefore be tempting to infer that poverty drives outmigration. However, that conclusion is problematic because on the one hand it oversimplifies parents' motives by pegging them exclusively to immediate needs, while on the other hand it ignores the fact that migration typically requires capital and relies on social networks. Because the level of benefits one can derive from a social network is often associated with wealth and prestige—two factors long thought to be linked with mobility (Lin 1999)—we suspect that children from families with higher economic status in Nubri are more likely than others to gain admission to Tibetan-run boarding schools.

Using a methodology for investigating emic perceptions of relative wealth (Grandin 1988), we asked knowledgeable Nubri residents to rank households in their respective villages from one (wealthiest) to five (poorest). In follow-up interviews our interlocutors could easily distinguish gradations in affluence among their neighbors based on "external wealth" *(chiyi nor),* or visible assets such as landholdings and cattle, and "internal wealth" *(nangi nor)* consisting of gold, jewelry, and other assets that are kept within the confines of the home but sometimes displayed during public events. Nubri residents understand that they live in a society with considerable economic variation between households. In contrast, some schools' funding appeals project an image of undifferentiated poverty in Nepal's highlands. For example, the following text appeared on a school's website:

> Our students come from the high mountains of Nepal, from villages that have no electricity, no toilets, no sanitation, no telecommunications, no hospitals, no roads and no schools. They come from villages that are 6 to 14 days' trek from the nearest road, villages that lie above 10,000 feet (3000 m). Getting to and from the villages is often dangerous because of treacherous trails, falling rock, landslides and avalanches. . . . We know the children

before they come to us. . . . In any case, their backgrounds are well-known. They are means-tested by virtue of their Himalayan origins.

School administrators may be tempted to depict Himalayan communities as desperately poor because doing so makes it easier to solicit financial support from foreign donors. Nevertheless, the funding appeal portrays communities as they may have appeared to outsiders two or three decades ago, but not today.[6] The "means-tested" claim is misleading because it implies all families are uniformly poor. Our analysis shows that among households with children aged five to nineteen, those who have placed at least one in a boarding school rank slightly higher on the relative wealth scale than those who did not do so. It is therefore possible that the most preferred boarding schools have unwittingly admitted more children from relatively wealthy households. If this is the case, the reproduction of existing socioeconomic differences in Nubri may be counteracting the potential leveling effect of educational migration.

We started this chapter with a case study to illustrate some of the challenges parents faced in the early years of educational migration, and gender dynamics that paved an easier educational pathway for sons than daughters. We also emphasized that the people of Nubri have a history of valuing education, just not the secular type that today's modernity discourse venerates. Parents, embarrassed by adversities engendered by their own illiteracy and inability to speak Nepali, recognize secular education as a means for their children to avoid lives circumscribed by agricultural toil. Foreign patrons, as weak ties, provide the financial means for parents to send their children to school. Meanwhile urban-based monks, as strong ties, facilitate educational migration through their access to gatekeepers in the school admission process. We do not mean to imply that all children are helped by monastic brethren; the connections parents use to gain admission for their children are as varied as the institutions where they end up. Nevertheless, monks as a migration vanguard contribute to cumulative causation whereby "each act of migration alters the social context within which subsequent migration decisions are made" (Massey et al. 1993:451). In this case monks—especially those in the capacity of school administrators—effectively reduced the risks and costs of migration for their kin and thereby played a role in increasing the magnitude of outmigration.

In chapters 5–7 we analyzed the motives and means for moving children out of the village and into urban monasteries and schools. The fact that the majority of children are now being raised in institutions rather than their natal households is strong evidence that the cumulative weight of parental decisions has generated a culture of migration. This raises vexing issues that we address in chapter 8. What incentives do educational migrants have to return to the village, and how do parents induce some of their children to return home so they can contribute to the reproduction of the household and Nubri society?

The Household Succession Quandary

A MONK RETURNS

Walking through Rö one day we spotted a young man drinking a cup of tea outside a store beside the pathway. Yeshi's pale complexion and clean clothing were incongruous with villagers of his age group. We stopped, engaged him in conversation, and quickly confirmed our suspicion that he is a former monk who had just returned to the village. Yeshi explained how this happened:

> My parents sent me to school in Manang [the neighboring valley]. Usually when you finish that school you move on to the city. But my father died so my mother requested many times that I return because there was nobody who could do the work at home. But once here I became very sick and didn't recover for a long time. Lamas were consulted. They did a divination that revealed I should embárk on a religious pathway. So I went before a local lama who made me a monk.
>
> My health still did not improve so I went to Kathmandu to receive treatment from a lama. Once recovered, I joined his monastery. Actually, I had wanted to become a monk from a very young age. My mother told me to return home, but I didn't want to. I wanted to stay at the monastery. My maternal uncles were there. They helped me get admitted to the monastery, where I stayed for seven years.
>
> I progressed with my studies and eventually the monastery sent me for training in Tibetan medicine. But my mother had been telling me to return time and time again, so eventually I came back. I have two brothers. One of them died. The other, who is younger than me, is a monk in Kathmandu. I got the responsibility [to be the household's successor]. Because I have been

told over and over to return, I came here three weeks ago to have a look. Our house is very old and needs to be repaired, and my mother feels uncomfortable because she has been staying at my uncle's home for a long time.

I will remain here and assume the role of my father. My lama told me to study Tibetan medicine for six years and then serve the monastery for three years. Now I feel very uncomfortable. My aim was to remain a monk and finish my medical studies. Now I've lost the opportunity. I wanted to stay at and serve the monastery until death. I told this to my mother, but she kept telling me the problems that she is facing and that there is no one to look after her. My mother is quite old and my brother is young so he can't do much. I have no other option.

Despite wanting to remain a monk, Yeshi felt obligated to follow his mother's entreaties and abandon monastic life. It was his duty, as the eldest surviving son in the family, to assist his mother and become the kyimdag (head of household). The needs of the family superseded his desire to continue monastic education. But Yeshi is not the only *dralog* (monk who returned [to lay status]) in his village. In chapter 5 we foreshadowed that mass monasticism can lead to mass defections. In the past, dralog were rare and somewhat stigmatized in Nubri society. Nowadays they constitute 36 percent of the males aged fifteen to twenty-four who live full-time in Yeshi's village. Many of them are married.

We begin and end this chapter with a focus on the dralog because today he may represent the most reliable and viable candidate for household successor. In between, we explore the challenges parents face in trying to arrange marriages for children who have attained secular education. The objective of this chapter is to demonstrate the adaptability of Nubri's family system in a rapidly changing society.

THE EDUCATED SON CONUNDRUM

Until the 1990s secular education was rare, and nonfarming occupations nearly unattainable in Nubri. Parents therefore held considerable sway over children's' life courses and had a relatively easy task ensuring that one of their sons, preferably the eldest, would become the new kyimdag. High fertility helped. If a woman bears six children (roughly the norm for Nubri in the 1990s), there is a very high probability that at least one of them will be male (Guilmoto 2009:532). However, the vicissitudes of mortality meant that any family could be left without a son. Some parents bore witness to the death of all their sons, leaving them without a successor.

The greatest obstacle to household succession is no longer the peril of mortality. Rather, it is the very real possibility that a son will not return home after completing his education. Born in a village but raised in an urban environment, a son may anticipate a life course that extricates him from agro-pastoral subsistence. He becomes somewhat estranged from village life and develops intentions about marriage and reproduction that may diverge from his parents' aims. Succession becomes tenuous when parents relinquish the role of habituating their children to village life.

How do parents arrange for a household successor when their sons are raised in an environment that is so alien to village life? Some convince a son to return by appealing to filial obligations. For example, Lhakpa completed twelfth grade and now lives in his natal village. When asked what prompted him to return, Lhakpa replied in a matter-of-fact manner, "I am the oldest son. My father and mother are getting old and needed me to take over the household." He now shares a house with his parents, wife, and small children. But not all parents are so successful. Coaxing a son back to a village where there are few jobs commensurate with his skills is a tricky proposition. Arranging his marriage adds another layer of complexity, as the following cases illustrate.

Tenzin is his parents' only son. Prior to commencing tenth grade at a boarding school in Kathmandu, his parents informed Tenzin that they were arranging his marriage to Diki. Although from the same village, Tenzin did not know Diki very well because he had spent most of his life at a boarding school in the city. She had been raised in the village. Tenzin told his parents he did not want to get married, especially to someone who was uneducated. He even let Diki know that he was not interested in marrying her. As their only son, Tenzin's parents insisted he return to the village following tenth grade and marry, but, Tenzin said, despite pressure to "take all the village responsibilities like my father," he "really didn't have an interest in marriage."

After returning to the village, Tenzin commenced training as the future kyimdag. His father sent him to village meetings so he could learn the administrative system and how to represent the household in communal matters. Soon afterward, Tenzin and Diki married in a formal ceremony. But after a few weeks Tenzin moved back to Kathmandu to pursue further studies. When Diki eventually tracked him down, Tenzin informed her that he felt no love for her and wanted a divorce. She reluctantly agreed, thus ending a brief and unsuccessful marriage. Tenzin's father became adamant that he would never again try to arrange a marriage for his son.

Norbu, the eldest of two sons, was sent to a boarding school in Kathmandu at age eight. After completing twelfth grade, he returned home. Recognizing that years of education in boarding school made their son less familiar with—and perhaps resistant to—arranged marriage, Norbu's parents tried to condition him to traditional expectations over the course of two years. According to Norbu,

> At that time [shortly after returning to the village] they thought that I am not used to the [marriage] traditions. They were trying to get me used to the traditions through a slow process. Knowing that it is a tradition here to get married at an early age, I was thinking, "Why are they not telling me to get married?" They were slowly getting me used to that tradition so I would not run away from the village. When I first came back to the village, if they said, "You must marry," I might have run away.
>
> After two years, they did exactly what I was thinking they would do. I saw it coming. They got me used to the tradition and told me, "So, it is time for you to get married." I said, "This is not the time for me to get married because I still want to study further." They said, "You can take a wife and study at the same time. You can keep your wife at home; we will look after her. You can continue to study." They told me that they can arrange my marriage, and they told me the girl's name. But I said, "No."
>
> It's not that I didn't like the girl; it was just too early for me to get married. I still needed to continue with my education. If I got married, then I'd be focusing most of my time on my wife and kids. The time was not right. Plus, she doesn't know how to read. I don't need a girl who is too educated. But they chose one who is not educated at all. I was thinking about, maybe, like a love marriage.

Norbu rejected his parents' choice of spouse and, one year later, informed them that he would like to marry Sangmo, a woman he first met while a student in Kathmandu. They liked her and became supportive of their son's plan, but Sangmo's parents had already promised her to another man. In a dramatic turn of events Sangmo thwarted her unwanted suitor by fleeing the village until it was safe to return. Once back in the village, Norbu married her in what he termed *gyankham* (literally, wander off to a distant place), a form of elopement he described as "when the parents don't agree but the couple goes together and says, 'We are married.'" Whereas Norbu's parents were happy with the marriage, Sangmo's still had strong reservations. Only through the intervention of Sangmo's brother, a monk living in Kathmandu, did the marriage finally become accepted by both families. Now the couple lives with their toddler son in Norbu's parents' house.

These two cases provide glimpses into how parents are losing influence over who and when their sons marry. Whereas Tenzin reluctantly agreed to a marriage that he immediately regretted, Norbu resisted his parents' designs so he could marry a woman of his own choosing. The stories are compelling evidence that parents in Nubri are being forced to reconsider intergenerational power dynamics and the strategies they use to carry out household succession.

THE EDUCATED DAUGHTER DILEMMA

Marriage in Nubri has traditionally been predicated on long-term exchange principles similar to those found in other Himalayan societies (Levine 1988:59; Holmberg 1989:58–59; Fricke 1994:135–37; March 2002:168–71). A family that receives a bride is counted on to reciprocate by giving a bride in a subsequent generation. The expectation is represented symbolically at the wedding feast, where the family of the bride is accorded the highest position of respect and feted first with food and drink. The groom's family, which has just incurred a social debt, is served last. The expectation of reciprocity places pressure on parents to induce a daughter back to the village for marriage.

Arranging a marriage for a daughter who attends school is a major challenge. In the first place, getting her to return to the village—even for a visit—is complicated by bride capture.[1] This involves a man abducting a woman and holding her in his home or a secret locale until she or her family agrees to a marriage. The custom is not new. One fifty-year-old woman recalled how a man she did not want to marry confined her in his home. Refusing to eat for several days, she forced the abductor to release her or explain how she died of starvation under his captivity. In a more recent incident, which occurred while we were conducting field-work in 2014, a suitor abducted a young woman while she was working in his village. Coincidentally, a film crew was in the valley making a documentary on arranged marriages and bride capture. They interviewed the woman, who said, "I had gone to [name of village] to sell some alcohol. They caught me when I was returning. There were many of them. They came and jumped me all at once. I was helpless."[2] Many young women living in Kathmandu are aware of the practice, and in some cases stated that the specter of bride capture is why they are reluctant to visit Nubri.

Another disincentive for a daughter to return is the fact that she is usually ineligible to inherit the bulk of her father's property. Due to the norm of patrilocal residence, parents expect her to marry into another household, where she will contribute labor and reproduction. The gendered disparity in wealth and power has not escaped the younger generation raised in Kathmandu. When we solicited comments on the position of women in Nubri society, one young lady replied, "Women don't get free rights; they are still under their husbands. The husbands are like, 'We are the head of the family. You are under us, you can't go above us.'" Another said, "In the village, women are like inferior, men are superior." A third framed her response around gender, power, and reproduction: "Because both the husband and wife are uneducated, they have many children. Even if the wife says it is enough children, the husband would not listen. There are instances where women are forced to produce more children. I see many such cases and it is very sad. The wives have no choice but to listen to their husbands and cannot exercise their own wishes. Ideally, the husband and wife should discuss and come to an agreement. In the village, however, they would not discuss and listen to each other."

The awareness of gendered power dynamics raises the question, How can parents coax or coerce an educated daughter back to the village? Sometimes they resort to subterfuge. Young women are sometimes asked to return home during a school holiday only to unwittingly walk into marriages planned by their parents. For example, one recent graduate told us the fate of her classmates: "There were a few girls who were taken in the middle of the school semester. They were taken away for marriage. The parents were very clever—they didn't say it was for marriage. Their kids wouldn't listen if they said that. I'm sure they would be against it. So the parents said something, and took them up, and made sure it was all arranged, and the girls never came back [to school]."

Some parents take the more direct approach of arranging a marriage for a daughter living in Kathmandu and then informing her of the wedding date. However, such plans can go awry. Tsering and Gyurme fell in love while students in Kathmandu. But when she finished tenth grade, Tsering's parents informed her they had accepted engagement beer (longchang) from another family and instructed her to return to the village to get married. Tsering's future in-laws had already incurred large expenses by arranging the upcoming wedding festivities. According to Gyurme,

> Two days before she was going to the village I received a message, so I called Tsering. She told me that she had to go to the village and explained the troubles to me. We met the next day. I asked her about her plans. She said she was not going to marry the boy. If they forced her, she wouldn't stay even if they cut her throat. She said she would leave. I told her in that case don't go

to the village at all. If you want to leave the boy, then don't marry him in the first place. If you leave after marriage, then it's considered bad. I told her the other choice is to leave him before marriage. She said she had to go to the village. There was no choice as the boy's family had started pressuring her family. I told her that I was coming along, and she said, "Let's go together and we will discuss the matter on the way." After reaching Nubri she stayed for a night at my home and then went to her parents' home [in another village] the next day. She said she wanted to go, so I let her.

Nobody knew the extent of the young couple's involvement, so Gyurme devised a ploy to go to Tsering's village. He managed to meet her surreptitiously, and the two ran away in the middle of the night to Gyurme's father's home. According to a cousin who was present at the time, "Late at night my uncle burst into my room yelling, 'Wake up, wake up! Gyurme brought home a wife!' I said, 'What?' He said, 'Yeah, yeah, wake up. You have a lot of work to do.' I got up immediately, washed, went to my uncle's house and, yeah, Gyurme had brought Tsering all the way from her village. Through the rest of the night we made preparations. In the morning everything was ready. We performed a brief ceremony, after which they were married."

After the dawn ceremony legitimized the couple's marriage, the family of the jilted man could do nothing but demand restitution.

In some ways Tsering and Gyurme's marriage resembles bride capture, albeit with a twist that the bride voluntarily slipped away rather than being forcibly ensnared by a suitor. Some people even told us that bride capture can be used as a culturally acceptable cover for elopement. A middle-aged woman explained, "People say that one knows in advance if such things [bride capture] are to happen. It happens usually in the case where parents have promised a girl to someone else, but she is not interested in the marriage because she likes another man. Sometimes when parents don't agree to a match, a girl runs away with a boy she likes. The girl or her parents somehow know about it in advance. One doesn't just steal a girl like that."

Another woman explained,

> In most cases [of bride capture] the girl might not want to marry the boy their parents chose. The general practice in the village is that even if the daughter does not wish to marry the boy, parents agree to the marriage if the boy's family is wealthy. The parents think that if they pressure their daughter, she will relent and marry into that household. But sometimes a girl likes another boy, and the two know that their parents will not allow them to marry. Therefore, they plan a scheme and the girl acts surprised when she is taken away.

Bride capture seems to both thwart and facilitate marital ambitions. On one hand, the fear of being forced into an unwanted marriage keeps some unmarried women away from the village, and single. On the other hand, a woman can exert agency over spousal selection by using bride capture as a subterfuge to circumvent her parents' arrangements.

The conundrums of a changing society are causing parents to reevaluate marital strategies for their daughters. Women we interviewed often stated that their parents would not think about arranging a marriage without asking them first. Several even spurned proposals on various grounds, including that years of city dwelling render them unfit for the physical toils of village life, immediate childbearing will disrupt education and derail employment aspirations, and men who are raised in the village may not be suitable companions. For example, after completing tenth grade and before moving on to higher studies, Pema worked as a teacher in her natal village. She received two marriage proposals. Both proposals went through her parents, as is customary, and in both cases her parents deferred to Pema for the final decision. Conversations with her uneducated married peers tempered Pema's views on joining a village man in matrimony. She said, "Some of them tell me their husbands are drinking lots of alcohol, and beating them. Most of them tell me that they must work in the field the whole day and it's very tiring. They say, 'It seems like you are so lucky, you don't have to do all these things.'"

Pema turned down both proposals. When we asked Pema's classmate whether anyone had sought her hand in marriage, she explained,

> Yeah, but I rejected him. The boy went through my parents, and they shared the news with me: "He asked you for marriage, so do you want to accept or not?" I said, "No, because I don't want to just waste my life." By *waste my life* I mean that if you marry at a very young age you don't know the full value of education, only half, so it is a waste of time. If I had said yes, I think right now I am having a child, working in the fields, really busy like in the village. And I think maybe I won't like my husband because I don't know him.

Sangye spoke of her reaction to a marriage proposal when visiting her natal village:

> During winter vacation we got a one-month holiday so I went home. There is one village guy who asked me to marry him. He came to my home. They all thought I was sleeping while his parents were talking with my parents. My parents talked about it like, "It is up to our daughter's wish." They said they would discuss it with me the next day. The guy's parents then put 10,000 rupees [$110] by my pillow. Early the next morning I woke up around four o'clock and packed all my stuff. I wrote a note saying I didn't

keep the money and asked my mom to take care of it. Then I ran right to Kathmandu. At the time I was so young. After that I didn't go back to the village for several years. Now the guy is married, so it is not a problem.

Our interviews with parents reveal several reasons why they are conceding marriage decisions to their educated daughters. Some are adamant that an arranged marriage will interrupt or even threaten her long-term prospects. Others admit that they do not understand the modern world their children are accessing through education, so it is best to refrain from interfering too much in their lives. A few mothers who experienced arranged marriages recalled the sufferings they endured when entering a household as a relative stranger with little power or authority, and stated that they do not want a similar fate for their daughter. Based on our household surveys, very few educated women are now married and living in Nubri. The majority (82.4 percent) of ever-married women aged fifteen to twenty-nine have no formal schooling at all. Clearly, parents have not had much success in enticing daughters back to the village. We suspect they recognize that forcing an educated daughter to marry against her will can create contentious relationships and embarrassing situations.

Despite the barriers outlined above, marriages still occur in Nubri. Some women find employment niches, like teaching and nursing, commensurate with their education and marry men who also have some schooling. Some former nuns have returned to Nubri and married even though they face social condemnation for abandoning their religious vows. But for the most part, recent marriages involve women who were held back in the village by parents. These are often the family's eldest daughter, whose labor was too critical to forfeit. Ironically, parents relied on such daughters to help raise younger siblings who they subsequently sent out for education.

UNBECOMING MONKS

During an interview we queried Angba about his succession plans. With household survey data in hand, we noted that he and his wife were in danger of being left alone because they had sent their only son to a monastery. Angba, however, was unfazed and explained, "It is good that my son learns religion. But he must come back to take care of the household since he is my only son. He will inherit the house and the land. The son is the successor who replaces his father [patsab bugyü]."

The phrase *patsab* (father's replacement) *bugyü* (by a son in the next generation of the lineage) encapsulates the merging of biological and material concerns through patrilineal descent and patrilocal residence. By accepting his father's property and role as head of household, a son is obliged to marry and perpetuate the lineage. But what happens when the most eligible successor is a monk who—at least technically—is destined for a life of celibacy?

By designating his monk-son as successor, Angba alludes to a practice that has become common as the first large cohort of boys sent to distant monasteries comes of age. Recent years have witnessed an upsurge in the number of dralog (monk who returned [to lay status]) fulfilling the role of household successor, and a normalizing of the practice. As a householder lama explains, "Because there are more dralog now, they are treated as normal and something ordinary. Some of them are recalled back by their parents, and so it is not really their fault. But some do not want to be monks anymore and return. Those who have disrobed due to major behavioral transgressions are looked down upon. Those who have disrobed for other reasons, and without committing misdeeds, are accepted as normal."

An ex-monk's comportment also determines how he will be judged, as one dralog explained, "After you disrobe, if you behave properly and stay with your parents, then people won't say anything. But if you drink alcohol and misbehave, then it is said to be more sinful, and people will comment about how the disrobed monk's behavior is even more shameful than a layman's behavior. Generally, if you behave appropriately, then people will not look down at a disrobed monk."

In some cases the dralog did not intend to renounce his monastic vocation but was forced to do so for reasons ranging from serious illness to inappropriate conduct. In other cases, he returned to lay life to fulfill his parents' family management strategy. Below we treat each situation separately.

The Unintended Dralog

We met Mingyur, the youngest of three brothers, at his brother's temple in Nubri. His eldest brother, a householder lama, inherited their parents' house, land, and cattle. The middle brother, a celibate monk, inherited the family's temple and attached fields. Mingyur was supposed to be a monk for life, so he inherited nothing. Today he is the temple's main caretaker, for which he receives food, lodging, and a modest stipend from his brother.

Mingyur became a monk at age eleven. His father had passed away, and his mother was struggling to raise the family alone. He recalled, "I was very young so I couldn't make the decision [to become a monk]. My father had passed away and my mother was responsible for everything. We were very poor. For this reason, and because my ancestors were very religious, she put me in the field of religion. My mother thought if she could position one of her sons to study religion, in the future Buddhism would not disappear and could still spread without any troubles."

Mingyur was ordained a monk at a monastery in Kathmandu where his grandfather's reincarnation resides. His middle brother also lived there and was tasked with overseeing Mingyur's upbringing and education. However, when his brother was scheduled to commence a three-year and three-month meditation retreat, he became concerned that Mingyur's naughty behavior would amplify in his absence. He therefore sent Mingyur to another monastery at a Tibetan settlement in south India.

Mingyur began to thrive at his new home, first through secular education that earned him an administrative position, and then as a student in a shedra (formal monastic study center). However, long nights of study began to take a toll on his body. Mingyur contracted tuberculosis and returned home to recuperate. Gradually he contravened monastic vows and recommenced life as a layman. Mingyur traced his path:

> After taking birth from your mother's womb, negative emotions like anger, hatred, and desire are common among everyone except those who are enlightened. Attachment and anger are not new to us. I began to flirt with girls. I lost my direction. I accepted my wrong action and gave up my monk's robes. I wore layman's clothing. I informed my brother that I had lost my vows. I had taken the vows of a monk under my lama. Now there were none of them in me. I realized that I couldn't continue like this. If I die there is no place except for hell. So I decided that I must seek forgiveness and after that lead a layman's life.
>
> Now I am a worldly man. I stay with a woman and soon I will have a child. My wife was married to someone else, but her husband is a mischievous alcoholic. For this reason she preferred me and I also became attracted to her. That's how we came together. What am I supposed to do now? It's not my stomach alone. I also have to fill my wife's belly, and my child's after he is born. Now I face so many troubles.

Illness derailed Mingyur's religious ambitions. Because his parents had planned for him to be a lifelong monk, he did not inherit any family property. He therefore must depend on the benevolence of his brother for subsistence. Mingyur laments leaving the relatively tension-free environment of the monastery and frets over providing for his wife and yet-to-be-born child.

Sangpo, by contrast, attributes his decision to leave the monastery to a lack of maturity. He is a soft-spoken, polite young man who spent only four years in a monastery before disrobing. Sangpo explained,

> My parents have six children, three sons and three daughters. I am the youngest. I wanted to stay at school but my parents wanted to make me a monk. They were right from their side. Today I regret not listening to them. I realized all this when my baby was born and I myself became a father.
>
> I became a monk at the age of twelve and returned at the age of sixteen. I became a dralog because I was not mature enough. I was happy in the monastery at first because we were all kids and I was very intelligent. After that I got spoiled. That's the truth. Maybe I had bad friends or maybe I was bad. I was looking at those who had left the monastery. They were leading free lives. I thought I would also live the same life. When I look back, I realize I was not able to think about my future. When I was a monk, I was looking at what others were doing and was always thinking to follow them. I was very young then. Now, thinking about why I became a dralog, I have many regrets. When I was in the monastery I didn't trust my teacher and my lama. I listened to other people instead of them. After being very bad for two years I became a dralog.
>
> When I became a dralog, I was not alone. There were many like me. Around twelve or thirteen of us returned that year to my village. For two years people bullied us a lot, calling us dralog all the time. Now they don't call us that so I feel better.

When Sangpo came back to the village, he initially lived with his parents who began looking for a suitable bride. Sangpo recalled,

> I didn't want to get married at that time. My parents were telling me to get married, but my plan was to get married at around twenty-eight or twenty-nine. They brought girls to me whose parents agreed [to the marriage], but I didn't agree. Eventually I got a bride for myself. But when I brought her here, my parents rejected her. They told me to go through the usual process of asking her parents to consent, but I just brought her home. Her brothers came [to take her back], so I said, "Whether or not she stays with me is her decision." I asked her to marry me—to consent or not was her choice.
>
> For one year we stayed with my parents. I told them that I didn't want to separate [i.e., live in separate households], but my parents didn't listen. Ours was a love marriage, so they said they had no control over my wife. Therefore, we had to separate. They said that they would cause fighting between me and my wife, and that wouldn't be good.

Like Mingyur, Sangpo left the monastery of his own volition. Neither man was designated to be his households' successors, so each had to carve a living from limited means. Both expressed a common sentiment that the relatively stable life of a monk has much to offer in contrast to the layman's travails. Yet their pathways to marriage were quite different. Mingyur was in his mid-thirties when he returned to Nubri. His parents were no longer alive and therefore could not ask another family for their daughter. In any event he was too old for an arranged marriage. Nevertheless, he managed to wed a woman who fled a miserable situation. Sangpo was still quite young when he came home. He rejected the brides his parents selected through the traditional procedures, and instead married a woman of his own choosing. After unanticipated returns to the village, neither man followed the regular route toward marriage and household succession. Both ended up forming neolocal households with their wives.

Dralog by Design

Not all monks leave their institutions due to health reasons or because they are not cut out for monastic life. Nowadays many parents recall a monk-son to the village so he can assume the role of kyimdag. For example, Gyaltsen was a monk for a few years, but his parents had second thoughts. Gyaltsen recalled,

> I was a monk for three years at a monastery in Sikkim. A lama from Nubri took me and some others to the monastery. If you stayed back in the village, you wouldn't learn anything, be it education or religious training. There was no chance of learning Nepali or English. So I went to Sikkim. After three years my father and mother asked me to return because they needed help in the fields. My father came to get me for a holiday and didn't send me back. Since I am the oldest son, I had to stay in the village. I was thirteen when I joined the monastery and sixteen when I quit. Well, I didn't quit just like that. It is wrong if I do not inform my lama properly. I informed him when he came from Sikkim to attend a religious ceremony here in Nubri.

As an impoverished man with little land and many children, Gyaltsen wonders why his parents yanked from his grasp the opportunity to remain a monk. Perhaps bitter about being denied a chance for an easier life, Gyaltsen sent all of his children to boarding schools. He does not intend to bring any of them back to the village.

Yönden, another returned monk, told us that he first underwent a hair-cutting ceremony and received basic religious training under a local lama. Afterward, his parents sent him to a monastery in Kathmandu where his maternal uncle *(ashang)* was a khenpo. Yönden recalled,

I didn't think about returning to the village because life is very good there at the monastery due to the kindness of the Rinpoche and others. It is like heaven. I could take leave to visit the village, but I returned only once, two years ago, and then went back to Kathmandu after six days. My main reason for being here now is that there is no one at home. My father died five years ago, so there is no one to take the responsibility and assume the head-of-household role. Besides me, my mother has six other children. All of them are younger than me. My mother needed someone to help take care of the family. That is why she and my siblings requested I return. I had no choice. I sought forgiveness [from the Rinpoche] and returned. Life is tough here. I don't know how to work since I don't have any experience.

Yönden, as the eldest son in his family, was obliged to resume life as a layman. He felt it would have been selfish, and even irresponsible, to continue living as a monk when his widowed mother and younger siblings requested that he return. His account also illustrates a dilemma faced by many young men and women who are raised outside the village. They are not habituated to long days of physical toil and therefore lack the conditioning required to make a living by farming and herding. Men like Yönden have little choice but to adapt because a lack of secular education limits their employability elsewhere. Many dralog now engage in the full range of village economic and social activities, and have become nearly indistinguishable from their peers who never left the valley for education.

MONKS AND THE EVOLVING FAMILY MANAGEMENT STRATEGY

In the pragmatic calculus of household succession, recalling a monk-son to the village makes more sense than one may expect. Until recently, lifelong celibacy was the exception rather than the rule in Nubri. There were no monasteries for celibate monks in the valley, and married lamas occupied the pinnacle of the religious hierarchy. Nevertheless, parents have long expected their successor to undergo some level of religious training. Adolescent boys and young men honed their literacy and liturgical skills by studying under lamas during the annual winter retreat. Some spent months or years apprenticing under astrologers and medical practitioners. Gradually, parents and lamas trained young men to be full participants in village economic and religious practices. The typical kyimdag is therefore adept at farming and herding, can read and write Tibetan, and possesses at least rudimentary liturgical skills so he can participate in communal rites. Likewise, the dralog is literate, versed in

Buddhist philosophy, and trained in ritual performance. Because the locale for religious training has shifted from the village to the monastery, upon return the former monk must learn aspects of rural living such as farming, managing a household, and participating in the local administrative system.

The dralog phenomenon adds a layer of ambiguity to monasticism. Entering a monastery and taking religious vows is supposed to set one on a life course of celibacy. Yet nowadays parents may send a son to a monastery with the premeditated aim of recalling him to the village once the need arises for a household successor. The arrangement is sometimes explicit, as one father explained:

> I gave my son to the monastery. I made him a monk but want to bring him back to take over the household. He will receive the patrilineal inheritance *[pashi]* and get married. I already informed the monastery that I have only one son. I plan to let him study for a few years, and then will bring him back to marry and continue the household. The lama has agreed. The matter is cleared. By staying at home he doesn't learn religion or anything, so sending him as a monk is good. He will stay for ten years. Three years have elapsed, so after another seven years he will take over the household.

Recently some institutions in Kathmandu and India have established branch monasteries in Nubri. The lamas in charge of some branches understand local circumstances and are amenable to the idea of temporary residence, especially for a son slated to be the future kyimdag. A father told us,

> The kids we send down [to Kathmandu and India] don't come back. Their minds are set to stay down. If we send them to a monastery in Nubri they will know the local customs, so there is a better chance they will stay. Our plan is to bring our son back [from a local monastery] when he is twenty. I decided to approach the abbot and offered to pay something. The abbot said, "I will accept him. As a monk, he contributes to spreading the Buddhist teachings. He has the Bodhisattva mind *[changchub semba]*." Our son is getting education, clothing, and food, so I feel like we are freeloading. We'll be taking him back, so I think I should make some donation to the monastery.

This father tempers the risk that his son will never return by sending him to a branch within the valley rather than to a monastery in the city. By making an explicit agreement with the abbot, he can feel reasonably secure that household succession is in order. In other cases, however, there is little if any consultation between parents and clerics. For example, Dolma found herself in a bind. Her husband migrated abroad for work and thus far has not remitted any support. Regarding her son who was residing in a monastery, she said, "I asked him to come home. I needed help to do the work here. My other son has gone to school and my daughter is a nun, so I am all alone. I didn't go to see the head lama, because he wouldn't let my son go. I didn't seek the monastery's permission, because they would only grant him a temporary release. They would later ask me to send him back to the monastery. So I just asked my son to come home."

Dolma's son was present at the time of the interview. He had just returned a few days before and clearly had not made the adjustment to lay life. After becoming attuned to a lifestyle of scholarship and prayer in a fellowship of urban-dwelling monks, he found himself forced to subsist in a highland environment through the unfamiliar vocations of farming and herding. During the interview he hardly uttered a word, and when he did speak, his wispy voice lacked any hint of confidence that characterizes more acclimated young men who sally forth each day to wrest a living from the surrounding landscape.

This chapter focused on a straightforward question: Who will return home? The answer is anything but simple because educational migration is loosening the authority parents exert over a child's life course. Persuading school-educated offspring back to the village is difficult because they often have, or at least envision, employment opportunities elsewhere and are not always keen on returning to marry a spouse chosen by parents. Withdrawing a son from a monastery has emerged as a relatively secure household succession strategy because it is laden with cultural and economic incentives. On the cultural side, village regulations obligate household heads to participate in regularly scheduled Buddhist rites. A young man with religious education is therefore fully qualified to represent his household at such events. On the economic side, besides managing the farm and herds, the returned monk can generate some income by performing rites at local households and, during winter months, among the Buddhist community in Kathmandu. In an environment of rapid social and cultural change, the dralog represents many parents' most promising avenue for succession even though it entails deviating from normative monastic expectations. The fact that some leaders of celibate institutions facilitate the succession scheme attests to the adaptability of the relationship between clerics and laypeople in Nubri society.

CHAPTER 9

The Transformative Potential of Educational Migration

THE LAMA GOES, THE LAMA RETURNS

We sat with Yungdrung at a tea shop in an alleyway radiating outward from the great stupa of Boudhanath, a major Buddhist site in Kathmandu. Through the break between buildings we could view a continuous stream of people passing by: elderly men and women spinning prayer wheels, beggars chasing tourists, youths with their eyes glued to mobile phone screens. We had just concluded a long interview with Yungdrung. His children are all in Kathmandu, some even plotting moves abroad as their school years round to a close. As we watched the jumble of people amble by, Yungdrung mused,

> In my opinion, a person should eventually return to their own village. It is said that a lama should go to another place to receive and practice religious teachings but return to his own village to establish a spiritual foundation. Likewise, students have to go to other places and endure lots of hardship to acquire education and a livelihood. Then they should help their own village. But without money, one cannot do anything meaningful back home. If one can go abroad and work for five to ten years, one can earn enough money to help schools, monasteries, elderly people, and one's own parents. Those who are unable to go abroad just go up and down the valley carrying loads, and that is about it. Without money, you are helpless. In earlier times, whether we had money or not, we managed to be self-sufficient. These days, people have been exposed to the outside world. Even if we tell our children to stay, they reply, "What is the use of staying in the village after all the education we have had?" That is true. They will remain poor like their parents if they

stay back in the village. So there is no choice. The best we can do is to make sure our children receive education so they can make their lives better. And, hopefully, they will return to help the village. But whether they return or not depends on the individual.

Yungdrung likens the current outmigration to the need for Nubri's lamas to travel elsewhere for religious instructions so they can return with new knowledge and capabilities. Likewise, he feels that young people can use education to aid their natal villages. But the situation is fundamentally different now. The itinerant lamas of yore were firmly entrenched in an agro-pastoral society where they could attain self-sufficiency through barter and exchange. In contrast, educational migrants are uprooted at a tender age, raised by relative strangers in an urban environment, tutored to function in a monetized economy, and enculturated with modern notions about everything from love to livelihoods. Yungdrung acknowledges that young people can benefit their communities only if they have the incentive and wherewithal to return. Given their exposure to the broader world and a scarcity of jobs in rural areas, his pessimism that few will return is well founded.

Education, career aspirations, and the seduction of life outside the village are detaching youths from their rural homesteads. Some of the results are predictable—for example, delayed marriage and an associated fertility decline that underscores the diminishing control parents exert over their children's lives. Other trends are not so easy to anticipate. To shed light on the evolving nature of family relationships, we first analyze educational migration as a form of fosterage whereby parents relinquish supervision of their children to an urban institution in order to provide them with opportunities that are not readily available in the village. We then explore how educational migration is driving a unique trajectory of population change that diverges in key ways from the forecasts of demographic transition theory. We then shift the focus to endogamy to illustrate how marital choices among Nubri's young people are expanding in conjunction with newfound ideologies and autonomy, but not without bounds due to the enduring influence of parents. We conclude by spotlighting the indistinct distinction between arranged marriages and unions of choice. Many scholars of family change view arranged marriage as an artifact of traditional, collectivist behavior that withers with the rise of individualistic attitudes driven by the forces of modernization. In contrast, our evidence points to a more complex reality that involves intergenerational negotiation and compromise. We argue that agents of social change in contemporary Nubri include both the educated youths with their urban acumen and global yearnings and their parents who never had access to secular schooling and whose lives remain firmly rooted in the village.

INDEPENDENT CHILD MIGRATION AND FOSTERAGE

Migration is not a new phenomenon in the Himalayan region.[1] What differs in Nubri is that most migrants are not adults seeking employment, but children sent for education.[2] Reviews of mobility in the Himalayan region and the social science literature on education and migration lead us to suspect that either the outmigration pattern in Nubri is highly unusual or similar patterns elsewhere have gone unnoticed. Most research on schooling and migration, exemplified by Corbett's study of rural Nova Scotia (2007), focuses on the propensity to migrate after attaining a certain level of education.[3] Although research on education and the inclination to migrate can help us understand what *may* happen to Nubri's children *after* they finish school, it does not provide a useful framework for analyzing migration that is geared toward gaining access to school. We therefore turn to other bodies of literature for insights.

Hashim defines the "independent child migrant" as "any child who migrates independently of his/her parents, although the decision to move may or may not be an autonomous one" (2007:911; see also Giani 2006; Hashim and Thorsen 2011), and delineates three categories of independent child migrants: "(1) where children enter a fostering arrangement in order to ensure their continued access to education or to a better education; (2) where children actively seek an apprenticeship opportunity; (3) where children travel to secure the resources to continue or to complete their education." (2007:919)

If we consider institutional residence analogous to fosterage, then Hashim's first category applies to Nubri's educational migrants. But first, a caveat. Fosterage in North American and European societies is often viewed as a pathology—the breakdown of family or the inability of parents to care for their own kids (Donner 1999; Alber 2003). Bowie points out that "it is so self-evident to most people in Euro-American society that children should be raised by their 'natural' parents that it might come as a surprise to learn that this is not always and everywhere the same" (2004:3). In fact, studies throughout the world show that fosterage comes in many forms and is pursued for a variety of reasons. It can be a means to solidify social ties, manage the size and composition of the family, and facilitate opportunities for young people (e.g., Goody

1982; Isiugo-Abanihe 1985; Bledsoe 1990, 1994; Eloundou-Enyegue and Stokes 2002; Leinaweaver 2008; Alber et al. 2013). When educational facilities and jobs are concentrated in cities, fosterage can be one of the better options for boosting rural children's life chances (Eloundou-Enyegue and Stokes 2002:278–79). The rural-urban opportunity discrepancy is evident in Nubri, where local schools cannot offer the same array of amenities as well-endowed urban institutions. As a result, parents view educational migration as a viable prospect even when weighed against depleting the household's labor force and the emotional burden of prolonged separation.

Eloundou-Enyegue and Stoke define fosterage as "the practice of sending children to live with relatives or friends for extended periods. In effect it is a transfer of guardianship of one's children to another individual or family. Unlike adoption, fosterage is a temporary, partial, and informal transfer: the children's primary loyalty is still to their parents; guardianship is temporary and can be terminated if any of the parties becomes dissatisfied with the arrangement; and the financial burden of rearing the child is often shared, with the biological parents occasionally bearing some of the schooling or health expenses" (2002:279).

With a few tweaks, the definition accurately depicts the situation in Nubri, which involves the sending of children to live in an institution (rather than with relatives or friends) and entails the transfer of guardianship to the institution (rather than to another individual or family). A boarding school only holds temporary guardianship because the child will eventually graduate, be expelled, or be withdrawn by parents.[4]

Upon gaining admission to a boarding school, a child enters a family-like structure where an array of adults who take on fictive kinship relationships tend to her needs. For example, one school that houses many children from Nubri assigns incoming students to a hostel managed by a woman they refer to as *amala* (mother). She is responsible for many of a village mother's domestic duties, such as rousting children from bed, cooking breakfast, supervising as they wash and brush their teeth, and making sure they dress properly before nudging them off to the first class. She then tidies the dorm, helps with lunch and dinner, and at the end of the day puts the kids to bed.

Male staff members, whom children call *pala* (father), play less of a nurturing role and more of a protective role; they are the guards, drivers, and maintenance workers. A pala can discipline children—for example, by shooing them away from potentially hazardous areas and scolding those who act naughty in public spaces. Teachers also play a role in childcare with duties ranging from daily instructions to maintaining discipline in classrooms, the dining hall, and recess areas. Unlike the amala and pala, children refer to teachers using the nonkinship English terms *sir* and *miss*, a reflection of their elevated status as educators.

Another person who has a significant impact on a child's upbringing is the *jindag* (patron; sponsor). In chapter 7 we introduced the jindag as a weak tie who facilitates migration by covering tuition, room and board, and other expenses. Originally the term *jindag* referred to "the householder who, in the Buddhist structure of society, offers alms . . . to a monk" (Ruegg 1991:858). In a Tibetan religious context the jindag is generally a lay benefactor who forms a "priest and patron" *(chöyön)* relationship with a cleric. The affiliation is seen as mutually advantageous: the patron supports religious endeavors that the priest transforms into spiritual benefits. As Diemberger notes, the jindag concept has evolved to cover "a wide range of relationships that imply providing material support for something collective, usually but not exclusively with a religious connotation" (2007:42).[5] In a secular educational context assistance is delivered to an individual rather than collective. In this case Tibetans (including people from Nubri) call the foreigner who provides a sponsorship jindag. Some jindags assume a quasi-parenting role by maintaining regular communications with a child, visiting Nepal regularly, discussing academic progress with teachers, and taking the child out for some personal time. In letters and in person a sponsorship recipient is encouraged to address the jindag as mom or dad.

To summarize, similar to fosterage, in a boarding school people other than biological parents assume parental responsibilities, including the nurturing role of the amala, the protective service of the pala, the educational duty of the teacher, and the financial support of the jindag. Some relationships are coded in kinship terminology that distinguishes between ethnic Tibetans (pala and amala) and foreigners (mom and dad). Collectively the foster parents provide an opportunity for the child to achieve a level of socioeconomic mobility that would be difficult to realize in the village.

In the case of monasteries, the cultural ideal of "renouncing one's house for a state of homelessness"[6] makes the parallel to fosterage less obvious, especially since a boy is supposed to remain in the institution for life. Yet similar to boarding schools, monks form kinshiplike relationships in a monastery. Generally parents request an older monk who is a relative or acquaintance to accept their child as his disciple. We saw this in the case of many Nubri monks who were cared for by an uncle (see also Gyatso 2003; Mills 2003). If parents are unable to find such a caretaker, the monastery assigns the role to an older, unrelated monk.[7] Referred to as *gyegen* (teacher), he lives with and takes on a parenting role with the disciple. A familial bond based on reciprocity can develop over time whereby the gyegen raises and helps educate the young monk, who in turn is expected to care for him in old age. Finally, the relationship with one's primary religious instructor, referred to as the *tsewey lama* (principle teacher), assumes a spiritual father-son affinity. The Tibetan monk Tashi Khedrup, who entered Sera Monastery in Tibet as a child, mentions this type of bond: "For me the Lama was a second father and I remember him always with deep affection" (Tashi Khedrup 1998:10). Tibetans encapsulate the kinship principle in the phrase *gyalwa yabse* (victorious father and sons), which they use to describe the relationship between highly accomplished masters and their main disciples.[8]

Monasticism resembles fosterage because parents transfer the obligation to raise their child to members of an institution who are responsible for his education and for providing him a valued position in society. The similarity is even more evident in cases where monastic residence is temporary rather than lifelong. In chapter 5 we discussed how difficult it is for the religious practitioner to disentangle from family obligations, and in chapter 8 we explained how parents can send a son to a monastery with the expectation that they can recall him at a certain age. Withdrawing a son from the monastery so he can become the kyimdag is perhaps an extreme example of Mills's point that a monk's attachment to his natal household remains more or less intact for life (2009).

Although transferring a child to the care of others is nothing new in Tibetan societies, what makes Nubri's situation so unique is the scale of the phenomenon.[9] With close to 75 percent percent of the population aged ten to nineteen living in boarding schools and monasteries, Nubri eclipses by a wide margin Tibet of the 1950s when 10–30 percent of the male population consisted of monks (Goldstein 2009:3). Additionally, the percentage is far greater than in African societies, where fosterage is most common yet the proportion of children living away from parents rarely exceeds one-third (Isiugo-Abanihe 1985:61–63; Caldwell and Caldwell 1987).[10] Based on the sheer magnitude of the phenomenon, outmigration and institutional fosterage are destined to exert a major influence on demographic trends and social changes in Nubri. We will deal with the demographic ramifications first.

EDUCATIONAL MIGRATION AND DEMOGRAPHIC CHANGE

As a "dispersed cooperative breeding strategy," fosterage, assert Scelza and Silk, has a positive impact on a mother's reproductive success by buffering the costs of high fertility. They posit that fosterage is "especially advantageous for mothers who are able to terminate investment in certain offspring and reallocate investment to others, positively impacting their overall fitness [ability to produce offspring who survive to reproductive age]" (Scelza and Silk 2014:462). Caldwell and Caldwell made a similar point using an economic rationale by noting, "the institution [of fosterage] so weakens the link between biological parentage and the number of children being raised that much of the discussion in economic demography about fertility decision making and its concern with the value and cost of children is rendered meaningless" (1987:419). In both cases the scholars argue that fosterage can bolster fertility by alleviating the costs parents incur in raising children.[11]

In chapter 4 we documented that Nubri's fertility decline commenced well after parents began sending children to boarding schools and monasteries. The temporal sequence suggests that Nubri's version of a dispersed child-rearing strategy may have helped maintain high fertility. Some parents told us that raising many offspring in the village is difficult due to limited resources. That they continued having children under trying economic conditions suggests that their ability to transfer child-rearing costs to an institution moderated the incentive to limit fertility. However, as Brunson notes, childbearing decisions occur over time and under continuously shifting circumstances (2016:113–21). When educational migration was gaining momentum in Nubri, modern contraception was not readily available, infant and childhood mortality were still very high, and securing seats in institutions less certain. Therefore we simply cannot determine if parents decided to have many children because they were confident they could defray child-rearing costs by enrolling them in schools and monasteries.

Although fosterage may have reinforced high fertility in Nubri, at least during the early days of the outmigration phenomenon, educational migration is now causing a fertility decline. In 1997 parents had sent only about 10 percent of girls out of their households for education. Most were still young at that time, so their effect on fertility would have been negligible. Today the situation is different because a large percentage of women in or nearing their prime reproductive years live outside the valley. Their impacts on fertility will come through several routes. For one, it is reasonable to expect that the nearly universal correlation between female education and lower fertility will hold true for Nubri. To cite just one example, consider that in 1996 women in Nepal who had some secondary education experienced much lower fertility than women with no education (2.5 vs. 5.1 births per woman; Pradhan et al. 1997:38). The difference persisted in 2011 even as fertility declined across the nation (1.7 vs. 3.7 births per women; Ministry of Health and Population et al. 2012:76). Furthermore, evidence suggests that women who migrate to cities experience lower fertility than their counterparts in the village. Demographers argue that the difference may be related to migrant selectivity (movers are less inclined to have children), disruption (movers may experience temporary separation from partners), or adaptation (movers assimilate to the low fertility norm of city residents) (Jensen and Ahlburg 2004; cf. Kulu 2005). Although it is too early to fully analyze rural-urban fertility differences among Nubri women, at this point it is clear that educational migration is associated with a rise in the age at marriage, and perhaps an increase in the percentage who never marry. Figure 12 compares the percentage of Nubri's never married women by age and year. In 1997, 52 percent aged twenty to twenty-four and 25 percent aged twenty-five to twenty-nine had never married. By 2013 the proportions had risen to 68 percent and 39 percent.[12]

Figure 13 compares the marital status of women who reside in Nubri with those who live elsewhere. The vast majority of women living outside of Nubri have never married, a percentage that is elevated by the fact that many are nuns. Educational migration is therefore driving fertility downward through a combination of an older practice (religious celibacy) and a newer phenomenon (delayed marriage). The nuns we interviewed never intend to marry, while most laywomen expressed a quandary that may prove difficult to resolve: they consider financial independence a prerequisite for marriage but see marriage as an impediment to achieving financial independence. As one young woman responded when we asked if she was considering marriage, "It's like taking away your freedom. Once you are married, you are committed to your husband. You are then bound to have children and not have your own life. You don't have opportunities to study and support yourself or your family in a better way." When we asked another woman what she would do if her parents entertained a marriage proposal, she stated with conviction, "I would say no to the proposal. In Nepal today having a tenth-grade education is not enough; you need more

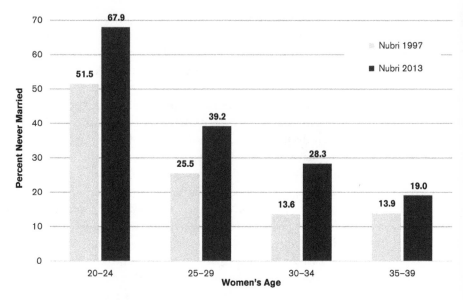

FIGURE 12. Never Married Women by Age, Nubri 1997 and 2013
Sources: Childs 1997 Household Demographic Survey; Beall, Childs, and Craig 2012 Household Demographic Survey; Quinn and Childs 2013 Household Demographic Survey.

education. Without further education you cannot really earn good income to repay your parents.[13] It is good if you are able to stand on your own feet."

In summary, Nubri is undergoing substantial demographic changes. As detailed in chapter 4, a demographic transition is underway that began in the early 2000s with a decline in infant mortality at a time when fertility remained high. Births outpaced deaths, resulting in population growth. We presented longitudinal data from our household surveys to demonstrate that the de jure population increased between 1997 and 2013 while the de facto population decreased due to outmigration. Delayed marriage, nonmarriage, and contraceptive usage are causing a reduction in fertility that, in combination with outmigration, will accelerate population decline. According to our projection, Nubri's population is likely to decrease by over 50 percent in the next fifty years (Childs et al. 2014:90–91).

Changes in Nubri's population trends are playing out somewhat differently than the classic model of demographic transition would suggest. Lee and Reher summarize the impacts a demographic transition typically has on a society: "The transition transforms the demography

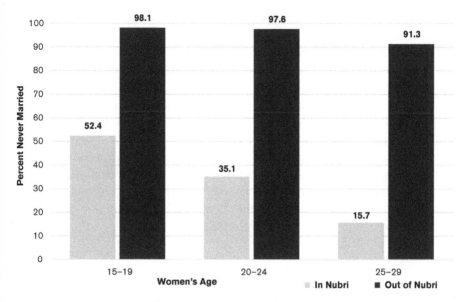

FIGURE 13. Never Married Women by Age and Residence, Nubri 2013
Sources: Childs 1997 Household Demographic Survey; Beall, Childs, and Craig 2012
Household Demographic Survey; Quinn and Childs 2013 Household Demographic
Survey.

of societies from many children and few elderly to few children and
many elderly; from short life to long; from life-long demands on women
to raise young children to the concentration of these demands in a small
part of adulthood; from horizontally rich kin networks to vertically rich
ones. The transition made possible the radical change in women's economic and social roles; the invention of retirement as the third stage of
life; and a demographic efficiency that fostered heavy investment in the
human capital of fewer but longer-lived children" (2011:1).

Nubri's demographic transition both converges with and diverges
from Lee and Reher's assessment. The most obvious resemblance is that
outmigration has already aged Nubri's resident population. If we dis-
count infants and children under the age of five (i.e., those who are too
young to be sent away), then the mean and median ages of those who
live full time in the valley are 37.0 and 37 years. If nobody had moved
out, then the mean and median ages would be 30.5 and 26 years. In
1997 people aged ten to twenty-four comprised 24 percent of Nubri's
resident population, but now they constitute less than 15 percent. If
nobody had moved out, those aged ten to twenty-four would represent
30 percent of the resident population.

On the other hand, Nubri's fertility decline is still in a nascent stage, so childbearing has not yet truncated into a short time span. Most mothers continue to bear children over the course of many years and only start using birth control in their thirties. What has changed is that parents are spending less time raising each child. Once beyond the toddler stage, they transfer child-rearing responsibilities to the boarding schools and monasteries. Furthermore, contrary to the demographic transition creating the "invention of retirement as a third stage of life," the opposite is occurring. As we discuss in the concluding chapter, educational migration is compromising the capacity for many elderly people to retire in a culturally appropriate manner. Far from the predictable outcomes implied by Lee and Reher, Nubri's demographic transition is moving along several unanticipated trajectories.

MARITAL ENDOGAMY AND THE MARGINS OF CHOICE

We now turn to marital choice and endogamy as means to explore the evolving nature of intergenerational relations. Endogamy refers to the preference or expectation to marry someone within a specific social group, usually defined on the basis of ethnicity, religion, and other variables. In the past marital choices in Nubri were geographically constrained because people interacted with a relatively small set of potential spouses, mainly those living in close proximity. According to our 1997 household survey, 87 percent of ever-married women in Rö and Lö had wed within their natal village. In other words, almost everyone formed a union with a person from the same village who had a similar ethnic background (Nubri Tibetan) and religious affiliation (Buddhist).

Marrying a person from the same village, or even the same valley, is no longer inevitable because schooling and urban residence have increased young people's independence and expanded their social networks. Most of the educated individuals we interviewed feel it is appropriate in today's society to choose one's own spouse and would balk at a marriage arranged by parents. In the previous chapter we presented several cases to illustrate how young adults resist or even reject their parents' schemes in order to marry a favored partner, usually someone who has life experiences similar to their own. Today's youths typically mention a comparable level of education as a preferred spousal trait and state that schooling facilitates mutual understanding. For example, one woman explained, "If I talk to him [an uneducated husband] about science, he won't know what I'm talking about. He will think I am crazy."

Another expressed a desire to marry someone with knowledge of the modern world and an outlook that extends beyond the village. Also, recall the cases in chapter 8. Tenzin reluctantly married the uneducated Diki but almost immediately dissolved the union, while Norbu rejected the spouse his parents chose partly on the basis that she had never attended school. The emergence of education as a favorable spousal characteristic should come as no surprise given that research on "educational assortative marriage" finds that people tend to wed others with a similar schooling background (Blossfeld 2009).

Physical separation from the village and the expansion of social networks does not mean that everyone becomes fair game for marriage or that young people can act with impunity. In fact, the young people we interviewed expressed preferences that converge with the marital propensities of their parents. They consistently mentioned a desire to form a union with someone of a similar religious affiliation and ethnic background. In the case of ethnicity, they no longer restrict the pool of eligible partners to people from Nubri. Potential spouses can come from a greater assortment of Nepal's highlanders who speak Tibetan dialects and practice Buddhism—in other words, people of similar cultural background. Furthermore, most expressed the importance of marrying someone who meets their parents' approval. One woman explained, "I want fifty percent from my side and fifty percent from my parents' side. If I have a love marriage, they won't be happy. If they are not happy with that guy, I won't be happy either. All I need is for both sides to be happy."

Ethnic and religious factors feature prominently in parental approval. We asked young men and women how their parents would react if they married a *rongba* (lowlander; a term that implies a non-Tibetan Hindu). A few responded that they personally could envision such a match, but their parents would find it problematic. One said her parents would "kick her out" of the family if she married a rongba. Another claimed his parents would object because "when getting married one must consider ethnicity."[14] One woman explained, "People from Nubri traditionally believe that since we are Buddhists, we should marry a person who is Buddhist. We regard people like rongpas as low caste. If someone marries a rongpa, Nubri people don't eat together with them."[15] Another woman recalled her mother's ultimatum, "If you ever get married to a lower caste person, like Nepali, Bahun-Chhetri, and all of those, then don't call me mom." She clarified that her parents would accept marriage to a Sherpa because he would be Buddhist. When we pointed out that many Newars are also Buddhist, she said, "Yeah, but I think my mom won't agree. She'll look at him as Nepali." Another young woman told us that her mother advised, "Don't marry a rongba or someone who is not related to our caste." When pressed on what she meant by caste, she replied, "We can marry Lama or Sherpa [Buddhist highlanders culturally affiliated with Tibetans], but not Tamang or Gurung [ethnic groups that speak Tibeto-Burman languages but are considered distinct from Tibetans]."[16] Similarly, another said, "My parents advise, 'Marry a boy from Nubri. He can understand more about you and your life, and about village life.' If I marry a Bahun [Brahmin] boy, he will not treat me well because whenever he sees my parents in dirty clothing he would say, 'Hey, I don't like your parents. They are so dirty.' If I marry a boy from Nubri, someone whom I like, he will know my situation. My parents also told me, 'It is fine if you marry a boy from the Himalayan region.' Tibetans are okay, they are like us."

These statements attest that educational migration has stretched marital possibilities beyond the confines of Nubri's boundaries but not to the point that it includes everyone. The pool of potential mates is still for the most part a subset of the region's population, namely, Himalayan highlanders who speak Tibetan dialects, practice Buddhism, and share the contours of a pan-Tibetan ethnic identity. Parents continue to sway decisions by making a clear point: if you want to maintain family relations, do not marry someone of a different cultural heritage. Because so few educated individuals have married thus far, it is premature to determine if young adults will fall in line with the elder generation's ultimatum. We suspect that many will balance personal preferences with deference to parents, which would complicate the prediction that modernization leads people to reject collective marital considerations in favor of individualistic choices.

MARRIAGE AND THE MISAPPROPRIATION OF MODERNITY

In a study of secular education and demographic change, John Caldwell argues that schooling leads people astray from traditional norms. He writes, "The main message of the school is not spelled out in textbooks. It is assumed by teachers, pupils, and even parents. They all know that school attendance means acceptance of a way of life at variance with the strictly traditional. Many school children no longer realize just how great that variance is or just what strictly traditional behavior is" (Caldwell 1980:241).

Caldwell's appraisal of education and culture change aligns with the tenets of modernization theory that draw a sharp distinction between traditional and modern behaviors. In demography, the dichotomy is epitomized by Cleland and Wilson's statement on ideational changes that play a role in demographic changes. They argue, "An important consequence of the structural modernization of societies . . . is a psychological shift from . . . fatalism to a sense of control of destiny, from passivity to the active pursuit of achievement, from a religious, tradition-bound and parochial view of the world to a more secular, rational, and cosmopolitan one."

Cleland and Wilson see modernization as a force that unshackles people from cultural restraints preventing them from pursuing a more rational approach to family formation and reproduction. As Allendorf and Pandian note, proponents of modernization theory predict that industrialization, urbanization, and education will transform family arrangements across the world in ways that converge with the Western norms of choice marriage and low fertility (2016:435), trends that are supported by survey research across the globe. Educated women are less likely to have an arranged marriage (Fox 1975; Xu and Whyte 1990; Barber 2004; Ghimire et al. 2006; Emran et al. 2014) and more likely to marry at a later age.[17] Many scholars interpret a drift toward marriages of choice (often termed love marriages) as evidence that traditional norms are giving way to modern behaviors.

The notion that modernization or globalization propels people across the world toward a uniform practice of companionate marriage has received a fair share of criticism, notably from scholars who have engaged in comparative research on love and intimacy (Hirsch and Wardlow 2006; Padilla et al. 2007a; Hirsch et al. 2010). Although people in many societies now prefer to form marriages based on intimacy and trust rather than familial obligation, local cultural filters continue to shape contemporary unions in diverse ways (Padilla et al. 2007b; Hirsch 2007). Furthermore, Arland Thornton points to a critical flaw in modernization theory's linear prediction of social change that is rooted in a peculiar methodology he labels "reading history sideways," that is, comparing societies on the assumption that they represent different stages along a common developmental trajectory. Reading history sideways recalls the methodology deployed by proponents of unilineal evolution, notably anthropology's nineteenth-century precursors Lewis Henry Morgan (1871) and Edward Burnett Tylor (1889). Despite being debunked long ago by Boas in his turn to historical particularism (1896) and discarded as a futile exercise by British social anthropologists like Radcliffe-Brown (1940), assumptions derived from reading history sideways continue to plague social scientific research. One route is via "developmental idealism" which entails four propositions: "(1) modern society is good and attainable; (2) the modern family is good and attainable; (3) the modern family is a cause as well as an effect of a modern society; and (4) individuals have the right to be free and equal, with social relationships being based on consent" (Thornton 2005:8).

In the perspectives of demography, international development, and the family planning movement, the modern family is nuclear, neolocal, and founded by consenting adults. It enlarges at carefully planned intervals regulated by contraceptive usage. In contrast, the traditional family involves arranged marriages at early ages, partilocal or matrilocal residence, multiple generations living under the same roof, and the absence of reproductive control. Thornton argues, "the acceptance of developmental idealism undermines indigenous family forms by suggesting that they are traditional rather than modern and that they are impediments to socioeconomic development" (2001:457).[18] In other words, reading history sideways results in the stereotyping of many family arrangements as stubborn relics that hinder individual liberty and progress.

To illustrate how imprecise the distinction is between traditional and modern marriage, consider the case of Tibetan societies that are renowned for accommodating an assortment of arrangements.[19] Polyandry (one wife with two or more husbands) is practiced alongside polygyny (one husband with two or more wives). Patrilocal residence is the ideal in arranged marriages, but matrilocal residence is possible when a family has no male heir, and neolocality is common in cases where partners marry out of love. Tibetans even have a linguistic means to discern a formally arranged match involving inter-familial negotiations culminating in an elaborate ceremony (*changsa*, literally "drinking gathering") from a less formal union that begins with affection (*khatug*, meeting of the mouths). The two are not mutually exclusive. Parents often commence matrimonial formalities after a couple falls in love and expresses their desire to marry. Many polyandrous unions begin with a "meeting of the mouths" between two lovers. Prior to the wedding ceremony the groom's parents arrange for his brother(s) to join in the marriage (see Urgyen Nyima's case, chapter 5). The coexistence of arranged and love unions in the same society renders absurd any attempt to label one traditional and the other modern. Both can be found in the past and present (and sometimes even in the same marriage!) albeit at varying frequencies.

Turning to Nepal, many sociological studies of family change seem wedded to core tenets of modernization theory, especially policy-oriented papers that advocate education as a means to boost the age at marriage and encourage spousal choice (e.g., Caltabiano and Castiglioni 2008; Ghimire and Samuels 2014).[20] Studies have revealed associations between modernization and a rising age at marriage and the propensity for people to marry partners of their own choosing. Barber and Axinn (2004) argue that exposure to mass media is associated with ideational changes about marriage and family life. Ghimire and colleagues (2006) link choice marriages to the spread of new social organizations (e.g., schools, employment, markets) that lessen the influence parents exert over the lives of their children. They conclude that education changes the decision-making dynamics within families in a way that gives the younger generation more latitude in choosing spouses. Barber (2004) posits that education is not the sole driver of a shift toward individualistic attitudes toward marriage. Proximity to schools, employment opportunities, transportation infrastructure, and markets also play a role. Fricke and colleagues foreshadowed these conclusions by demonstrating a correlation between experiences outside of the family (e.g., wage labor) and a woman's role in spousal choice (Fricke and Teachman 1993; Fricke 1994; Fricke et al. 1998; Axinn and Fricke 1996).

In Nubri 92 percent of female respondents to our reproductive history survey stated that their first marriage had been arranged. Meanwhile, personal narratives presented in the previous chapter show that many young people are resisting parental control over their engagements. Therefore, if we were to detect a decline in the percentage of marriages that are arranged by parents, the evidence would suggest that the modernizing potency of education is disrupting traditional norms. But how does one meaningfully document changing marital practices?

As a methodology for assessing marital change, social scientists often use arranged marriage as a proxy for traditional, collective behavior, and interpret any shift toward marriages of choice as evidence that modern ideas and individualistic behavior are making headway. Operationalizing the variables for tracking change, however, is not so straightforward. For example, in a study centering on Chithwan, a multiethnic area in southern Nepal, Barber finds evidence that "living near nonfamily institutions during childhood is associated with individualistic attitudes toward marriage, or with positive attitudes toward individual rather than family control of marriage" (2004:253). The concept of individualism was operationalized through seven survey questions linked to a fourfold Likert scale (from strongly agree to strongly disagree). To assess "individually controlled aspects of marriage," participants responded to prompts such as, "It is better to have no children than to have a child who marries a spouse of a different caste," and, "If a husband and wife cannot get along, they should get divorced." To assess "family-controlled aspects of marriage," participants responded to prompts such as, "Parents should always choose a spouse for their child," and, "After coming to her husband's home, a daughter-in-law should be obedient to her mother-in-law." These constructs and probes presume the existence of a normative marriage system that offers a limited set of options to which people customarily adhere. A person who responds in a way that diverges from the proxies for tradition is coded as one who has an individualistic attitude.

While a cross-sectional survey instrument can be used to assess attitudes, which was Barber's intention, the lack of a longitudinal dimension hinders its ability to determine whether the traditional preference was ever the statistical norm. How many women in the older cohorts played a role in choosing her own spouse, married a man of a different caste, or disobeyed her mother-in-law? Even asking those questions is problematic because an affirmative response may cause discomfiture by contradicting normative expectations. The more sensitive the survey question, the more unreliable the answer (Bleek 1987; Tourangeau and Yan 2007).

The issues raised above are not trivial in Nepal's socially complex environment.[21] Brunson reminds us that the expectation for women to adhere to strict gender norms varies by caste and socioeconomic status, and that distinguishing individual choice from family control over marriage is a complicated proposition. In a peri-urban society near Kathmandu, where people pursue modern lifestyles and increasingly marry spouses of their own choice (individualistic behavior), patrilocal residence (family control) remains resilient because it continues to confer social and economic advantages (Brunson 2016). Furthermore, arranged and love marriages have coexisted for a long time in Nepal. Five decades ago Pignède noted that Gurung couples were gaining more freedom to make their own decisions about marriage (1993:226). Similarly, Macfarlane reported that young Gurungs could get married based on mutual attraction, and argued that "the 'romantic love complex' effectively weakens the link between the economic structure and age at marriage" (1976:223–24). Ahearn's data shows that, prior to 1960, close to 15 percent of Magar men in her fieldwork site selected their own spouse without parental input, while another 25 percent had some say in the matter (2001:79). Fricke documents a Tamang preference for arranged marriages in which a significant percentage of brides had input (Fricke 1994). March's interviews with elderly women demonstrate that the entanglement of love and family involvement in marriage has been around for a long time in Tamang society (2002).

We do not dispute that there is a positive association between education and age at marriage, or a negative association between schooling and the tendency for parents to arrange marriages. But we do contest the notion that one can draw a meaningful distinction between so-called traditional (arranged by family) and modern (individualistic choice) marriages. For one, marital norms have been in flux since the day scholars started studying families in Nepal. Sometimes the baseline for assessing change is an assumed yet unsubstantiated adherence to traditional norms, as is the case in some cross-sectional studies. In the case of longitudinal studies, the baseline may be a snapshot of a society that is already undergoing change. In either case a presumed shift to individualism implies that behavior in traditional societies is culturally determined, decision-making resides primarily in the hands of parents, and only through modernization do young people gain the agency to select their own spouses. Young people are regarded as agents of change who circumvent the cultural inertia of their parents.

Education does play a role in giving young people more latitude in marital decision-making, a point that is beyond dispute. But the dichotomy between arranged and choice marriage glosses over the actuality that both generations exert varying degrees of influence in both the past and present. Caldwell recognized this when he argued it is difficult to clearly distinguish love from arranged marriages in societies where a romantic affair can evolve into a formal wedding with a full complement of economic exchanges between families (1980:244). Fricke and colleagues find that choice marriages among Tamangs continue to retain an "interfamilial component," that is, parents do not entirely relinquish influence over their children's unions (Fricke et al. 1998:233). Barber acknowledges that even with a shift toward more marriages of choice, "children still are subject to strong social pressure to obey their parents and other family elders in deciding when to marry, whom to marry, to what caste that marriage partner should belong" (2004:254). In a comprehensive longitudinal study of marital change in India, Allendorf and Pandian find modernization has not led to the large-scale abandonment of arranged marriages. They observe, "Rather than displacing their parents in the decision process, young women joined their parents in choosing husbands" (2016:457). We agree with Rindfuss and Morgan that it is better to view arranged and choice marriages as a continuum of possibilities rather than a strict dichotomy (1983:269).

The cases presented in the previous chapter support the conclusion that education is influencing the way many young people in Nubri approach matrimony. Tenzin grudgingly accepted a marriage arranged by his parents, but then divorced within months because he could not envision life with an uneducated partner he did not love. Tsering, on the brink of entering into an arranged marriage, preempted her parents' plan by eloping with Gyurme. Norbu and Sangmo used different tactics to resist arranged marriages; he just said no while she fled the village. Pema's parents entertained two proposals for their daughter but left the final decision to her. Sangye's parents also seemed willing to allow her to accept or reject a proposal, but she took no chances by fleeing the village before dawn. Yet the younger generation has not completely usurped the power of their parents, who, after all, still have an incentive to exert control over at least some of their children's marriages. Parents partially cede marital decision-making to some of their children while insisting that marrying someone of similar ethnic and religious heritage is a condition for maintaining family relations. In other cases, parents concoct a ruse that brings a girl home to an unexpected wedding so she can fulfill the pragmatic needs of social and biological reproduction. To secure household succession many parents now enroll a son in a monastery with the intention of withdrawing him when the time arrives to pass the responsibility. Characterizing contemporary developments as a predictable outcome of modernization or as a progressive trek toward individual choice is therefore misleading. Evidence points to an evolving situation that includes intergenerational skirmishes and détente.

In this chapter we have taken to task the postulate that the first generation of people to attain secular education will be the primary agents of social change. One can draw such a conclusion only in the absence of a diachronic perspective and a deeper understanding of intergenerational conciliation. In the case of Nubri, it was parents who made the decision to send their children to schools and monasteries. They may not have foreseen all of the consequences, but they no doubt knew that they were forging radically different life courses for their offspring, pathways that would inevitably lead to social and cultural transformations. Parents candidly express their premonitions of change in the oft-repeated assertion "Better a pen in the hand than a rope across the forehead." The younger generation would never be in a position to wield that pen if not for decisions made by their parents. It is the parents who never went to school—not just their children—who should be considered agents of change.

CHAPTER 10

Nubri Futures?

Sweat mingling with droplets of rain trickled down our foreheads as we ascended the final steps of the hour-long climb from Trok. We were entering Oong, a cluster of temples and houses for elderly retirees set within a forest of ancient oak trees. Smoke wafting through the wooden shingles let us know that Tsering Lhamo was home. We did not have to raise our voices to announce our presence because the settlement, which used to team with the elderly, their caretakers, and an assortment of religious practitioners, is now nearly deserted. "Please enter," Tsering Lhamo said from within when she heard our footsteps. Seated beside the hearth, she deftly replaced a pot of boiling potatoes with a smaller vessel containing arak.

You met Tsering Lhamo at the beginning of this book. She is the woman we encountered back in the village struggling under a load of milled grain, a harbinger of challenges that emerge when educational opportunities take children far from home. Tsering Lhamo splits her time between a village house in Trok and the temple of her deceased husband at Oong. Over a cup of the warming arak, she began to detail the damage the earthquake of April 2015 caused to the temple. After drinks and a meal, she took us for a tour.

The mud-plastered exterior walls of the temple resembled shattered glass with fissures radiating from deep holes. Parts of one wall bowed outward, straining to remain erect under the weight of the wooden beams and slate shingles. Inside, the damage was even worse, but it also told a story of decay that preceded the catastrophe. Evidence of the earthquake was visible in the debris scattered about the floor and the misaligned wooden panels adorned with paintings of Buddhas and lamas of yore. Yet many of the paintings showed signs of prolonged neglect, the images fading under dust and the erosive scouring of water leaks. Tsering Lhamo told us that the earthquake is not the main culprit of her temple's deterioration. Rather, it is a lack of people in the village who can provide material support, a decrease in the number of Oong's religious practitioners who used to pray within, and the absence of an heir who can take full-time responsibility for maintenance.

After parting with Tsering Lhamo we descended a trail that was being consumed by the encroaching forest, scrambled over crumbling terraces demarcating fields overrun by weeds, and walked through the desolate settlement. Gaping cavities in roofs allowed the drizzling rain to soak everything inside dwellings where elderly residents used to spend their waning years spinning prayer wheels and contemplating future lives. The front wall of one structure had collapsed, making us feel like voyeurs gazing into the tousled remnants of domestic life: shelving cleared of all wares, tattered fragments of bamboo baskets, rusting pieces of a metal stove, and a rotting wooden barrel previously used for fermenting grain. Oong is empty not because there are fewer old people. To the contrary, because of youth outmigration, the elderly constitute a higher percentage of the valley's population than ever before. Oong's abandonment is a result of the diminishing household labor force, which has left families struggling to manage a village household while maintaining a retirement home for the aged. A place that brimmed with retirees in the 1990s is now occupied by one couple, a bachelor, and sometimes Tsering Lhamo.

The gradual desertion of Oong is symptomatic of changes wrought by educational migration. While Tsering Lhamo's situation illustrates how educational migration can affect a parent's life, the dilapidated retirement houses and decrepit temples exemplify the cumulative impacts outmigration has on a community. In this chapter we use Oong as a starting point to illustrate how demographic transformations are affecting elder care, reconfiguring religious life, and compromising villagers' ability to maintain the ritual cycle. We then introduce the concept of "disembedding" to discuss the pros and cons of a migration phenomenon that distances youths from their places of birth while enhancing

FIGURE 14. The last couple residing at Oong.
Photo by Geoff Childs.

their capacity to function in a complex and evolving society. We conclude with a young migrant's appreciation for the sacrifices her parents made so that she can lead a more comfortable life.

THE PREDICAMENT OF AGING

People from Nubri are fully aware that major changes are underway in their homeland. The monk Karma Chögyal expressed his apprehension about the potential long-term consequences of outmigration:

> There is a real possibility that our people [mirik] might go extinct.[1] However, there is no way that we can stop people from leaving. As more young people leave Nubri, they are caught between two very different societies. Some stay in Kathmandu for good after they get married and start a family. Those who return to the village have a very hard time adjusting to village life. As a result, there is a possibility that our society will follow what happened in Limi [a highland community in western Nepal]. I heard that only old people live in some Limi villages, and once they die, the villages will be empty. A friend from Limi told me about this just recently. There are a few villages inhabited only by old people who stay because they want to die in the same place they were born. The rest of the people have moved to Kathmandu and sent their children abroad. As the old people die, there is a danger the village society will go extinct in the coming decades. Our society is also approaching a similar situation. It might not take long for such a thing to occur.

Karma Chögyal comprehends the magnitude of the population-aging trend that we analyzed in chapter 4 and likens it to another highland area of Nepal that is nearly deserted now except for the elderly. What he does not mention, however, is a vexing question. Who will take care of the elderly if this demographic trajectory continues?

Gerontologists use various terms to assess the aging process including *successful aging, productive aging,* and *aging well* (Depp and Jeste 2006). They strive to measure more than just the health and physical abilities of older adults, but also cognitive skills, social functioning (Rowe and Kahn 1997), and the capacity to adapt to changes associated with aging (Schulz and Heckhausen 1996; Baltes 1997). In a review of the literature on successful aging, Depp and Jeste point out that "there is no consensus about whether successful aging should be defined objectively by others or subjectively by older adults themselves" (2006:7). We fall in the subjectively defined camp because any attempt to derive an objective definition runs the risk of obscuring how people in a society like Nubri view and understand the aging process. Simply put, successful aging is a cultural construct. Any assessment of successful aging therefore needs to consider local beliefs, behaviors, and relationships that exemplify meaningful ways of living the final years of life (Lamb 2017).

For Tibetan Buddhists, life is an endless cycle of suffering characterized by birth, death, and rebirth. The only way to escape the cycle is to attain enlightenment. Three interlinked themes frequently arise in Buddhist teachings: to be born human is a precious opportunity because only humans are capable of attaining enlightenment, death is inevitable and can occur unpredictably at any moment, so one must not squander the potential to attain enlightenment by neglecting religious practice. Commenting on the importance of these three themes, Tibet's thirteenth Dalai Lama Tubten Gyatso (1876–1933) stated in a sermon to clerics and laypeople, "Consider also how rare is the human life form in comparison to the immeasurably large number of animals, insects and so forth. At the moment we have all the opportunities of human existence at our disposal, but if we ignore them for transient, worldly pursuits, there is not much hope that after our death we will regain an auspicious rebirth. Those who die bereft of spiritual training have little hope of happiness in the hereafter" (Mullin 1998:53).

Despite compelling rationales for pursuing esoteric Buddhist training, the religious practices of most young and middle-aged laypeople in Nubri center on rituals that protect the household and ward off misfortune.

The situation changes with the aging process. Once parents bequeath the household head position to their son, they gain leeway to begin withdrawing from everyday economic engagements so they can dedicate more time to prayer and contemplation. The relationship between cause and effect (*ley;* generally glossed as "karma") is foremost in the minds of the elderly who recognize that a lifetime of committing morally errant acts can catalyze an unfavorable rebirth. Although most elderly in Nubri believe that enlightenment is beyond their reach, they do not resign themselves to an unalterable fate. To the contrary, they draw upon various means from prayer to the cultivation of a compassionate mindset that can influence future lives by mitigating the effects of past actions.

In chapter 5 we discussed the distinction between the Realm of Worldly Sufferers (jigtenpey yul) and the Realm of Religious Practitioners (chöpey yul). The latter, usually a temple complex physically separated from the village, is the ideal retirement place for Nubri's elderly. Oong is one such Realm of Religious Practitioners where, ideally, old people live in small houses and dedicate their days to spiritual endeavors. Some receive support from adult children who dwell in the village, others from a daughter who, decades ago, they designated to be a nun so that one day she could be their caretaker.[2] Culturally appropriate aging in Nubri therefore involves (1) a belief that reincarnation is influenced by the tally of positive and negative actions, (2) a gradual cessation of subsistence activities so one can devote time and energy to religious practices that positively affect future rebirths, (3) a place of residence removed from the bustle of village life so one can concentrate on religious practices, and (4) a caretaker who can provide the types of support, like food and physical assistance, that enables withdrawal from village life.

Educational migration is having an enormous impact on factors that allow the elderly to retire in a culturally appropriate manner. First, many parents can no longer ensure a caretaker and grow more infirm each day under the fading hope that an adult child will return to the village. Some parents still envision the nun-caretaker option, which was common in the not-so-distant past (see chapter 6). For example, Dawa and her husband have five children. Their eldest daughter, now in her twenties, studies at a nunnery in Kathmandu. When we asked about future plans for their daughter, Dawa said, "She will live with us. But what to do if she has lived in the city for too long and doesn't return to the village? It is our custom to ordain the eldest daughter as a nun so that she may serve her parents in old age. Besides caring for her parents, there is nothing much for her to do in the village. It is up to her whether to come back to the village or stay in the city. If she thinks about us, then she will come. If she doesn't care, then she won't come."

Dawa has a husband and several children she potentially can count on for support. Widows, however, face heightened insecurity as they age. Not only are they without male partners—the ones who inherit and thereby own the majority of household assets—but they often have fewer children because spousal death curtailed their reproduction. Nyima, fifty-one, became a widow when her three children were young. She recalled, "When my husband passed away my daughter could see my poor condition, so she joined a nunnery." When we asked who should take care of her in old age, Nyima responded, "My daughter will take care of me when I become old. She should. If everything goes well, we will move to the gomba [i.e., the temple complex above the village]. If I call her back now and disrupt her studies, maybe she won't come. But when I become old and infirm, yes, she will come to see me. I know that she cares for me."

Nyima's plan to retire at the temple complex is contingent on her daughter's agreement to fulfill the role of caretaker. But bear in mind that the nuns we interviewed in Kathmandu generally oppose the idea of returning to the village as full-time residents. By recognizing the excellent opportunities for their daughters in Kathmandu's nunneries, parents may have inadvertently sacrificed their own well-being in old age.

Yangchen, a forty-nine-year-old woman who has four children with two former husbands (she divorced the first, and the second died), discussed the dilemma she will face in the future. Her eldest child, a daughter, is a nun in Kathmandu. When we asked Yangchen what the benefits are of making a daughter a nun, she responded bluntly, "So she can serve her parents." Yangchen then explained that her daughter has a medical condition that makes it difficult to breathe at high altitude, so she can never return to the village. Her next eldest child eloped and now lives in Kathmandu, and her youngest daughter is at a boarding school. As for her son, who is a monk, she said, "It is up to him whether he wants to help me or not. So far, he is not helpful. He does not even visit. He should return when he is around twenty-one or twenty-two years old. He has to help me take care of this household." Because Yangchen cannot count on her daughters, her hope rests on the possibility that her son will renounce his religious calling and return to the village. She is not confident that he will do so.

Buti, widowed two decades ago while still in her twenties, has one son and one daughter. Nowadays she manages the fields on her own through labor exchange and performs all her household's communal obligations. Her son is a monk in Kathmandu, and her daughter attends a boarding school. When we asked which child will take care of her in old age, Buti responded, "I hope my son stays in the village. I didn't tell him to come back, but he is my son and must take care of the household. It is his obligation to fulfill all the household's community obligations." When we asked what she will do if her son does not return, Buti shrugged and said, "I have relatives who help me. But in the future, who knows if they will help." Many of Buti's contemporaries will face similar dilemmas over old-age care. If they have trouble securing care for themselves, will they be able to assist others like Buti?

Not everyone is pessimistic about the future. Pemba explained,

> I think in old age our children will take care of us because of the way they are brought up as Buddhists. They have a firm belief in the law of cause and effect. Whether they will actually look after us depends upon each individual child. As Buddhists, when we grow old we believe in seizing the opportunity [of being born as a human being] to engage in spiritual and meritorious deeds as a way of preparing for the next life. A good heart and compassionate disposition are two important characteristics that are highly regarded in our way of life. Elderly Tibetans are more spiritually devoted and try to spend much time reciting prayers and earning merit. I have four children. While I do not or cannot expect all of them to be nice to us and perfect, I also do not think all of them will be bad and useless. So, I hope one of them will look after us.

Importantly, Pemba is married and has succeeded in getting his four children into high-quality schools in Kathmandu. He is also well versed in Buddhist philosophy. Perhaps these factors help explain why he is confident that one of his children will care for him and his wife in old age.

The abandonment of Oong exemplifies how culturally appropriate aging is becoming increasingly difficult to achieve in Nubri. Educational migration is eroding the foundation of an unstated yet customarily accepted intergenerational contract—a caretaker from the younger generation will assist aging parents. As a result, more and more elderly people continue dwelling in the Realm of Worldly Sufferers rather than the Realm of Religious Practitioners. Some still work the fields when, ideally, they should be sequestered at Oong devoting time to prayer. Rather than demographic transition leading to "the invention of retirement as the third stage of life" (Lee and Reher 2011:1), population trends in Nubri are hindering the capacity for many elderly people to spend the waning years in the culturally resonant manner of their ancestors.

FROM HOUSEHOLDER LAMAS TO CELIBATE MONKS

There are several temples at Oong, like Tsering Lhamo's, that are privately owned by ngagpa (householder lamas) but are falling into disuse and disrepair. Declining religious activity at Oong is affected by two related trends: a shift toward celibate monasticism and a decline of the ngagpa tradition. Both trends are ultimately tied to the widespread practice of sending sons to distant monasteries.

In the 1840s the intrepid Bonpo pilgrim Karu Drubwang Tenzin Rinchen traveled through Nubri and neighboring Tsum. In his autobiography he describes the people he met and relates how incredulous they were that anyone would want to pursue a life of celibacy. Karu wrote,

> With the exception of true siblings they behave quite unashamedly with one another, and speak without reserve. There are no lamas or monks, ordained or otherwise, who observe rules, but all are tantric householders who frequent women. They belong to the rNying ma pa [Nyingmapa] and bKa' brgyud pa [Kagyüpa] schools. Consequently, if you tell the people in this area that you're an ordained monk, they'll think it's a complete fabrication, because to be a lama you need to be a member of the appropriate clan; and since monks therefore have to maintain their patrilineages, anyone who says he doesn't sleep with women is regarded as a liar. To say that you don't need a woman is very badly considered, or else an indication that you're sterile or homosexual. It causes utter revulsion. Or else, if you say you've given up women they think you're making it up, and guffaw loudly—everyone just laughs in amazement. (Ramble 2009:499–500).

Karu's remarks attest to how deeply embedded householder lamas were in Nubri during the 1840s. The situation had not changed much by the 1990s, when ngagpa still dominated village religious life. There were a few celibate monks, but even their dalliances with women were tolerated.

The life courses of Rö's most senior Ngadag lineage members epitomize the importance of perpetuating the lineage through marriage. They represent the last generation of men who underwent religious training in Tibet, primarily at the borderland monastery Dragkar Taso. Tashi Dorje (1919–2017) had a desire to become a celibate monk but, out of concern for continuing the lineage, his father insisted that he marry and remain a ngagpa (Childs 2004:65–67). Tashi Dorje's cousin, Yönten Gyatso (1938–2012), was also expected to marry. He recalled,

> I first got married at the age of fifteen. While staying with my brother at Dragkar Taso Monastery, Dragkar Rinpoche [the head lama of Dragkar Taso] asked me to come up and study at his place. I stayed there for one

month. Around that time, his eldest daughter was given to me and my brother as a bride.

After returning home for one month, we went back to her father's monastery. Soon there was trouble in the marriage because she wanted me to stay in her father's household as a *magpa* [matrilocally resident husband]. She said she feels lonely in Nubri and misses her family. I said there is no way I could stay there as a magpa. Dragkar Rinpoche had no sons, only three daughters, and his elder brother is a monk. There were no male heirs to carry forward their great lineage. Dragkar Rinpoche suggested that, since we are two brothers, one of us could stay with him as a magpa. But we insisted that there is no way either of us could stay as a magpa. In the end, the marriage did not work out.

Another marriage was arranged for me and my brother. I left the marriage after two years due to some disagreements. She and my brother stayed together. I then met my current wife who has a long story of personal suffering, but let's not discuss it. Whatever the past, we were very compatible and have been together since then. We have two sons and one daughter. (Childs 2015)

Tashi Dorje and Yönten Gyatso came of age at a time when celibacy was uncommon among Nubri's religious practitioners. Tashi Dorje's ambition to become a monk was trumped by his responsibility to preserve the lineage. Meanwhile, Yönten Gyatso had a somewhat bumpy marital history involving two arranged polyandrous unions followed by a wife of his choosing. Despite being high-level practitioners at the pinnacle of the local religious hierarchy, they were never expected to lead the life of celibate monks.

With the rise of educational migration and mass monasticism, the situation has changed. Tsering Lhamo's son, Dzamling Dorje, is the only male offspring of his ngagpa father. As we quoted him saying in the opening of this book, "Since I belong to a lama's lineage, if I don't marry, our lineage will come to an end." He further explained,

In the past it was a part of our tradition in Nubri for the lamas living in the village to marry while still carrying out their religious duties. But I became a celibate monk at a very young age, and I have developed a strong commitment to this celibate way of religious study. I have a strong apprehension that I would never be able to continue proper religious study if I marry. It will mean that I will be involved in lay life, such as taking care of my own children and managing the family estate. Although I might still be interested in religious matters and find some time for study, I am afraid that I would never be able to dedicate my life fully and purely to religious activities. That is why I worry about taking on a layman's duties.

Despite the pressure to marry and keep his lineage intact through procreation, Dzamling Dorje is reluctant to renounce his monastic vows.

FIGURE 15. A ngagpa (householder lama) whose son is a monk.
Photo by Geoff Childs.

He has well-founded reasons to believe that the responsibilities a layperson shoulders would detract from his ambition to study and practice Buddhism at the highest level.

Karma Chögyal is also the son of a householder lama. Unlike Dzamling Dorje, Karma Chögyal faces no pressure to abandon celibacy, because his father has another son in the village, Rabgye, who married and has children. Here we can see a generational difference. The father, as a ngagpa, simultaneously fulfilled his religious role as a lama and his social role as a husband and father. Those duties are now divided among his sons. Karma Chögyal is a fully ordained monk who has become a highly regarded scholar and teacher; Rabgye has less religious training than his brother, yet as a male member of the lama lineage is fully qualified to propagate the bloodline. One lives in Kathmandu, the other in the village.

Although there are still ngagpa residing full-time in Nubri, they are generally above age forty. Those who are most highly respected have either passed away in recent years, like Tashi Dorje and Yönten Gyatso, or are being compelled by advancing age to reduce their engagement in local religious events. Few of them currently train novices during the annual winter retreat. It is now the abbots of monasteries and their entourage of monks, rather than ngagpa, who are instructing the next generation of religious practitioners. They do so in urban monasteries and, increasingly, in recently established branch institutions in Nubri. In the 1990s there was only one indigenous monastery in the valley that housed a few celibate monks. Now there are three more institutions, extensions of "mother" monasteries in India and Kathmandu—the very institutions that have successfully recruited scores of monks from Nubri. The closely cropped stubble of the celibate monk supplanting the braided locks of the ngagpa signals that a major shift in the social organization of religion is underway in Nubri.

THE COMMUNAL OBLIGATION IMPASSE

In addition to private temples like the one owned by Tsering Lhamo's family, Oong is also where one of Trok's five communal temples is located. Called Oong Gomba, it is the site of two of the rituals described in chapter 3, including the one that closes the annual cycle. Keeping these rituals viable and vibrant is becoming increasingly difficult. Dzamling Dorje explains,

> People are feeling burdened by the religious obligations these days. In the past people were more religious minded. The lamas are known as the chief spiritual advisors [wulag].[3] Everyone must abide by whatever they say either out of faith or because it is the law. They are the kings, the lamas, and the leading authorities. Over time these lamas have made certain regulations in the belief that the laypeople would automatically engage in religious activities. That is why there are many religious ceremonies that require people to frequently perform the role of caretaker. However, times have changed. People are less religious minded these days, and thus have less respect for these traditions. Further, people are hard pressed for time due to development and other changes. Therefore, people find these religious obligations too burdensome and time consuming.
>
> It is rare for laypeople these days to understand the rituals as acts of gaining merit and dispelling obstacles.[4] They see the role of caretaker more as a burden and less as a meritorious act. Since these obligations are part of the community regulations, some people suggest that they should be reduced. Despite such opinions, thus far the village elders have persisted and maintained these communal religious activities. From one perspective, it is good that these practices are maintained. If we give in to such complaints, it might gradually lead to a scenario when there is no community activity. But, if viewed from a different perspective, forcing people to perform these religious activities without their genuine interest will generate less merit. Also, it does not appear right to force people to do something that they are not really interested in. That is the current reality.

Dzamling Dorje acknowledges a quandary spawned by outmigration. On one hand, fewer helping hands in the village creates more onerous obligations for those who remain. On the other hand, compelling people to participate or contribute more of their scarce time and labor risks diminishing the merit the rites are designed to generate. Although we are not in a position to comment on whether piety among villagers is on the wane, we can address the pressing question, Why is religious activity becoming more of a burden?

The answer is related to specific impacts outmigration has on agricultural production. In chapter 3 we described Trok's tax system, which generates produce and labor for the annual ritual cycle. Some villages have already curtailed the system, others appear to be on the road to abandoning it. As Dzamling Dorje notes, so far Trok is holding onto its traditions, but the future is in doubt. We heard grumblings from several folks about the expensive and time-consuming duties associated with the ritual cycle. Many grievances are directly related to the fact that people now struggle to produce the surplus grain needed to meet tax obligations. One village leader in Trok told us that the burden of responsibilities is why "everyone complains that they no longer want to be classified as drongchen households." By petitioning to be reclassified as smaller households, Trok residents seek to reduce their communal obligations. The reason they are so inclined to make the shift is that educational migration affects farm production. As one man observed, "The leaving of young people for education in schools and monasteries is having a negative impact. In Trok you can see that many fields have turned into pastures because there is a shortage of labor."

Trok's temples own a disproportionate number of the fields that people are allowing to lie fallow. As described in chapter 3, a sharecropping household must relinquish a specified amount of produce from each temple field to support the annual rituals. However, the arrangement is contingent on the household agreeing to farm these fields. With educational migration depleting the labor force, many now struggle to sow and harvest even the fields they personally own. Fewer mouths to feed diminishes both the incentive and the requisite hands to sharecrop temple land. The predictable outcome is that many fields now lie fallow. According to beyig documents, the temple land area farmed to support Trok's two most elaborate rituals, the Kanjur reading and Dumje, has declined by nearly 12 percent in recent years. Most of the fallow fields lie on the fringe of village territory and therefore are difficult to defend against marauding animals, a task that parents used to delegate to young people. As one man put it, "Planting those fields is not worth my time. I only end up feeding the bears and monkeys." The fact that fewer families are farming temple lands is evidence that outmigration is weakening the ritual system's funding mechanism.

The situation is complicated by the fact that many children raised away from the village struggle to comprehend the local administrative system. Any intricate system is best learned through participation. A person who lives in the village can read the documents, contribute to regular debates about procedural matters, and partake in fifteen communal rituals every year. A child who comes of age in a boarding school has no opportunity to internalize the complexities of village administration. As a local leader commented while we were photographing the corpus of loan manuscripts, "If we don't take proper care, these documents will be lost forever. With the younger generation going down to Kathmandu, people later will have a hard time understanding these regulations since they are so unfamiliar with the traditions."

Trok's annual cycle of communal rituals is still intact but is frayed at the edges and in danger of unraveling. Although this is not the first time a Himalayan community has adjusted its administrative mechanisms to changing circumstance (Ramble 2008; Ramble and Drandul 2017), educational migration presents a novel convergence of challenges. It reduces the household labor force, which in turn diminishes the ability to produce surplus grain and contribute time and effort to rituals. Temple fields, a critical source of funding, are the first to be abandoned. Children raised outside of the community become strangers to the ritual cycle. Current leaders, who are mostly in their sixties, are adamant in their desire to continue Trok's religious traditions. But will their successors have the means and motivation to do so?

In summary, Oong's status as a retirement settlement is compromised by the increasing difficulty families face in supporting two houses, one of which is for the elderly so they can retire in a culturally appropriate manner. The settlement's role as a religious retreat is declining with the gradual replacement of the householder lama tradition with celibate monasticism. And if people are no longer willing or able to support the annual ritual cycle, the communal temple at Oong risks falling into disuse. The situation is unlikely to reverse soon because of impediments to return that arise the moment children are separated from their natal homes.

DISEMBEDDING THE YOUNGER GENERATION

In his analysis of education and mobility in rural Nova Scotia, Corbett argues that schools are institutions of "disembedding" because they facilitate a form of outmigration that loosens ties between individuals and their places of birth (Corbett 2007). That is precisely what is happening in Nubri, albeit with a major difference. In rural Nova Scotia young people are educated in their natal communities and then leave. In Nubri children move elsewhere—often at very young ages and across great distances—to gain access to education. The disembedding effect is thereby magnified because most young people spend few of their formative years in a village where they would be exposed to the local vernacular and customs, all the while embedded in a dense network of kin. As the monk Dzamling Dorje explained, "There is a big social distance between parents and their children these days. When children return home and interact with their parents, there is always some tension. First, many cannot speak the local dialect. Second, even if they speak the local dialect, a problem occurs because the children cannot understand at all what their parents tell them about a way of life that has continued since the time of their ancestors."

Karma Chögyal expressed a similar sentiment, "There is definitely a problem when you take young children so far away from the village. We know very well that they will lose the knowledge of local language, culture, history, and society. For example, a few young educated people have recently returned to Nubri and are working as teachers. However, they don't have any knowledge of Nubri culture and society [*drotang*, literally, "way of doing things"]. Everyone is deeply concerned about this big problem."

Yungdrung, an influential village leader, also worries about the affect educational migration is having on Nubri culture. In his opinion, "Those who go to boarding schools don't know about cultural practices like making daily water offerings. They don't know who should sit where in a house, and who sits above and below [i.e., seating hierarchy]. They are so confused. If this continues, we will lose our culture."

All three men see a direct connection between disembedding youths from their natal villages and the loss of cultural knowledge. Yungdrung was quite specific in pointing out that they lose the ability to discern fundamental social conventions such as how gender, age, and social status determine where one should sit at a public event or when visiting another's home. If the younger generation does not learn basic rules of behavior, then the unique "way of doing things" in Nubri is in jeopardy.

Regarding the loss of language, Karma Chögyal mused,

> I understand that sending children to schools is very good because it means a better future for them. However, modern education alone is not enough.

There is also a need for traditional education, in particular, Tibetan culture and language. This is essential because it is the main spoken language of the region. Today there are many parents who are not able to afford the fees for the standard Tibetan schools, and they end up sending their children to ordinary Nepali schools. And these children become unable to speak Tibetan, which means that they can't even communicate with their parents. Under such circumstances, how will parents communicate with their children?

He has a point. Children who are sent to Nepali schools are at a disadvantage when it comes to reengagement with their home communities. But those who attend Tibetan schools also face difficulties. Most are fluent in Tibetan, albeit a standardized school form that is not always mutually intelligible with the Nubri dialect. Even in everyday interactions, the younger generation prefers—and seems more comfortable—speaking to each other in Nepali. This should come as no surprise since they live in the nation's capital, where competence in the lingua franca is indispensable. Yet it entails a hefty cost, namely, the diminishing ability of children to communicate effectively with their parents. One young migrant lamented, "I don't know much of my native language, so when I visit Nubri I feel lost. My mother knows some Nepali language, so I stay with her and talk with her. In the beginning I used to talk in Nubri language because I didn't want to make her upset or something, so I get started with Nubri language. But in the end, we speak in Nepali language."

Daily interactions are one thing. Trying to participate in village life when unable to speak the Nubri dialect is another matter altogether. Several young men told us that they understand virtually nothing when they return to the valley and attend village council meetings—the very gatherings where details of the administrative system and ritual cycle are often discussed. As one young man explained, "When I visited the village, my father insisted that I attend the village council meetings. I tried to speak Nubri language, but I somehow speak differently. The villagers could not understand me." Cultural reproduction is difficult to accomplish if the younger generation loses the ability to communicate in the local vernacular. After all, managing core village activities is dependent on understanding concepts expressed verbally in the Nubri dialect and in writing using the Tibetan script. Even many of the written terms are specific to Nubri or even a village like Trok, so literacy alone is insufficient for understanding how the system operates. Cultural continuity depends on lived experience.

Karma Chögyal also frets that living in an urban environment leads to the disintegration of tightly knit communities. He explained,

In general, people in Nubri have enough to eat, drink, and wear, and the way of thinking is quite good. People are not greedy and they have strong affection for their parents and relatives. This strong sense of community is very rare in today's world, and I think this is a very positive aspect of Nubri society. For instance, if a person falls sick, everyone—even adversaries—would pay a visit and inquire about the sick person. They would take along some arak to show concern. Such social behaviors are characteristic of a human society. Otherwise we are not that different from animals, who are driven more by the instinct of self-survival. We see some of these individualistic attitudes in the cities, where people keep to themselves and do not bother about each other's welfare. In Nubri there is a strong sense of community. In cities, people don't know who their next-door neighbor is or what that person does for a living. People just don't care about these things.

Karma Chögyal captures a concern shared by many Nubri residents, especially the elderly who feel lost amid a sea of unfamiliar faces in the city. Urbanization is often associated with modernity. Yet Karma Chögyal feels that population density prompts regression toward a dog-eat-dog world where people are mainly concerned about their own welfare. For him, disembedding youths through rural to urban migration can lead to alienation and a loss of community cohesion.

The liminality Nubri's youths encounter—living in a city detached from natal villages—positions them as "double outsiders."[5] We have seen how some become estranged from rural communities because they do not understand customs and struggle with the local vernacular. Meanwhile, in Kathmandu they live in a society dominated by people of a different religion, Hinduism, who often relegate them to a low status. One girl vividly recalled feeling marginalized when she and her classmates were bused to a Nepali school to take an exam. Some of the high caste teachers demanded, "Who let these bhotey into our school?" As noted before, *bhotey* is a Nepali term for ethnic Tibetans that is often used with pejorative intent. The ambiguous status of educational migrants also manifests in questions of ethnic identity. For example, when we asked Dolma how classmates at her college view her, she responded, "They usually think I am Gurung or from Manang."[6] Döndrul, a college student, told us, "Most of the students in my school are Bahun [Brahmin]. They ask, 'Are you Sherpa?' Because I look like a Sherpa I say, 'I am Sherpa.' Others ask, 'Where are you from?' But I usually don't tell them because if I say, 'I am from Nubri. My culture is Nubri,' they don't know what that is. I sometimes say, 'I am from Gorkha. Do you know Mount Manaslu?' They recognize that, so then

I tell them, 'I am bhotey lama, but I'm not from Tibet. I am from Nepal, Gorkha.'"

Note how Döndrul uses the term *bhotey* knowing that his classmates will recognize it, yet quickly distances himself from Tibetan exiles to establish his credential as a native of Nepal. He seems compelled to qualify that he is not a foreigner. Meanwhile, Lhamo chuckled when we asked her the same question and said, "Some think of me as a Sherpa, and some tell me I am Chinese. I don't know why. My friend and I speak Tibetan [in school]; they think it is Chinese language. They always tell us, 'You guys are speaking Chinese language.' They call us 'Chinese girls.'" Lhamo's classmate Tsechu confirmed the story and added, "In my college when friends ask me where I am from, and I say, 'I am from Gorkha.' They say, 'Are you Chinese? You look like Chinese.' Then I pretend I am Chinese so they keep asking me to speak Chinese language. When my friend and I say we are Tibetan, they don't really believe us. They say, 'You look Chinese. You are from China.' They ask us to teach them Chinese language, so we teach them some Tibetan and say it is Chinese language."

The interpersonal politics of ethnicity underscores the perception that Nubri's youths are outsiders in a city like Kathmandu. Some classmates assume they are Sherpa, Buddhist highlanders who have achieved fame, wealth, and status through mountaineering prowess. Others mistake them for members of ethnic groups such as Gurung. But some look at them as more than just ethnic others. By assuming that they are Tibetan exiles or Chinese, high caste Nepalis mark young people from Nubri as aliens in the very nation of their birth.

Educational migration has generated positive outcomes as well. Recall that many parents said they feel like lemba (deaf mutes) when traveling outside the valley because they speak nothing but their own dialect. Their children do not suffer the same embarrassment. Most are now trilingual in Nepali, Tibetan, and English. Habitual code-switching illustrates how comfortable they are navigating the complexities of a multilingual society. In an interview with Lhakpa about a project that captured people's experiences of the April 2015 earthquake, he interspersed three languages in one sentence when he said, "Data [English] ma ong par la [Tibetan] future reference [English] ko lagi [Nepali]," or, "The data can be used for future reference."[7] Linguistic competence expands the range of employment opportunities for Nubri's youths. Our participant researchers from Nubri have no problem interviewing in Tibetan, filling out survey forms in English, and negotiating permits with government officials in Nepali. Language acquisition, albeit coming at the partial expense of one's mother tongue, confers an array of social and economic advantages in contemporary society.

On another positive note, Nubri's youths are by no means becoming lost or completely assimilated within an alien urban environment. Many are adapting quite well to the multi-ethnic melting pot of Kathmandu. One young man is the only member from a highland community of a city-league cricket team. Others regularly post images of themselves hanging out at restaurants and parks with former college friends who hail from all over Nepal. Furthermore, Nubri's youths are keeping in touch with each other and forming new communities the same way young people across the world do—through social media. They have launched Facebook pages and WeChat groups in which they regularly exchange thoughts, feelings, and personal updates about their whereabouts and undertakings. Affection for Nubri is evident in the somewhat romanticized depictions of the physical beauty and unique culture that come through in selfies using mountains, alpine lakes, and colorful festivals as backdrops. Through such postings they signal a connection to their place of origin and prolong the duration of a brief visit by keeping it visible through digital means.

On the other hand, interactions through social media and intermittent visits can never usurp the attachment to a place formed through full-time residence. Despite expressing love for their homeland, precious few young people state an intention to settle either short-term or permanently in the village. Their main impediment is not related to identity, language loss, or the alienating effect of disembedding. Rather, it is simply the lack of job opportunities. Dzamling Dorje acknowledged the dilemma when he commented,

> To say that everyone should stay in the village and not go outside for education is not right at all. When the whole world understands the importance of education and everyone is trying to get education, it does not make sense for us to say that we will forsake education in order to maintain our farms. We must continue to send our children for education. What is badly needed is employment opportunities for these educated people back in Nubri. It would be great if meaningful employment opportunities existed. At present I think there is a huge missing link with parents working hard in the village while their children are away getting education. Even if the children have very good educational skills, they are not in a position to undertake a big project that will create employment opportunities back home and attract more young educated people. If an educated person returns to the village, the most attractive job at present is that of a teacher. Not everyone can be employed

as a teacher because there are only a certain number of schools that need teachers. So, young people are caught in a bind. It is a problem if they go back to the village, and it is also a problem if they don't go back. If they work in Kathmandu, they might get a good salaried job, but there is not much they can do to change the situation back home. Overall, I think sending children to school is good even though the parents have to undergo hardships. What is really needed is some new development in Nubri whereby these young people can be gainfully employed after they complete their education. In that case, those who leave for education could return to the village, resulting in a circular movement of people. At present, because there are no such opportunities, it becomes a one-way movement with no possibility of return.

Most young men and women view the prospect of pursuing an agrarian lifestyle as a reversion to something they evaded through education. Those who do return are lured by the few jobs that pay good wages, income that some hope to parlay into a future move abroad. Like rural Japan (Knight and Traphagan 2003), Nubri is no longer a lifecourse space where residents spend the entirety of their lives. Educational migration has transformed the valley into a lifephase space for youths who are born in the village and sent out at a young age. They still consider Nubri home and make occasional visits that help instill an emotional attachment to the valley, but most are unlikely to settle upon the soil that their ancestors have cultivated for generations.

PARTING THOUGHTS

In this study we built upon the research of our predecessors in anthropological demography by framing educational migration as part of a family management strategy in which Nubri's parents manipulate the composition of their households (a short-term goal) and enhance the prospects for family members to diversify their socioeconomic activities (a long-term goal). We used migration network theory as a heuristic tool to understand how long-standing religious connections shaped pathways for sending children to specific institutions, and argued that monks, as a vanguard for rural-to-urban migration, expedited cumulative causation by using information about and connections within the city to increase migration intensity. The outcome is today's culture of migration. Moving away from the village for education is now normative behavior bolstered by economic rationales and laden with social status implications.

As practitioners of anthropological demography, we have integrated ethnographic and statistical methodologies in order to generate insights that would never be possible when employing one to the exclusion of the other. However, bridging epistemological chasms remains a challenge. Proponents of statistically driven studies are often skeptical about the value of ethnographic research. The two most common criticisms we encounter are that ethnography is better at generating anecdotes than hard facts, and conclusions drawn from qualitative fieldwork cannot be generalized. On the second point we partially agree, but only because the depth of knowledge ethnography can produce makes us reluctant to render analysis amenable to comparison by way of reduction and simplification. It is better to present a robust story with complicated refractions than a linear one that mines conclusions from a database denuded of social context. As for ethnography being anecdotal, we have taken pains to demonstrate the efficacy of interpreting statistical trends in dialogue with qualitative evidence. Participant observation, informal conversations, and in-depth interviews do far more than beget a string of just-so stories of dubious veracity. Together these methodologies reveal patterns, motivations, and meanings expressed through the cultural lens of people who are central players in a migration phenomenon that is affecting their livelihoods and transforming their communities. A strict reliance on survey data would conceal the evocative nuances of lives in transition.

On the flip side we disagree with those anthropologists who dismiss quantitative measures on the grounds that they are mere social constructs or that they reside at the far end of the "lies, damn lies, and statistics" falsehood spectrum. Numbers can and do provide tangible insights about social processes. In the absence of our own survey data, any observations about demographic trends in Nubri would have been unsubstantiated and, quite frankly, anecdotal. Analyzing reproductive history data led to the hypothesis that a fertility rate disparity between Nubri residents and Tibetan exiles helps explain why Nepal's highland communities became major recruiting grounds for monasteries and schools that depend on a steady supply of novices to remain viable. We supported that suspicion with testimonies from various actors to argue that demographic trends help drive outmigration through a supply-and-demand chain linking urban institutions with rural communities. In addition, data from the household surveys not only enabled us to quantify the age-sex composition and magnitude of outmigration, but also to uncover prominent sending destinations. This revelation opened a route for exploring social connections that help explain why a disproportionate number of youths end up in particular schools and religious institutions. Furthermore, we analyzed data on fertility, mortality, and marriage to document an emerging demographic transition, and then turned to ethnographic data to investigate how Nubri's population trends are generating social outcomes that differ from those predicted by modernization and demographic transition theories. As foreshadowed in chapter 1, we have used quantitative data to answer *what is happening* with demographic trends, and qualitative data to address *why it is happening*. The final question we ask is, *Why does it matter?*

We share Corbett's mixed sentiment about education and outmigration when he writes, "I am deeply ambivalent about the way that young people in isolated and rural communities are put in a situation where a serious engagement with formal education pretty much always leads away from home. Education failure and immobility is often tragic at the individual level in contemporary Canada, but so too is education success and the depopulation of rural places" (Corbett 2007:5).

Like rural Nova Scotia, Nubri society is at a crossroad. Education provides Nubri's children with new opportunities but also depletes communities of an energetic and productive generation that has the training and capabilities to operate in a rapidly changing society. The cumulative weight of parents' decisions to secure brighter futures for their children through educational migration catalyzed a range of societal changes, both positive and negative. Consequences include the very real specter of population decline, the diminishing ability of Nubri's elderly to retire in a culturally appropriate manner, and the potential demise of an elegant cultural system that evolved over centuries to forge communities through shared endeavors. On the positive side, young people are gaining the skills and connections to improve living conditions for their kin in Nubri. This became especially evident in the wake of the April 2015 earthquake, which leveled nearly every structure in the valley and disrupted the lifeline of trails connecting Nubri to the rest of Nepal. Young people immediately banded together to form Tsum Nubri Relief Center to coordinate humanitarian aid and rebuilding efforts.[8] But even before the earthquake, a trickle of people had returned to provide vital services. A young man worked for several years as a teacher at a local primary school, then convinced a foreign organization to build a school in one of the poorest villages in the valley. He is now managing the construction and heading the school board. Another man also returned to his village as a teacher, then garnered the support of several nonprofit organizations so he can spearhead development initiatives. Two women completed nursing school and were hired by an organization that builds and manages rural health posts. They became the first-ever practitioners of allopathic medicine from Nubri to work in Nubri. One young woman spent a "gap year" doing a service-oriented project in the valley. Reflecting on the experience, she said,

> For me it was big honor, a privilege to go to my own village. I was born there, and it was a great experience for me, to stay there for one year, helping the kids as much as I can. The kids were so happy to see me. They gave me more respect when I wore a *chuba* [garment worn by Tibetan women]. And at the same time, I was helping my parents after school finished. I felt so sad whenever I walked to school and saw them working in the field, under the hot sun, so it just came naturally from my heart to help them as much as I can. I helped them with physical chores, like working in the fields, grazing the cattle, cutting the grass for the cattle, preparing food—all those things. It was so fun. When I went back [to Kathmandu] my parents were crying, "Oh no, we don't have anyone to help us." When I left I also felt like crying. I am in touch with the kids over there, and the beautiful places. It is still underdeveloped. I really want to go there to help my village after I finish my further studies.

Even though most educational migrants will seek their fortunes elsewhere, some will return to Nubri as intermittent visitors, a few as full-time residents. The quality of those who come back will partially compensate for the quantity of those who leave. By reengaging with the village, many young people acquire a deep appreciation for Nubri culture and society. They also develop sincere compassion for their parents' hardships, which were amplified by sacrifices made so the younger generation could reach for a brighter future. To illustrate this point, we conclude with a daughter's expression of gratitude to her parents. Yangzom recently informed us that she had interviewed her mother and graciously gave us permission to print her thoughts and feelings. Here is what she sent us, carefully handwritten on the pages of a lined notebook:

> She is born around 1960 (animal year is Mouse). She is the eldest child in her family. She is hardworking and kindhearted. Due to some problem in her family nobody in the village was allowed to talk to her or enter her parents' house (and vice versa). They treated her family like a blacksmith.[9] So her parents left for another village, leaving her alone in the village with one of their servants, who could not hear or speak well. At that time she was only ten years old.
> Poor girl who was only ten years old had no one to play with and speak with. Her parents gave her the responsibility for the whole house and all the

FIGURE 16. Educational migrants from figure 11 who returned to work in Nubri. Photos by Geoff Childs.

activities of the village. At the age of going to school she was forced to take all the responsibilities of the house. Her days were passed by working in the fields with one of the old servants, and nights were passed with open eyes whole night due to fear of losing things. The whole night she used to cry because she was deeply hurt. But there was no one to speak and share with, and no one to help her.

When she was sixteen she got married with rich family member's sons. Their marriage was zasum [polyandry] which means two husbands and one wife. At that time her husbands' father was powerful. So all the villagers respected them and obeyed them. Her older husband was quite smart and a business-minded type, and the younger was hardworking and not that smart. And later on due to some problems, she got divorced from older husband and lived with younger husband. So they divided all the things with the older husband that they had before. But unfortunately she and her husband got only a big bowl for storing water. So they got lots and lots of problems. They had no pots to cook food, no cups and plates for eating, and no blankets and mattress for sleeping. They got only one pot for cooking. So they cooked everything in that one pot turnwise.

Every year she got pregnant and every year her child used to die. Altogether she gave birth to ten children, and now only four of them are alive and six already died in small age. Villagers were also tired of coming for her children's funerals. They used to backbite like, "Let's go in next time like it's a funeral because every year we have to go like that." When she heard this, she was very hurt. But what to do? There was nothing to do but just cry and feel little bit light. They worked really hard and added the things they needed one by one.

Now they have quite a happy life. They got altogether four children, one son and three daughters. This "she" is my mother (amala). Lastly I wish my pala (father) and amala a happy and prosperous life ahead.

On a separate page Yangzom conveyed her feelings after hearing her mother's story: "Tears dropped from my eyes continuously and I became speechless for a while. I felt myself lucky compared to her life. I wish for happy and prosperous life for my father and mother in the future. I want to treat you well and thank you for giving me birth. Yes, I feel proud to be your daughter. Thank you lots and lots and love you 4ever."

Appendix

The Population of Nubri

To describe Nubri's population we first need to distinguish the de facto population (those present at the time of a demographic survey) from the de jure population (those who hold some claim to belong to the area even if not physically present at the time of the survey). According to Nepal's 2011 census, Nubri's de facto population is 2,502 individuals. An additional 167 people are recorded as "absentee," which brings the de jure population to 2,669.[1] However, the census data reveals extremely small cohorts aged ten to fourteen and fifteen to nineteen. Clearly, the census did not enumerate children living elsewhere.[2]

Comparing villages enumerated in the 2011 Nepal census with our own household surveys, we find that the de facto populations are roughly the same but our de jure population is 32.4 percent larger than the census's de jure population. Therefore, to derive a reliable estimate of Nubri's entire population, we use our de facto and de jure population data for Samdo, Rö, Lö, Li, and Trok. For villages not included in our surveys, we multiply the Nepal de facto census figures by 1.324, which is the difference (32.4 percent) between the census tally and our own de jure enumeration. We thereby estimate the de facto and de jure populations of Nubri to be 2,452 and 3,491 respectively (table 9). The magnitude of outmigration is evident—over 1,000 individuals, or roughly 30 percent of the population, no longer live in their natal villages.

TABLE 9. ESTIMATE OF NUBRI'S POPULATION

Location		HH Surveys		Nepal Census		De Jure Multiplier	Best Estimate	
VDC	Village (wards)	de facto	de jure	de facto	de jure	x 1.324	de facto	de jure
Sama	Rö (1–6)	470	604	–	–	–	470	604
	Samdo (7–9)	95	174	–	–	–	95	174
	Sama VDC Total	**565**	**778**	**–**	**–**	**–**	**565**	**778**
Lho	Li (1–2)	169	273	–	–	–	169	273
	Sho (3–4)	–	–	188	210	278	188	278
	Lö (5–9)	357	527	–	–	–	357	527
	Lho VDC Total	**526**	**800**	**188**	**210**	**278**	**714**	**1,078**
Prok	Trok (1–3)	197	314	–	–	–	197	314
	Kwak (4–5)	–	–	142	148	196	142	196
	Tsak (6–7)	–	–	128	135	179	128	179
	Namrung (8–9)	–	–	94	100	132	94	132
	Prok VDC Total	**197**	**314**	**364**	**383**	**507**	**561**	**821**
Bihi	**Bihi VDC Total**	**197**	**314**	**612**	**615**	**814**	**612**	**814**
	NUBRI TOTAL						**2,452**	**3,491**

SOURCES: Nepal's Central Bureau of Statistics (http://www.cbs.gov.np/); Beall, Childs, and Craig 2012 Household Demographic Survey; Quinn and Childs 2013 Household Demographic Survey.

Notes

1. All names in the book are pseudonyms except for historical figures and oral history sources.

2. *Ngagpa* is sometimes translated as "tantric practitioner" or "married lama." We gloss the term "householder lama" because it accurately represents the dual status of a religious practitioner who is also head of a household. It is a hereditary position attained through the combination of birth in a lama lineage and Buddhist education. Many spend several years in monasteries or retreat centers under the tutelage of senior Buddhist masters, and complete meditation retreats ranging from a year to three years and three months. Ngagpa do not take vows of celibacy, because they are expected to marry in order to perpetuate their patriline. They are especially common in Nyingmapa communities. Clarke contrasts the householder lama and celibate monk traditions as a difference between a "world embracer" and a "world renouncer" (1990:169), which is not entirely accurate because many ngagpa engage in high-level studies of esoteric Buddhism.

3. See the appendix for a breakdown of Nubri's population by village.

4. The Tibetan term *rku* means "thief." Some locals say that the name *Kutang* has nothing to do with thievery, but derives from the Tibetan terms *sku* (statue) and *thang* (plain). The toponym Plain of Statues refers to the extraordinary number of stone carvings one finds in the area (personal communication with ethnomusicologist Mason Brown).

5. http://www.himalayangtrekking.com.au/trek-manaslu.php. http://www.ethichimalaya.com/nepal/trekking-in-nepal/manaslu-trekking.php. Accessed 8/1/15.

6. http://allnepal.com/nepal/restricted_manaslu.php (accessed 7/30/15). To demonstrate how widely disseminated these images of Nubri have become, a

Google search containing the two terms "Manaslu" and "medieval" yielded fifty-two thousand results.

7. On herbal contraceptives in premodern societies see Hern 1976, Riddle 1994 and 1999, and Yarmohammadi et al. 2013; on coitus interruptus see Santow 1995 and Schneider and Schneider 1995; on emmenagogues and abortifacients see Conway and Slocumb 1979, Riddle 1991, and van de Walle and Renne 2001; on infanticide see Howell 1979, Chagnon, Flinn and Melancon 1979, Scrimshaw 1983, Patterson 1985, Harris and Ross 1987, and Lee and Wang 1999; on abandonment see Ransel 1988 and Kertzer 1993; and on "aggressive neglect" see Scrimshaw 1978, Levine 1987, Das Gupta 1987, and Scheper-Hughes 1997.

8. In demographic terms, people who move within a country are classified as outmigrants (from a place of origin) and inmigrants (to a destination) to distinguish them from international movers who are labeled emigrants and immigrants.

9. https://youtube.com/watch?v=7jcKkchLY_g. The interview is part of the World Oral Literature Project archive (http://oralliterature.org/).

10. See Beall and Leslie (2014) for a methodological discussion of the reproductive history survey.

11. The research was supported by a Washington University Summer Research Grant.

12. The project Genes and Fertility of Tibetan Women at High Altitude in Nepal was supported by the National Science Foundation (award 1153911).

13. The project Infant Growth, Milk Composition, and Maternal Energetics in a High Altitude Environment was originally supported by grants from the Wenner-Gren and Leakey foundations, and later by a more substantial grant from the National Science Foundation (award 1518013).

14. The Shelley and Donald Rubin Foundation and Washington University provided funding for this research.

2. MOVING IN BEFORE MOVING OUT

1. de rjes skad mi gcig gis phyogs la byon/ rnal 'byor phug tu zla ba gcig bzhugs nas/ mi ma yin mang po la chos gsungs/ mi'i gdul bya snod ldan yod dam gzigs pas/ dud 'gro lta bu min pa gcig kyang mi 'dug pas/ thugs nges par 'byung ste mgur 'di bzhes so/ ma rig mun sel lo tsA ba/ mar ston chos rje'i zhabs la 'dud/ dam chos nyi ma med pa yi/ mtha' 'khob mun pa'i smag rum na/ rten mi yi gzugs su 'dug na 'ang/ yid rnam par zhes pa'i rgyu ba la/ zas btung ba longs spyod ma gtogs pa/ chos don du gnyer mkhan mi 'dug bas/ yid nges par 'byung ba'i glu 'di la/ khyed mi min lha 'dre nyan par bgyi/ sdon las ngan bsags pas lus ngan thob/ lus ngan blangs nas yang dang ni/ las ngan bsags nas ngan 'gror 'gro/ 'di 'dra'i mi lus dud 'gro'i sems/ mthong bas bdag yid nges par 'byung/ yid gong nas snying rje skyes na yang/ phan 'dogs kyi bya sa mi 'dug pas/ bdag mngon par byang chub thob pa'i tshe/ 'di rnams bdag gi gdul byar shog/ rnal 'byor gyi phug la gnas pa yi/ gzhi bdag 'khor dang bcas pa khyed/ dkar phyogs skyong la brtson par gyis/ zhes gsungs te/ skad mi gcig pa'i yul nar 'dul ba mjad cing byon pas/ phal cher rje btsun chen po mthong ba dang bros

'gro yin 'dug ku bod kyi mi thams cad la byams pa chen po'i ting nge 'dzin bsgoms kyin las kyi 'brel ba bzhag nas/ smon lam rnam dag mdzad kyin btsum smad nar byon pas sngar dang 'dra bar 'dug/

2. Others have translated *takob (mtha' 'khob)* as "barbarous frontier region" or "beyond the pale." Although these translations capture the essence of how Tibetans view outlying regions and their inhabitants, in the absence of associated adjectives we prefer to translate takob as peripheral region.

The great Indian philosopher Nagarjuna (2nd century BCE) listed birth as a barbarian in a peripheral land as one of the eight unfree or inopportune states that prevent one from practicing Buddhism (Nagarjuna 2013; Engle 2009:n.148). As Huber argues, authors of early Tibetan histories often applied the term takob to describe their own homeland. However, "when the Tibetans were confidently Buddhist, they of course portrayed themselves as an extension of this superiority and their non-Buddhist neighbors were then cast as the barbarians instead" (2008:82).

3. Personal communication, Mark Donohue, June 2016. Ghale is a Tibeto-Burman language spoken in several villages in Gorkha District, notably Barpak (Paudel 2008).

4. The only disyllabic village names in the Tibetan-speaking part of Nubri are Namdru and Samdo. One spelling of Namdru that appears in local documents is *rnam ru* which has no apparent meaning, while another, *gnam sgrug*, means something like "gather the heavens." As for Samdo, the village was only founded in the early 1960s by Tibetans fleeing China's oppressive policies and therefore should have the most unambiguous name. One person who wrote about the village claims the proper spelling is sa mdo which he translates as "Confluence of Rivers." He even uses that interpretation to title his book *Where Rivers Meet* (Rogers 2008). The syllable mdo does connote a confluence and is used in toponyms, for example Chamdo (spelled chab mdo) where *chab* is a formal term for water. But *sa* means "earth," so if sa mdo is the proper spelling, it is unclear what type of confluence is implied. On the other hand, Lobpön Gyurme says that the proper name of the village is Tsamto (spelled mtshams tho), or "Border Signpost." The name refers to a signpost erected decades ago to mark the border between the territory controlled by Rö and settlements across the mountain passes to the north. The exhaustive Tibetan map compiled by scholars at the Amnye Machen Institute in Dharamsala, India, also uses the spelling mtshams tho. Border Signpost is the most probable origin of the village's name.

5. de'i phu na bod kyi skad smra/ mdo na skad rigs mi mthun pa mang po yod/

6. gung thang gi dbus nub ri gzar zhing mtho ba/ g.yas ri rgyal po khri la bzhugs pa lta bu/ g.yon ri btsun mo bu khur 'dra ba/ . . . gcen lha mchog lde'i sku rings su mnga' thang yang sngar las 'phel bar gyur cing/ gshongs dbus nub ri steng po che dar yol bres pa lta bur pho brang phyis khab gong du grags pa sku mkhar lcags 'ob dang bcas pa byas/

7. nub ri mtha' 'khob kha gnon du/ rod kyi brag rdzong nag po brtsigs/

8. See Surkhang 1966 and 1986 for descriptions of Tibet's pre-1959 tax system.

9. The prophecy Tashi Dorje cites comes from the autobiography completed between 1614 and 1624 of Lodro Gyaltsen titled *How I Myself Turned Back the Mongols, [Written] in Order to Benefit Those Who Will Turn Back Mongols in the Future* (slan chad kyang sog bzlog mdzad pa po rnams la phan pa'i phyir du rang nyid kyi sog bzlog bgyis tshul/). Tashi Dorje cites his source as Soglo's biography (sog blo'i rnam thar), which is a misspelling of Lodro Gyaltsen's designation as the Mongol Repeller (sog bzlog). The passage reads as follows (p. 234) with Tashi Dorje's rendering in parenthesis (p. 12): me spre'u (sprel) bya la stod du 'khrugs/ dmag dpon gsum gyis (gyi) rdzong kha (khag) 'joms/ dmag gi rnga chen rnam gsum brdung/ lha sras gdung rgyud (brgyud) gtsang ma kun/ skyid mo lung dang ku thang tsums (tsum)/ rong btsan kun la gnas chos shig

Lodro Gyaltsen (1552–1624) was a disciple of Zhigpolingpa (1524–83), a specialist in rituals to thwart enemy invasions. Lodro Gyaltsen was also involved in the search for hidden valleys (Gentry 2014:65, 105–16), or sanctuaries where descendants of the medieval emperors (i.e., Ngadag lineage members) could go during a time of social and political upheaval. One of the prophesized signs that it is time to seek the hidden land is when invaders slay the rulers of Gungtang (Childs 1999).

10. The fort built around 1280 by the Gungtang king.

11. lam phyed tsam 'khyol zhing skabs der lam 'di yi nye 'gram du grub thob phug zhes bya ba bya skyibs brjed nyams dang ldan zhing rnal 'byor pa'i yid la 'jo ba'i ri khrod 'di nyid dang mjal bas der mnga' bdag bkris rnam rgyal mchog dgong mo gcig bzhugs par brtsam pas/ skabs 'dir/ mtshan lam du nub ri rod kyi gnas mchog gangs ri spung rgyan gyi gnas bdag rdo rje brag skyed nyid dngos su phebs te de ltar/ khyed phyi rol du ma phebs bzhugs na dge/ khyed phyi rol phebs na bar chad yod/ gnas 'di ru bzhugs na 'gro don byung/ khyed ma 'ongs pa'i gdul bya 'di ru yod/ zhes lung bstan cing bshol btab pa la brten slar nub ri 'dir bzhugs rgyu'i spro ba 'phel/ grub thob 'di nyid gnas 'dir bzhugs na bzang ngan gyi mtshan ma brtags pa'i phyir ram rten 'brel 'grig min gyi sa dpyad gnang skabs rod kyi brag rdzong nag po'i rgyab ri de'i steng la sgrub chu gcig bar la sgrub chu gcig 'og la'ang sgrub chu gcig bcas byung bas ya mtshan rmad du byung ba'i rten 'brel 'grig par brten sngar gyi rnal 'byor pa 'di nyid kyi zhal nas kyang/ mgna' bdag khyed gnas 'dir bzhugs na bkris shing 'gro don che/ bdag re zhig sbas yul skyid mo lung sogs gnas nges med rnams su 'byol nas 'gro zhes gsung nas gnas gzhan du phebs/ de nas mnga' bdag nyid chos phyogs kyi bya ba kho nar dus gda' bzhin sgrub pa 'ba' zhig la gzhol kyang nam zhig gi tshe bod 'bangs rnams la thugs brtse yal bar 'dor ma nus nas pha tshab bu dang/ chos tshab gdung la dmigs te nub ri smad kyi sa khul krog zhes pa'i yul lung der/ rdzong dpon ye shes kyi sras mo gnas skya pu sprin zhes mkha' 'gro ma'i mtshan dang ldan pa sngon nas las 'phro yod pa zhig sku mtshams la bzhugs yod pa 'di nyid gsang thabs su btsun mor bsus nas krog nas rod yul du rdzu 'phul ya ma zung du ma zhig bstan nas phebs par mi kun gyi mthong thos su 'gyur/ de nas krog yul nas rdzong dpon ye shes kyi gtsos mi ser du ma zhig rod yul du bcar bas mnga' bdag gi gnas tshul rnams gsal por go rtogs byung bas/ de rnams kun mgon po gang nyid kyi slob mar 'gyur zhing dad dam 'gyur med thog ji srid nam gnas kyi bar slob mar gzung ba'i gsol 'debs zhus/ slad nas rdzong dpon ye shes gtsos pa'i mnga' 'og mi ser bcas nas rod kyi sa sbal sa gnya'

thang gi steng der rod bla brang dga' skyid khang gsar brten dang bcas pa gsar du bzhengs/

12. The only threat to succession occurred when Tashi Namgyal's only son, Senge Namgyal, had no son of his own. According to Tashi Dorje's account, "Drubtob Tashi Namgyal had a consort [*tsunmo zurpa*; literally, a wife on the side] named Pema Tsomo, who was the daughter of the dzongpön of Koren in Tibet named Dawa. Their eldest son, Pema Tutob, took up residence at Shari. Their youngest son, Sonam Chöpel, became the head of Shelpug Monastery, the place of the treasure revealer Garwang Dorje. Their middle son, Sonam Tenzin, came to Nubri to assume the position as the head of the Rö Labrang. The consort's son became the third in the line of Rö's succession" (Tashi Dorje 2010:22).

13. See Belleza's account of ancient inscriptions at www.tibetarchaeology. com/june-2016/. Accessed 7/1/17. On the Kyungpo lineage, see also Stein (1959 and 1972) and Vitalli (1996).

14. According to a history of the lineage written by Chogtrul Karma Migyur Dorje (2017:82–113), he was born during the twelfth sixty-year cycle of the Tibetan calendar (1687–1746). Chökyi Nyima, born in 1953, was the eleventh successor in the lineage. Assuming a generational gap between father and son of twenty-five years, Chökyi Gyaltsen was born around 1703, which falls within the twelfth cycle. The chronology makes sense given that the sixth lineage successor, Sherab Sangpo, reportedly met the king of Nepal, who granted his temple tax-exempt status. The twenty-five-year generational gap would place Sherab Sangpo's birth around 1828, in which case he would have been twenty-eight years old when the Kingdom of Nepal incorporated Nubri into its domain.

15. See Clarke (1980) for details on how lama lineages in Yolmo spread through a similar process.

16. The text is titled bka' 'gyur rin po che'i dkar chags ye shes gsal sgron. We are indebted to Dorje Gyaltsen for allowing us to photograph it.

17. Śākya Śrī' (1853–1919) was born in Kham and attained considerable fame as an accomplished yogin. He spent time in Kathmandu renovating Buddhist sites, and many of his disciples were from the Himalayan region. See http://treasuryoflives.org/biographies/view/Shakya-Shri/8782 Accessed 6/28/16.

18. spyod lam thams cad mu stegs ha la bzhin/ ri la gnas pa'i ri dag thams cad bsod/ lung la bcas ba'i ra lug rnams ma lus gri kha'i ngang la btang/ gzhi bdag dkar phyogs skyong mkhan yang nag po srog bcod dbang du song/ yul khag re la 'bon nag re/ pho mo rgan gzhon thams cad yang bsam pa sdig pas phyogs la 'gyur/ lha klu bdud btsan thams cad la srog bcod rgyun gyis 'thun bzung nas/ ston mo sha 'gyed khrag 'gyed byed/ skyid lung sbas 'dabs yin 'gyur kyang/ rong khung mun pa'i mtha' khob 'dra/

19. Prohibitions do not guarantee that everyone will refrain from hunting. The same lama told us that a few years ago, some people were caught laying snares to trap wild animals. They were flogged and fined.

20. bzhi'i mchog 'gyur lho phyogs 'dzam bu'i gling/ dam chos dar ba gangs can bod yul dbus/ de yi cha zhabs nub ri ku thang zhes/ bskyed rdzogs bsgyer sgom bstan pa dar ba'i cha/ kun gyi yid smon bkra shis krog gi yul/ rgan sgo rnams ni dge bcu khrims la brtson/ stag shar tsher ma la [hole in paper] sang dag 'ngul/ a ma mtsho sman 'dra bas zas bcud spel/ na chung me tog 'dra ba glu

gar mkhas/ byis pa lha phran 'dra ba rtse cho mangs/ 'di 'dri'i yul na bsod nams bsags pa yi/ mi don chen rnams la lta ji smon/

21. According to Snellgrove, the term *Thakuri* derives from the Sanskrit term *thakkura,* which means "diety" or "lord," and "was originally a title claimed by warriors of lordly rank" (1989:19). As Hindu "wearers of the holy cord" *(tāgādhāri)* they rank just below Brahmins and ahead of all other Chhetri groups in Nepal's complex caste system. Nepal's pre-1990 constitution stipulated that the King of Nepal must be a Thakuri member of the ruling Shah dynasty (Sharma 1978:2; Höfer 1979:7–9; Whelpton 2005:10–11).

22. As another example of flexibility: prior to the Gorkha conquest a local headman (termed *gowa* in Tibetan) wielded the authority to collect taxes and adjudicate disputes in Walungchung, northeastern Nepal. After the conquest Walungchung's gowa retained his role, but rather than being a local chieftain he became an officer of the Kingdom of Nepal tasked with the responsibilities of tax collector *(tālukdār)* and chief of justice *(amal)* (Steinmann 1991).

23. http://info-buddhism.com/Khunu-Rinpoche-Negi-Lama-Tenzin-Gyaltsen-Dodin.html. Accessed 3/10/16.

24. *Bhotey* is a Nepali term, laden with negative connotations, for people of Tibetan ethnicity (see Ramble 1993).

25. Throughout Nepal there are many examples of Thakuris intermixing with other ethnic groups (Sharma 1978:8). For example, James Fisher notes that a single Thakuri clan living in a predominantly Magar community practices clan exogamy, so members must always marry a Magar. They no longer wear the sacred thread of the high-caste Hindu and have modified their clan name from Thakuri to Thakula, which "simultaneously suggests their high-caste origins and their present fallen status." Culturally and linguistically they have assimilated to such an extent that they are indistinguishable from fellow villagers (J. Fisher 1986:41, 157). Elsewhere other groups claim Thakuri status in an effort to ascend the caste hierarchy. For example, the Thakalis of Tukche, who have a long history of interacting with different ethnic groups through trade, have distanced their social and linguistic bonds with Tibetans by claiming Thakuri status. They claim that their Chan clan is the same as the Thakuri Chand clan (W. Fisher 2001:33, 50). Fürer-Haimendorf argues that the Thakali practice of modifying clan names to include a *chan* ending (a well-known Thakuri clan name) "was part of a still continuing movement to justify a claim to a higher status in the caste-hierarchy of Nepal" (1981:3). Given the history of fluid ethnic identities in the complex social matrix of Nepal, finding that Thakuris have assimilated to Nubri society comes as no surprise.

26. rgyal khrims gser gyi gnya' shing/ yul khrims lcags kyi a long/ chos khrims dar gyi mdud pa/

27. The manuscript was photographed and archived by members of the German-Nepal Manuscript Preservation Project. Running number L10379, reel number L1211/9.

28. The obligation contract follows rather precisely the language and configuration of a standard Tibetan legal formula analyzed by Schneider (2002; see also Bischoff 2017; Ramble and Drandul 2017). It starts by listing the date, followed by the standard inscription, introduction protocol, and formula leading into the

narratio (*don rtsa*, "basis of the legal act"). The agreements in the dispositio are also commonly found in Tibetan obligation contracts translated by Schneider. We have therefore followed some of Schneider's and Bischoff's (2017) translations.

29. By merging religious and secular administration into the hands of the magistrate, the people of Trok follow a Tibetan template called *chösri nyitrel* ("religion and political affairs joined together") that became fully elaborated under the rule of the Dalai Lamas from the mid-1600s to 1959. The government not only controlled secular affairs but also acted as a major patron of religion (Goldstein 1989:1–37).

30. Unorthodox spellings make this manuscript difficult to interpret, so our translation is somewhat tentative. shing glang zla 9 tshes 7 la lugs nyid gong ma khrim dag rin po che'i zhabs drung du zhu ba/ dag ming stag khung sham sal nas po nas rlos glang mi gyur bis gen gya tsang mar phul bis snying por lag/ nub khams rnams [smudge] rdzong kar khral sprod yin ba rnams zhur rig dbor tsang logs yong ba la stan nas nub ris spyis khyabs/ go mang la' gob stad zhus bis rlar nas nub ris khral khung la zhug ston tsa go mang nas mis nga [smudge] yul gyis khung rlag byes ba grang ma bis rgyu kyen dug bas/ zla tshes nas zung/ khrim spo kyu rgyu ngas khung rlag/ ngan ba ris mang med ba/ chogs mig gas tshang/ yul thog stan tshang/ la gya la gom zha [smudge] la la/ mar shar pag/ cho cho phur phur/ chogs mis nas kor ma stog zhag ras nas tshang spyar sa med ba dang/ rang zas zas cing/ mi' stam med ba rang rang yul sa nas du cha/ 'u lag tho ko ba [smudge] ga/ ma ba kar lis tsho nyas sgrig zhu sgyu . . . mi ser nyam sgrig la gal rig pu tsam med pa/ yul spyis nyen lam tsan/ khyen gyed bo/ sta tshes nas zung/ gong tsheg bris ston la gal rig pu tsam shar tshes/ yul spyis le khris yod ba ma tsher/ [smudge] mang gang sung zhu sgyu/ phyis su bren stam ra kyed/ nog sting rlang/ ris kyul tsho gyoms/ nga min khi min/ pang sted nag thog/ pon stag khur/ ngan ba khog [smudge] lha sam rnams dag/ tsos ba gyen rlog med ba/ gong tshig la gal tshes ba ser stang 5/ zhu ngo stes rgyu med ba go ba so nam kyis stags/ [list of the others who affixed their seals]

31. German-Nepal Manuscript Preservation Project. Running number L10373, reel number L1211/3.

32. sa 'brul zla 9 tshes 3 la/ lugs gnyis gong ma khrim dag rin po che'i zhabs drung du zhu ba/ bdag ming rtags khung gsham gsal rnams nas blos blangs mi sgyur ba'i gan gya gtsang 'bul pa'i snying don rtsa/ blod rigs 'dzin dbang grangs gyis sprog spe rang gam zhing bre rgyod sa gong bzhi de byam nas sding rtsong du rnam ru bsod nams tshes ring la rtsong zhing/ rin babs yang gtsang bdag 'byung zhing du gong du zhus pa'i don tshig la/ nga min kho min spangs brod nag thog/ snyog pa sting blog/ dpon rtags khur sogs mi zhu zhu ba dang/ 'gal te su thod nas smi gnyen pa'i brang skad rtsam/ til 'bru rtsam zhu ba shar tshes gong khrim zhabs su 'ba' gser sprang gsum zhu ngo gron sgyur med pa bul lam zhus chog pa/ bdag rigs 'dzin dbang grags gyis rtags/ [list of the others who affixed their seals]

33. The etymology of *miser* is unclear in this context. Miser is a term used in Tibet's pre-1959 administrative system that refers to subjects who were bound to estates managed by the government, a monastery, or a noble family. Here, it implies a leadership position of lesser rank than the gowa. Nowadays most people use the Nepali administrative terms *attache* and *sattache*.

34. lugs gnyis gong ma la/ khrims bdag rin po che/ zhabs drung du zhu gsol/ bdag ming gtogs khongs blos bslangs mi 'gyur phul snying don rtsa/

3. EMBEDDING THE HOUSEHOLD IN THE VILLAGE

1. See Karmay 1998 for a detailed description of the origin of purification rituals in Tibet, and Nālandā Translation Committee 1997 for a brief discussion of lhabsang and the translation of one text used in such a rite.

2. The text is titled rlung rta skyed thabs dang dar shing 'dubs thabs yul lha phrin col, or *Means for Strengthening the Wind Horse and Erecting the Flag Pole to Honor the Local Protector Deity.* See Karmay 1993 for details on the history of the wind horse and the various symbols that comprise the flag.

3. kye kye dar shing sa la btsugs pa yis/ dkor nor sa bzhi khyab bar shog/ dar shing gangs la btsugs la yis/ mi ngo gangs las dkar bar shog/ dar shing chu la btsugs pa yis/ mi brgyud chu las ring bar shog/ dar shing me la btsugs pa yis/ bsod nams me ltar 'bar bar shog/ dar shing rlung la btsugs pa yis/ snyan grags rlung ltar khyab par shog/ dar shing brag la btsugs pa yis/ tshe srog brag las sra bar shog/ dar shing spangs la btsugs pa yis/ mi nor spangs rtsa'i ltar bur rgyes pa shog/ lha klu sde brgyad la sog pa'i/ de bzhin gzhi bdag 'byung pa'i tshogs/ gnod pa skad cig ma byed cing/ bsam pa chos bzhin 'grub pa dang/ tshe srog bsod nams dpal 'byor dang/ snyan grags mda' thang longs spyod dang/ dbang thang rlung rta yar ngo'i zla ltar bskyed/ bkra shis phun sum tshogs par shog/ ki ki bswo lha rgyal lo/

4. Trok's household classification resembles the system in Ladakh where the major distinction is between *khangchen* (large household) and *khangchung* (small household). The former is the major productive unit inhabited by younger individuals; the latter is generally occupied by elderly residents and their caretakers (Mills 2003).

5. sa pho stag lho leb ngos ma yig yin/

6. Trok's drongchen are divided into three sections called *pakor* (spelled pa dkor in local documents). Although the etymology is uncertain, it may be pha dkor which can denote ancestral property. The three pakor are Yurungsang (G.yu rung gsang), Kyangpo (Kyang po), and Böchag (Bod chags). Yurungsang is the name of the lineage that, according to legend, first settled in Trok. People are uncertain about the origin of the term *Kyangpo,* but speculate that it was the name of a prominent household in the past. Böchag refers to households headed by relatively recent migrants from Tibet, that is, within the last century or two such as Gowa Sonam's descendants.

7. Units of measure in Nubri are kay, dey, and phulu. One kay = 20 dey, and 1 dey = 6 phulu. Dey is used as a measure of both volume and land area. Trok residents have a special cup to measure one dey (volume) of grain, which is approximately 1.35 pounds (Surkhang 1966:18). One dey is also a measure of the land area on which one dey of seed is sown.

8. One coin (*tam,* an old term for half a rupee) is owed for every four people and cattle, and one small measure of grain (*phulu*) for each person or bovine above a multiple of four. For example, a household has six members, four cows, and two female yaks for a total of 12 taxable units. The household's annual tax

payment is therefore three coins (4 x 3 = 12). Another has four people, five cows, and two female yaks for a total of 11 taxable units. Their annual assessment is therefore two coins and three small measures of grain (4 x 2 = 8 + 3 = 11). The annual assessment for all of Trok came to 79 coins and 78 measures of grain. Village leaders conceded that, due to the continual devaluation of the rupee, the tax had become a pittance that cannot even cover the expense of conducting the household review. Therefore, in 2016 they revised the system. Each household is now assessed a tax of 10 rupees on each member and female head of cattle. So the two households listed above are now obligated to pay 120 and 110 rupees respectively (about $1.20 and $1.10).

9. We base the dating on the recognition that none of the listed household heads were alive at the time of our 1997 household survey, and that some were the great-grandfathers of current household heads.

10. rgya yul khral legs ma yig bzhugs/

11. rig 'dzin dbang dus khyim gcig mi lnga zhing bre zhi bcu zhe drug tram rgyad bre drug/

12. Areas under Lhasa's authority prior to 1959 were divided into districts, referred to as *dzong*. The government classified most commoners as *miser* (subjects, which has also been glossed as serfs, see Goldstein 1986). Those who held a formal document, referred to as a *treten* (tax basis), were called *treba* (taxpayers). A household holding a treten retained the right to farm a specified amount of land and could only lose that right by failing to fulfill its tax obligations (Surkhang 1966, 1986; Goldstein 1971; Dargyay 1982). These included a land tax paid during the tenth month of the Tibetan calendar, which falls in November and December shortly after the harvest. The tax was paid in grain according to the amount of taxable land specified in one's lease. Every third year, each of Tibet's *dzongpön* (district commissioner) was required to conduct a full enumeration of all households under his jurisdiction (Surkhang 1966). See Childs (2008, chap 3) for how this system was administered in Kyirong District during the 1950s. The compiled data for all districts was called a *zhibzhung* (detailed register), as in the Iron-Monkey (1830) Zhibzhung (see Tsultrim et al. 1989).

13. Both definitions are from https://unstats.un.org/unsd/demographic/scon-cerns/fam/fammethods.htm. Accessed 6/29/17. For census purposes Nepal's Central Bureau of Statistics defines a household as "a group of persons who live together in a housing unit and share a kitchen," and a family as two or more people who are related through birth, marriage, or adoption (Pokhrel 2014:224). The US Census Bureau's definition focuses exclusively on co-residence: "A household includes all the people who occupy a housing unit (such as a house or apartment) as their usual place of residence." It defines of family as "any two or more people (not necessarily including a householder) residing together, and related by birth, marriage, or adoption." https://www.census.gov/programs-surveys/cps/technical-documentation/subject-definitions. Accessed 6/24/17.

14. Even Sanjek's more nuanced ethnological approach does not reflect the situation in Nubri. Sanjek posits that households in most settings share certain activities and functions. They are "crucibles of identity, primary locations in which life cycle phases are enacted (childhood, family establishment, elderhood), rites of passage celebrated and planned, inheritance decided, and

ancestors . . . venerated" (1996:359). In a situation of limited mobility, such as Nubri prior to the onset of educational migration, this may hold true. But in a culture of migration where the village is a lifephase rather than a lifecourse space, the urban institutional setting becomes the locus of identity formation for youths, parental control over rites of passage such as marriage diminishes, and norms of inheritance must be renegotiated.

15. To illustrate this point, Purbu is listed in Trok's household register as the kyimdag of a household that has six members. We know from our reproductive history survey that Purbu and his wife have six living children. The two eldest daughters are married within the village, so for administrative purposes they are members of their husbands' households. Among the other four, one is a monk, two are students in Kathmandu, and the youngest still lives at home. The six officially recognized members of Purbu's household therefore include three who are full-time residents of the village and three who currently reside in Kathmandu. Tamdin is listed in the register as the kyimdag of a household with four members. Among their only two living children, an unmarried, disabled, middle-aged daughter lives with them, while an unmarried adult son graduated from school and holds a full-time job in Kathmandu. In Tamdin's case the register counts three residents of the village household and one nonresident. We designed our household survey based on knowledge of the indigenous classification system, so in both cases we enumerated the exact same household members that are counted in the register.

16. Trok residents distinguish between private *(ger)* temples, which are hereditary possessions of lamas, and communal *(yul)* temples. The five communal temples are Khaltso, Oong, Palri, Chökhang, and Kani. The fifteen rituals are the following. First month of the year: Mani Dungyur Yum (Reading of the Prajñāpāramitā at the Great Mani) and Monlam (Great Prayer Feast Offering Assembly). Second month: Menchang Tsog (Medicinal Beer Feast Offering). Third month: Kanjur (Reading of the Kanjur). Fourth month: Nyungne (Fasting and Silence Retreat), Oong Gomba Kuchö (Commemoration Service at Oong Gomba), and Tsokhor (Circumambulation of the Lake, Khaltso). Fifth month: Palri Gomba Kuchö (Commemoration Service at Palri Gomba). Sixth month: Drugpa Tseshi (Fourth Day of the Sixth Month, a commemoration of the Buddha's first sermon). Seventh month: Tulku Kuchö (Commemoration Service of the Reincarnate Lama). Eighth month: Dasai Chöpa (Dasai Offering). Ninth month: Lhabab Duchen (Celebration of Buddha's Descent from the Realm of Deities). Tenth month: Dumje (Offering of Accomplishment). Eleventh month: Chökhang Chöbul (Offering at Chökhang Gomba). Twelfth month: Oong Gomba Zhibcu (Offering at Oong Gomba to close the ritual cycle).

17. The nine households rotate every year so that one acts as *chötrimpa* [(head of) religious law] and the others as *nyerpa* (caretakers). For each ritual they collect and allocate resources, manage the supporting labor force, and hold participants to the liturgical schedule. At the end of the year, when the chötrimpa position is passed to the next household in the rotation, they conduct a full accounting of all ritual implements and materials held by the five temples. The outgoing chötrimpa is obligated to replace, at his personal expense, any items that are missing. Thus the position entails a considerable time commitment and

financial risk. Because the duties can be onerous, chötrim households are exempt from some, but not all, yultrim obligation.

18. thog mar zhing sbe dkor la/ sha khang zhing bre 10 sa la sbe bre 80/ spang cug zhing bre 6 sa la sbe bre 7/ 'bru sbe bskor la/ grong chen la bre 6 dngos yod/ skye bre 2 len gos yod/ pho rang mo rang bre 3 dngos yod/ skye bre 1 len gos yod/ po cod bre 1 dang phul 3 dngos yod/ skye phul 3 len gos yod/

19. Similar systems are found elsewhere in Nepal's highlands. For example, in Yolmo full village membership requires a household to take a loan from the temple; annual interest payments support communal rituals. The two associated statuses of village membership are patron *(jiwa)* and priest *(lama)*. The former position rotates among the households that provide logistical support for communal rites, the latter position is open to any individual who can read Tibetan and thereby participate in the rites (Clarke 1980; see also Lim 2008 on the land tenure and communal obligation system in Langtang, Nepal).

20. *Torma* are ritual objects made from flour and butter, usually in a conical shape, which are placed on a shrine and dedicated to particular deities.

21. drug pa tshe bzhi la/ tshogs rgya 3 mar rgya 3 gtor ldan bre 8 bum ldan bre 1/ bu ram phul 4/ gom ldan 'debs 1 yod/

22. The Kanjur (bka' 'gyur) is a collection of texts that contain the translated teachings of the Buddha. During the annual ritual men collectively read the corpus before carrying all the texts around the village's territory. Dumje (sgrub mchod; Offering of Accomplishment) is a weeklong ritual to generate merit for the entire community.

23. Several families jointly own the water mills. They are responsible for the upkeep of the mills and for providing wood to make a fire for roasting the grain. In return, those who grind their grain must pay a nominal fee. One owner claimed that the profit from mill ownership is negligible once expenses and gomba grain procurements are deducted.

24. Forty-five dey out of 66 dey and 4 phulu in the case of a drongchen.

25. For example, residents of Rö are relatively wealthy because of three income sources associated with the village's position at the higher end of the valley. First, every year foreign alpinists attempt to scale the summit of Gang Pungyen (Mount Manaslu, elev. 26,759 ft.). Japanese climbers made the first attempts in the 1950s (Takagi 1954; Maki and Imanishi 1957). A relic of the early expeditions is that foreigners are still called "japen" in the local vernacular. Rö controls access to the mountain, so local leaders instituted a policy whereby only village residents are allowed to carry supplies to base camp. They also set the rate at 2,500 Rs ($25) per load. Second, in 2011 Nepal changed its tourism policy in the area so that trekkers are now permitted to stay in tea houses. A lodge building boom ensued. Because Rö is an ideal site to acclimatize and take side trips, trekkers inject a significant amount of cash into the village economy by spending two or more nights. Third, Rö's most substantial income is derived from trade. Since the early 2000s residents have benefitted from *yartsa gunbu* (ophiocordyceps sinensis) trade to earn unprecedented amounts of money (Childs and Choedup 2014). Now the village is the wealthiest in the valley.

26. Relative wealth survey is a methodology for measuring wealth differentials in smallholder communities (Grandin 1988) that involves standard ethnographic

techniques such as pile sorting, rank ordering, and paired comparisons (see Weller and Romney 1988; Bernard 2011). We asked knowledgeable individuals to rank each household on a scale from 1 (wealthy) to 5 (poor), and then asked the reasons behind each ranking. Continual probing generated insights on emic concepts of relative wealth.

27. On shabten rituals and literature see Cabezón (1996) and Lo Bue (2015).

28. The Prajñāpāramitā (Perfection of Wisdom) Sutras.

4. WHITHER THE YOUNG PEOPLE?

1. See Childs and Barkin 2006, Childs 2008, Schrempf 2008, Aengst 2013, and Craig et al. 2016.

2. The Total Fertility Rate (TFR) is a standardized measure of the average number of children that would be born to each woman if Age-Specific Fertility Rates remain constant. An Age-Specific Fertility Rate (ASFR) is a measure of births in a year to women aged x divided by the number of women aged x at midyear. The TFR is an estimate of the number of children that would be born to a hypothetical cohort of women, not to an actual cohort of women. To estimate fertility we used the own-children method (OCM), a reverse-survival technique designed to calculate the TFR in the absence of vital registry data (see Cho, Retherford, and Choe 1986). OCM has been applied to large data sets such as national censuses (e.g., Retherford, Cho, and Kim 1984; Haines 1989; Retherford and Thapa 1998) as well as household surveys to estimate fertility in small-scale populations (Schroeder and Retherford 1979; Childs 2003). Our data comes from three surveys: 1997 Nubri Household and Reproductive History Survey (Childs), 2012 Nubri, Tsum, and Mustang Household and Reproductive History Survey (Beall, Childs, and Craig), and 2013 Nubri Household and Reproductive History Survey (Quinn and Childs).

3. Nepal SEEDS. Geoff Childs is one of the founding board members.

4. People in Nubri readily acknowledge the mortality decline by stating, "Our children no longer die [as frequently]." Regardless, an organization that runs health and education programs in the valley still proclaims, "Children from these areas are counted fortunate if they live to see their early adolescence. Research indicates that over half will die before reaching their eighth birthday, which is most vividly demonstrated by the gripping fact that many parents will not name their children until the child reaches the age of five. Statistics tell us that one out of every five children born in the remote areas of the Himalayas will die before the age of one." http://mountainchild.org/about. Accessed 10/20/16). The assertion testifies to the way that infant and childhood mortality continues to be used in funding appeals despite a significant decline. As the only social scientists who have conducted rigorous demographic studies in Nubri, we can comment with some authority on the allegations. First, the claim that "over half will die before reaching their eighth birthday" has never been documented to our knowledge and is higher than any level of mortality we ever reported (e.g., Childs 2008), and clearly much higher than the level of mortality today. Second, the "gripping fact that many parents will not name their children until the child reaches the age of five" is either a fabrication or a statement born of

ignorance. In Nubri, as in most Tibetan societies, a Buddhist lama typically names a child within five days of birth. The name is subsequently recorded in a natal horoscope composed by an astrologer. We have not only witnessed infant naming ceremonies, but have also examined and translated natal horoscopes (Childs and Walter 2000). Furthermore, in our comprehensive household surveys parents told us the name of every single child—even the newborns. If parents did not name their children until age five, our data set would contain scores of empty cells where names should be entered.

5. The empirical trend of demographic transition (from high birth and death rates to low birth and death rates) typically begins with a decline in the death rate that prompts population growth because the birth rate subsequently exceeds the death rate. Eventually the birth rate declines, slowing the rate of population growth. In the final phase, the birth and death rates stabilize at low levels so that population growth is negligible. Demographic transition is an understudied topic in most Himalayan communities even though Nepal has been undergoing the process for decades (Caldwell 1998; Retherford and Thapa 1998; Feeney et al. 2001). As some historians have pointed out, scholars tend to underestimate the societal impacts of demographic transitions that are "every bit as dramatic as two other great transformations, urbanization and industrialization" (Gillis et al. 1992:1).

6. With respect to the European demographic transition, Reher points out that the ensuing population growth stimulated internal and international migration. He argues, "The population pressure created by higher population growth rates was an unmistakable push factor for this process" (2011:15).

7. www.rinpoche.com/Nupri/englishletter.htm. Accessed 12/09/16.

8. See Caldwell's thesis on the inversion of the intergenerational wealth flow as a classic statement on the connection between parental investment in children and fertility transition (1976).

5. BECOMING MONKS

1. We would like to thank Martin Mills for providing us with his English version of the article.

2. *Khenpo* is a formal religious title conferred after one completes a rigorous course of study in the Kagyü and Nyingma traditions.

3. *Nyechungi sampa* is a concept that stresses how one recognizes the true significance of Buddhism through a mindset of weariness with life that leads to renunciation.

4. de nas bdag rang ni lo gsum bzhi lon tsam nas snang ba'i dran pa zin pa tsam yan chad la chos byas dgos bsam pa ma rtog pa'i gzhan gyi snang ba gang yang ma shar 'dug/ de nas byi ba gzhan rnams ni rtsed mo la yang bya bsad pa dang brnyed btsug pa dang khyi ra byed pa dang bu chung 'phang brdag pa dang 'da' rtse ba dang rtsa lngas pa dang shing bshags pa dang pho mo sbyor ba'i tshul dang nang gtsang bca' ba'i tshul la sogs byas gyin 'dug/ byis pa rang gi rtse mo ni dgon pa bzhengs ba dang mchod rten dang ka' ni bzhengs ba dang/ dpal gtor bca' ba dang gtor chen gtor chung mang po bca' ba dang/ sku bzhengs pa dang ma ni rtse ba dang cho ga gtang ba dang rnga bdung ba dang rdo leb

gyi bung chal dung ba dang/ 'dud 'gro'i byi ba'i gtor ma bzor gshams nas 'chams gyab pa dang gong re gzhin zor 'phangs pa la sogs brtses gyin 'dod/

5. Some of Tibet's largest institutions covered food and lodging for monks. The big three Gelukpa monasteries near Lhasa (Drepung, Sera, and Ganden) attracted thousands of monks from branch institutions across the Tibetan Plateau. Most were supported by the yield from the monastery's agricultural estate and donations from patrons (Goldstein 1989:21–37).

6. An anonymous reviewer pointed out that when pursuing Geshe degrees in Gelukpa monasteries, monks can incur large expenses that place economic hardships on their families. The reviewer's point serves as a reminder that costs incurred by monks vary by institution and educational attainment.

6. BECOMING NUNS

This chapter is a revised version of a previously published article (Childs and Choedup 2015). We would like to thank the Institute for Comparative Research in Human Culture, Norway, for permission to include the article in this book.

1. Many elderly people who have not traveled much outside the valley struggle to understand or even speak a basic form of Nepali, the national language.

2. It is impossible to determine how long the nun-as-caretaker phenomenon has been part of the family management strategy in Nubri. In 1995 there were several eighty-year-old village-resident nuns in Sama, so the practice dates to at least 1920, when these women were ordained.

3. The importance of offering both secular and religious education became evident when we interviewed parents in Nubri about why they selected a particular nunnery for their daughter. Many immediately mentioned the opportunity to study English and other subjects as a deciding factor. The trend apparently started through the Tibetan Nuns Project's revision of its curriculum in 2003 to include secular education (Tobler 2006:44).

4. Belt (2010:48–55) discusses reasons why the residents of a nunnery in Dolanji, India, became nuns, including "practical considerations" related to suffering associated with village life (watching their mothers struggle to raise children, witnessing siblings die in tragic accidents, etc.). Gender-based suffering is a theme found in the writings of Orgyan Chokyi (1675–1729) from Dolpo, who observed: "The steed follows yet another mare. When I see the shamelessness of men, [I think:] May I be born in a body that will sustain the precepts. When acts of desire are committed, suffering must follow. When I see the mare suffering, melancholia flares. Behold us with mercy, Lord of Compassion. Let me not be born a woman in all lives to come. When I ponder the suffering of beings, melancholia flares" (Schaeffer 2004:142; see also Tsomo 2004:345–49).

7. BECOMING STUDENTS

1. On the civil war between Maoist rebels and the government of Nepal that engulfed the country from 1996 to 2006, see Karki and Seddon 2003, Hutt 2004, and Pettigrew 2013. Nubri was less affected than many other areas.

2. Until recently people from Nubri's upper villages regularly exchanged salt for corn with people in the lower villages.

3. rkang rjes lag bsubs/

4. khyi sna khug la ru kog rdar/

5. http://www.mountainchild.org/education. The video is titled *Mountain-Child's 5 Core Issues: 3 – Education*. Viewed 10/15/16.

6. For the record, the first hydroelectric generator was installed in Nubri in 1995. Now almost every village has electricity, and, paradoxically, many people in Nubri enjoyed more daily hours of electricity than those who lived under Kathmandu's irksome load-shedding regime that only ended in 2016. Some households began constructing toilets in the 1990s, and a few years ago several villages used their annual cash allotment from the district government to build a toilet for every household. The government of Nepal installed satellite phones throughout Nubri a decade ago. With the recent addition of cell phone towers, people not only make frequent phone calls to Kathmandu, India, and beyond, but routinely call each other within the same village to arrange meetings or exchange information. Although there are no hospitals, several organizations have developed a network of health posts staffed by nurses and midwives. Schools, which range in quality from substandard to respectable, exist in most villages.

8. THE HOUSEHOLD SUCCESSION QUANDARY

1. Two terms are used in Nubri to describe bride capture: *nyesung* meaning "seize a bride," and *nyabsrung* meaning "grasp and keep." Both describe taking a bride by force. The practice seems to be widespread in the Himalayan borderlands, at least as a metaphor for elopement. Holmberg (1989:60–66) and March (2002:50) both note the cultural salience of bridal capture in Tamang society but point out that it rarely occurs.

2. The title of the documentary is *47 Grams Gold: A Cruel Culture*. Only the trailer was available at the time of writing (https://www.youtube.com/watch?v=fNMUw3DyKK4).

9. THE TRANSFORMATIVE POTENTIAL OF EDUCATIONAL MIGRATION

1. Sherpas and Thangmi began moving to Darjeeling in the 1800s to capitalize on British colonial labor needs (Ortner 1989; Shneiderman 2015a). Cyclical migrants from Helambu have long ventured to India for summer employment (Bishop 1998), while winter trade missions attracted people from Mustang and Manang to markets in low-lying areas of Nepal and India (van Spengan 2000). Today, migration is a defining feature of many contemporary Nepali communities. Mobility between Nepal, China, and India is a core element of Thangmi identity (Shneiderman 2015a). Baumgartner's longitudinal data reveals that new economic opportunities involving tourism and mountaineering prompted the outmigration of entire families from Rolwaling to Kathmandu. By 2010 only 20 percent of the former population was living permanently in the valley

(Baumgartner 2015:35–39). Similarly, Goodall documents a high rate of rural-to-urban migration among pastoralists families in Ladakh (2004). Meanwhile, many researchers are now exploring temporary labor migration to the Middle East and Southeast Asia (e.g., Seddon et al. 2002; Thieme and Wyss 2005; Lokshin et al. 2010; Adhikari and Hobley 2015), while migration to North America is garnering much-needed attention (Craig 2011; Mishra 2011).

2. For interesting perspectives on educational migration elsewhere in the Himalayan region, see the studies that focus on social and economic mobility among Himalayan students who attend universities in urban India (Smith and Gergan 2015; Williams-Oerberg 2016).

3. Williams (2009) reviews studies that find a positive effect of education on the inclination to migrate (e.g., Stark and Taylor 1991), others that find a negative effect (e.g., Massey and Espinoza 1997), and some that find no association at all (e.g., Curran and Rivero-Fuentes 2003). Williams concludes, "The literature appears to favor the prospect that educational attainment does increase the likelihood of migration," but notes that the causal mechanisms remain somewhat murky (2009:883).

4. There are several ways to classify fosterage. Esther Goody distinguishes crisis fostering, which usually occurs during a time of family disruption, from purposive fostering, which is done when the family is intact (Goody 1975, cited in Castle 1995:688). Some Nubri children are sent to schools and monasteries during a family crisis, notably when one or both parents pass away. But the majority are sent when their families are intact. Nubri's situation also fits the classification of "educational fostering," defined as sending a child elsewhere, usually an urban area, to pursue formal education (Isiugo-Abanihe 1985:58).

5. Ortner's analysis of relationships between foreign and Sherpa climbers is one example of how the jindag concept operates in a secular context. The jindag (or zhindag, as she spells it), as a Sherpa may see his expedition boss, does not "directly bestow success" but can help facilitate upward mobility by providing opportunities (1999:83–88). Several scholars point out that Tibetan exiles have adapted the priest-patron relational concept so that it covers foreign support for secular and religious institutions (Klieger 1992; Huber 2001; Frachette 2004; Moran 2004). In an interesting twist, Moran observes "that in the Tibetan idiom [i.e. a religious context] it is the donor who is ultimately tamed (and ideally, liberated) by the giving, whereas in Western aid programs, it is the recipient who is improved by the gifts" (2004:65). Moran's point applies to educational migration because the gift of schooling gives the jindag a means to uplift a child's prospects in life.

6. khyim nas khyim med par rab tu byung/

7. In the large monasteries of Central Tibet administrators placed a novice monk sent from afar in a regional house *(khangtsen)* populated by monks from his area of birth. A room teacher *(shag gi gyegen)* oversaw the monk's daily life (Dreyfus 2003:57–59).

8. The spiritual lineage tradition is deeply ingrained in Tibetan Buddhism. The classic examples from the Gelukpa tradition are the *je yabse sum* (the Master Tsongkhapa and his two main disciples) and the *gyalwa yabse* (the spiritual relationship between the Dalai Lama and Panchen Lama). There are similar examples in other sects.

9. For example, parents can send a child as a "substitute" son or daughter *(bu tsab; bumo tsab)* to a childless couple for assistance and to be their successor. Among Tibet's former nobility, parents often sent a son to live with relatives so he could attend a private school. Monastic institutions grew in population over the centuries in part because many families were obligated to send a son, but also because of a connection between monasticism and prestige as encapsulated in the saying "The worst in the religious life is better than the best in secular life" (Goldstein 2009:2).

10. Data from more recent surveys shows that the proportion of children aged ten to fourteen who do not live with either biological parent when both are alive in selected African nations ranges from 16 percent to 28 percent. See The Gambia Bureau of Statistics (GBOS) and ICF International 2014; Ghana Statistical Service (GSS) et al. 2015; Liberia Institute of Statistics and Geo-Information Services (LISGIS) et al. 2014; and Statistics Sierra Leone (SSL) and ICF International 2014.

11. Similarly, Castle argues that "the social regulation of family size and composition through fostering must be considered as an important mitigating factor in child-rearing and its associated expense" (1995:679). Other scholars have noted that fosterage can buttress high fertility by reducing the cost of raising children, which in turn diminishes the incentive to limit childbearing (Isiugo-Abanihe1985; Caldwell and Caldwell 1987; Lesthaeghe 1989; Stokes 1995; Eloundou-Enyegue and Stokes 2002).

12. We do not mean to imply that all currently nonmarried women are destined to remain single. As they adjust to urban lifestyles and livelihoods, many will no doubt settle down and form families. Nevertheless, female nonmarriage is a common phenomenon in Tibetan societies, where a high incidence of females who do not marry (a trend linked to polyandry) moderates fertility. In places where unions between two or more men (usually brothers) and one woman are common, many women remain unmarried (Goldstein 1981; Schuler 1987; Levine 1988; Childs 2008). In Nubri during the 1990s polyandry was not very common. However, in villages where parents designated a daughter to be a household-resident nun, religious celibacy moderated overall fertility (Childs 2001b). To illustrate how different the pattern of female marriage in Nubri is to the rest of Nepal, consider that in 2011 only 7.0 percent and 2.0 percent of women nationwide aged twenty-five to twenty-nine and thirty to thirty-four had never married (Ministry of Health and Population et al. 2012).

13. She used the term *drinlan jalgö*, which implies filial obligation.

14. He used the compound *riggyü*, where rig implies race or ethnicity and gyü connotes biological descent.

15. She used the Nepali term *jaath*, which can mean caste or ethnicity depending on the context. She said in Tibetan *khateygi marey*, which literally means they "don't share mouths" implying noncommensal relations. Interestingly, Nubri residents classify their southern neighbors in a way that resembles the Hindu notion of caste and purity. This is not to say that they have appropriated and inverted a hierarchical system imposed on them, via the Muluki Ain, after being subsumed under the Kingdom of Nepal in the 1850s. Nubri society, like Tibetans elsewhere, have long maintained tiered social divisions based on descent, status, and occupation (Oppitz 1968; Aziz 1978; Childs 2008).

Perhaps as a subtle act of resistance, they view themselves as superior to those who relegated them to the low status of "enslaveable alcohol drinkers."

16. In the first statement she used the English term *caste,* which many use as an equivalent for the Nepali term *jaath.* The second statement shows how caste and ethnicity become conflated under the term *jaath.*

17. Data from Demographic and Health Surveys show a consistent association between education and age at marriage. For example, women in Nepal with no education marry on average at age 16.6, while women who have completed tenth grade or higher marry at age 21.8 (Ministry of Health and Population et al. 2012). In Niger, the country with the highest fertility rate today, women with no education marry at 15.6 compared to women with secondary education, who marry at 21.1 (Institut National de la Statistique 2013).

18. Allendorf finds evidence that the tenets of developmental idealism can become widespread and internalized. People she interviewed in India portray arranged marriages as traditional or old behavior, as opposed to self-choice marriages, which they view as modern (2013:465).

19. On marriage and the Tibetan family system, see Goldstein 1971 and 1976, Schuler 1987, Levine 1988, Haddix 2001, and Childs 2008.

20. Modernization theory lies at the foundation of many studies of family change in Nepal that primarily rely on the statistical analysis of survey data (Niraula 1994; Axinn and Barber 2001; Hoelter, Axinn and Ghimire 2004; Maitra 2004; Yabiku 2004, 2005; Choe, Thapa, and Mishra 2005; Aryal 2006; Ghimire et al. 2006; Caltabiano and Castiglioni 2008). Studies that are based on qualitative data (Pignède 1993; Ahearn 2001; March 2002) or that integrate qualitative and quantitative methods (Macfarlane 1976; Dahal et al. 1993; Fricke and Teachman 1993; Fricke 1994; Axinn and Fricke 1996; Fricke et al. 1998; Barber and Axinn 2004) are less prone to advance the unilinear trajectories of social change implied by modernization theory.

21. Survey research in Nepal often uses ethnic categories that are inconsistent and make little logical sense. For example, by labeling the categories as "Religious/Ethnoracial groups" the designers of the survey Barber used conflate three variables (religion, ethnicity, and race), one of which (race) is a social construct that has no scientific validity (Sussman 2014). Two groups, "Higher-caste Hindus" and "Low-caste Hindus," are distinguished based on a combination of caste and religion. Two other groups, "Terai Tibeto-Burmese (Tharu)" and "Hill Tibeto-Burmese (Tamang)," are distinguished based on geographical origin (Terai vs. Hill), language family (Tibeto-Burman), and ethnic identity (Tharu vs. Tamang). The last group is simply "Newar." The fact that Newars speak a Tibeto-Burman language, yet some practice Buddhism while others practice Hinduism, further illustrates the illogical way that Nepal's "Religious/Ethnoracial groups" tend to be categorized for survey purposes.

10. NUBRI FUTURES?

1. Mirik (mi = people, rigs = type or kind), although sometimes glossed as race, is a term Tibetans generally use for a culturally and linguistically distinct group of people.

2. Other important temple retirement centers in Nubri include Pema Chöling Gomba above Rö, Trong Gomba across the river from Lö, and Hinang Gomba up a side valley from Li.

3. He used the term *wulag,* which in Nubri often connotes compulsory service that commoners must provide for a lama. In that case, it is spelled 'u lag. Another term with a similar pronunciation but different spelling (dbu bla) refers to "chief spiritual adviser." In this case, Dzamling Dorje seems to be pronouncing dbu bla as 'u lag to make a satirical point about how religious obligations are too burdensome.

4. He used the term *barchey* (bar chad). In a village setting, barchey are thought of as impediments to health and well-being that are often caused by obstructing spirits.

5. The term *double outsider* has been used to describe a woman in a patrilocal marriage who moves to a new community where she has limited social support, and into a new family where she has low status (Tan and Short 2004; Brunson 2011).

6. Gurungs and the residents of Manang speak Tibeto-Burman languages. Many have long-standing religious and cultural connections with Tibetan society.

7. The project titled Disaster Narratives was led by Kristine Hildebrandt and funded by a National Science Foundation Rapid grant (#1547377).

8. https://www.facebook.com/tsumnubri/

9. Yangzom implies that people shunned or ostracized them. Blacksmiths, considered defiled by virtue of their occupation, are relegated to the margins of society. Their social interactions are severely curtailed by marriage prohibitions with nonblacksmiths and rules of commensality that forbid them from entering another person's home or sharing drinking vessels and eating utensils. As Holmberg argues, relegating blacksmiths to the lower rung of the social strata "poses a contradiction to conventional representations" of egalitarian Himalayan societies (2007:126).

APPENDIX: THE POPULATION OF NUBRI

1. http://www.cbs.gov.np/

2. There are other problems with Nepal's census. For example, caste/ethnicity and mother tongue designators for Nubri are completely inaccurate. Ninety-four percent and 97 percent of Rö and Lö VDC populations are classified as Tamang; mother tongue for most is also listed as Tamang. People in those villages self-identify as Tibetan and speak Tibetan.

Glossary of Tibetan Terms

Term	Tibetan Spelling	Translation
agu	a gu	"Uncle": father's brother.
amji	am chi	"Physician": traditional Tibetan medical doctor.
ani lobpön	a ni slob dpon	"Nun spiritual master": title given to a nun who completes advanced Buddhist training.
arak	a rag	Distilled alcoholic beverage.
ashang	a zhang	"Uncle": mother's brother.
barchey	bar chad	Impediments to health and well-being that are often caused by obstructing spirits.
bardo	bar do	Intermediate state between death and rebirth.
beyig	bad yig	"Interest Document": specifies the interest households must repay and the amount of grain sharecroppers must remit to support communal rituals.
beyul	sbas yul	A hidden land or valley.
buyig	bu yig	"Son Document": abridged version of the Mother Document that lists each household's annual tax payment.
chang	chang	Fermented alcoholic beverage.
changsa	chang sa	"Drinking gathering": refers to a formal wedding ceremony.
chinlab	byin rlabs	"Blessing."
chiyi nor	phyi'i nor	"External wealth": land, animals, and other household assets that are visible to outsiders.

chögyü	chos rgyud	"Religious lineage": also used for religious sect.
chöpey yul	chos pa'i yul	"Realm of Religious Practitioners": a society of religious practitioners—for example those who dwell at a temple complex, cf. jigtenpey yul.
chösri nyitrel	chos srid gnyis 'brel	"Religion and political affairs joined together": the Tibetan system of merging religion and politics.
chötrim	chos khrims	"Religious law."
chötrimpa	chos khrims pa	The person tasked with managing communal rituals.
chöyön	chos yon	"Priest and patron."
dey	'bre	Common unit for measuring volume and land area.
digpa	sdig pa	Unvirtuous or harmful action, often translated as "sin."
dralog	grwa log	"A monk who returned (to lay status)": often because he has broken one of his main vows, such as celibacy.
drashag	grwa shag	"Monk's dwelling."
drongba	grong ba	"Household."
drongchen	grong chen	"Large household": an administrative designation for a household consisting of relatively young adults and their children.
drotang	'gro stangs	"Way of doing things": refers to the cultural and social customs of a particular society.
dungyü	gdung rgyud	Honorific term for patrilineal descent group, generally in reference to high-status families.
dzong	rdzong	"District": term used in pre-1959 for a district-level administrative unit.
dzongpön	rdzong dpon	"District commissioner": an administrative position in the pre-1959 Tibetan government.
gengya	gan rgya	"Obligation contract": a written legal agreement for resolving a dispute, documenting a land sale, and other matters.
gewa	dge ba	"Virtuous deed; merit."
gomba	dgon pa	"Monastery": in Nubri the term also applies to a village temple and its surrounding community of religious practitioners and retirees.
gowa	mgo ba	"Headman."
gyaltrim	rgyal khrims	"Royal or national law": the laws of a country.
gyankham	rgyang 'khyams	"Wander off to a distant place": meaning to run away or elope.
gyed	'gyed	Alms given to a monk.

gyegen	dge rgan	"Teacher": used in both secular and religious contexts.
gyüpa	rgyud pa	Patrilineal descent group.
jigtenpey yul	'jig rten pa'i yul	"Realm of Worldly Sufferers": a society of laypeople who engage in mundane activities. cf. chöpey yul.
jindag	sbyin bdag	"Sponsor, benefactor, patron."
kay	khal	Measure of volume, about twenty-five to thirty pounds of grain. One kay equals twenty dey.
khatug	kha thugs	"Mouths met": refers to a union based on mutual affection in contrast to an arranged marriage.
khenpo	mkhan po	"Preceptor, abbot, scholar": title awarded to one who completes higher studies in Nyingma and Kagyu traditions.
kor	dkor	"Donation, offering." Specifically, religious funds acquired through donations and offerings.
kukey	ku skad	"Language of Kutang."
kukpa	lkugs pa	"Deaf-mute": used pejoratively to connote someone who is stupid or an idiot.
kuyön	sku yon	"Honorarium": given by a patron to a religious practitioner for services rendered.
kyimdag	khyim bdag	"Head of household."
labrang	bla brang	Residence and estate of a high lama.
lebngö	sleb dgnos	A review of all households conducted every third year. The resulting document (mayig or zhibzhung) records each household's members, assets, and tax obligations.
lenba	glen pa	"Imbecile, simpleton." Term often refers to someone who is deaf and mute.
ley	las	"Karma; fate": the causeand-effect principle that every action produces results.
ley gyumdre	las rgyu 'bres	Law of cause and effect.
lhabsang	lha bsang	A purification ritual that involves burning juniper.
lobma	slob ma	"Disciple, student."
lobpön	slob dpon	"Religious master": title awarded to one who completes higher studies in Nyingma and Kagyü traditions.
longchang	slong chang	"Engagement beer": the chang that is offered to a bride's family when making a marriage proposal.
lungta	rlung rta	"Wind horse": a symbol associated with fortune, typically inscribed on a prayer flag.
magpa	mag pa	Matrilocally resident husband, son-in-law.

mangja	mang ja	Tea offering to the monastic community.
mayig	ma yig	"Mother Document": a recording of each household's members and assets, the basis for determining a household's annual tax payment to the village administration. Generally called zhibzhung in Tibet.
mirik	mi rigs	"Ethnic group." Sometimes glossed as "race," the term usually refers to a culturally and linguistically distinct group of people.
miser	mi ser	"Subject." In Nubri the term also refers to a village administrative position.
mitagpa nyid	mi rtag pa nyid	"Impermanence."
nama	mna' ma	"Bride, daughter-in-law."
nangi nor	nang gi nor	"Internal wealth": gold, jewelry, and other household assets that generally are not visible to outsiders.
namshey	rnam shes	"Consciousness principle": something that endures from one bodily incarnation to the next.
narak	na rag	A religious ceremony to prevent the deceased from going to the lowest realm of hell.
ngagpa	sngags pa	Householder lama.
nyabsrung	nyab srung	"Grab and keep": i.e., bride capture.
nyesung	gnyen zung	"Seize a marriage partner": i.e., bride capture.
nyerpa	gnyer pa	"Caretaker/manager": i.e., someone who is tasked with performing duties to support a ritual.
pashi	pha gzhis	"Patrilineal inheritance."
patsab bugyü	pha tshab bu rgyud	"Succession from father to son."
phulu	phul lu	A volume measure for grain: six phulu is equal to one dey.
pochö	pho mchod	"Male religious practitioner": an administrative designation for the poorest households.
porang morang	pho hrang mo hrang	"Single man and single woman": an administrative designation for a household consisting of elderly residents.
riggyü	rigs rgyud	"Ancestry, race."
rongba	rong ba	"Lowlander": usually refers to Nepali Hindus.
shabten	zhabs brtan	Prayer ceremony to promote long life, repel negative influences, or bring good fortune.
shagya	shag rgya	"Sealing decrees": issued by lamas to restrict human exploitation of certain resources or sacred landscapes.
shedra	bshad grwa	Formal monastic study center.

sodey	bsod bde	"Good fortune, luck."
takob	mtha' 'khob	"Peripheral region": a place that borders the central regions where Buddhism is firmly established.
tertön	gter ston	"Treasure revealer": one who discovers concealed books, teachings, and other items of religious significance.
timcha	khrims bcas	"Formulation of rules": usually religious regulations.
torma	gtor ma	Ritual objects made from flour and butter, usually in a conical shape, that are placed on a shrine and dedicated to particular deities.
tulku	sprul sku	A reincarnate lama.
tsam	mtshams	"Religious retreat."
tsewey lama	rtsa ba'i bla ma	Principal guru, one's main religious teacher.
tsipa	rtsis pa	"Astrologer."
tsokpa	tshogs pa	Religious gathering in which offerings are distributed.
tsunmo zurpa	btsun mo zur pa	"Wife on the side": a consort.
wang	dbang	"Empowerment ceremony": for laypeople, a religious blessing at the end of a ceremony. For monks and lamas, the conferring of authority to pursue a particular teaching or practice.
wulag	'u lag or dbu bla	Compulsory or corvée service, usually to a lama. "Chief spiritual adviser."
yang	g.yang	"Fortune, prosperity."
yartsa gunbu	dbyar rtswa dgun 'bu	"Summer grass, winter worm": ophiocordyceps sinsensis, a caterpillar-fungus complex popular in Tibetan and Chinese medicine.
yogmo	g.yog mo	"Female servant."
yul	yul	"Village": can also connote communal, as in a communal temple.
yultrim	yul khrims	"Village or local law."
zhibzhung	zhib gzhung	Main or detailed register. A recording of each household's members and assets, the basis for determining a household's annual tax payment to the village administration. Also called mayig in Nubri.

References

Abreu, Alexandre. 2012. The New Economics of Labor Migration: Beware of Neoclassicals Bearing Gifts. *Forum for Social Economics* 41(1): 46–67.

Adams, David W. 1995. *Education for Extinction: American Indians and the Boarding School Experience, 1875–1928*. Lawrence: University of Kansas Press.

Adams, Leah D., and Anna Kirova. 2006. *Global Migration and Education: Schools, Children, and Families*. New York: Routledge.

Adhikari, Jagannath, and Mary Hobley. 2015. "Everyone Is Leaving. Who Will Sow Our Fields?" The Livelihood Effects on Women of Male Migration from Khotang and Udaypur Districts, Nepal, to the Gulf Countries and Malaysia. *Himalaya* 35(1): 11–23.

Aengst, Jennifer. 2103. The Politics of Fertility: Population and Pronatalism in Ladakh. *Himalaya* 32(1): 23–33.

Ahearn, Laura M. 2001. *Invitations to Love Literacy, Love Letters, and Social Change in Nepal*. Ann Arbor: University of Michigan Press.

Alber, Erdmute. 2003. Denying Biological Parenthood: Fosterage in Northern Benin. *Ethnos* 68: 487–506.

Alber, Erdmute, Jeannett Martin, and Catrien Notermans. 2013. *Child Fostering in West Africa: New Perspectives on Theory and Practices*. Boston: Brill.

Allendorf, Keera. 2013. Schemas of Marital Change: From Arranged Marriages to Eloping for Love. *Journal of Marriage and the Family* 75: 453–69.

Allendorf, Keera, and Roshan K. Pandian. 2016. The Decline of Arranged Marriage? Marital Change and Continuity in India. *Population and Development Review* 42(3): 435–64.

Alter, George. 1992. Theories of Fertility Decline: A Nonspecialist's Guide to the Current Debate. In *The European Experience of Declining Fertility*,

1850–1970: The Quiet Revolution, ed. J. Gillis, L. Tilly, and D. Levine, 13–27. Cambridge: Blackwell.

Aris, M. 1975. Report on the University of California Expedition to Kutang and Nubri in Northern Nepal in Autumn 1973. *Contributions to Nepalese Studies* 2(2): 45–87.

Aris, M. 1979. *Bhutan*. Warminster: Aris and Phillips.

Aryal, Tika Ram. 2006. Age at First Marriage in Nepal: Differentials and Determinants. *Journal of Biosocial Science* 39: 693–706.

Avedon. John F. 1986. *In Exile from the Land of Snows*. New York: Vintage.

Axinn, William G., and Jennifer S. Barber. 2001. Mass Education and Fertility Transition. *American Sociological Review* 66(4): 481–505.

Axinn, William G., and Tom Fricke. 1996. Community Context, Women's Natal Kin Ties, and Demand for Children: Macro-Micro Linkages in Social Demography. *Rural Sociology* 61(2): 249–71.

Aziz, Barbara. 1978. *Tibetan Frontier Families*. New Delhi: Vikas.

Baláz, Vladimír, Allan M. Williams, and Daniel Kollá. 2004. Temporary versus Permanent Youth Brain Drain: Economic Implications. *International Migration* 42(4): 3–34.

Baltes, Paul B. 1997. On the Incomplete Architecture of Human Ontogeny: Selection, Optimization, and Compensation as Foundation of Developmental Theory. *American Psychologist* 52(4): 366–80.

Bangsbo, Ellen. 2004. The Tibetan Monastic Tradition in Exile: Secular and Monastic Schooling of Buddhist Monks and Nuns in Nepal. *The Tibet Journal* 29(2): 71–82.

Barber, Jennifer S. 2004. Community Social Context and Individualistic Attitudes toward Marriage. *Social Psychology Quarterly* 67(3): 236–56.

Barber, Jennifer S., and William G. Axinn. 2004. New Ideas and Fertility Limitation: The Role of Mass Media. *Journal of Marriage and Family* 66: 1180–1200.

Baumgartner, Ruedi. 2015. *Farewell to Yak and Yeti? The Sherpas of Rolwaling Facing a Globalised World*. Kathmandu: Vajra Books.

Beall, Cynthia M., and Paul Leslie. 2014. Collecting Women's Reproductive Histories. *American Journal of Human Biology* 26(5): 577–89.

Beckwith, Christopher I. 1987. *The Tibetan Empire in Central Asia*. Princeton: Princeton University Press.

Belt, Joke van de. 2010. *Ani-La: The Nuns from Redna Menling*. Leiden: Sidestone Press.

Bernard, H. Russell. 2011. *Research Methods in Anthropology: Qualitative and Quantitative Approaches*. Lanham: AltaMira Press.

Bischoff, Jeannine. 2017. Completely, Voluntarily and Unalterably? Values and Social Regulation among Central Tibetan *mi ser* during the Ganden Phodrang Period. In *Social Regulation: Case Studies from Tibetan History*, ed. Jeannine Bischoff and Saul Mullard, 151–80. Leiden: Brill.

Bishop, Naomi. 1998. *Himalayan Herders*. Fort Worth: Harcourt Brace and Company.

Bledsoe, Caroline. 1990. The Politics of Children: Fosterage and the Social Management of Fertility among the Mende of Sierra Leone. In *Births and Power*, ed. W. Penn Handwerker, 81–100. Boulder: Westview Press.

Bledsoe, Caroline. 1994. "Children Are Like Young Bamboo Trees": Potentiality and Reproduction in Sub-Saharan Africa. In *Population, Economic Development, and the Environment*, ed. Kerstin Lindahl-Kiessling and Hans Landberg, 105–38. Oxford: Oxford University Press.

Bleek, Wolf. 1987. Lying Informants: A Fieldwork Experience from Ghana. *Population and Development Review* 13(2): 314–22

Blossfeld, Hans-Peter. 2009. Educational Assortative Marriage in Comparative Perspective. *Annual Review of Sociology* 35: 513–30.

Boas, Franz. 1896. The Limitations of the Comparative Method in Anthropology. *Science* 4: 901–908.

Bowie, Fiona. 2004. Adoption and the Circulation of Children: A Comparative Perspective. In *Cross-Cultural Approaches to Adoption*, ed. F. Bowie, 3–20. New York: Routledge.

Brauen, Martin. 2013. *Dreamworld Tibet: Western Illusions*. Bangkok: Orchid Press.

Brettell, Caroline B. 2000. Theorizing Migration in Anthropology: The Social Construction of Networks, Identities, Communities, and Globalscapes. In *Migration Theory: Talking across Disciplines*, ed. C. Brettell and J. Hollifield, 97–136. New York: Routledge.

Brettel, Caroline. 2003. Migration Stories: Agency and the Individual in the Study of Migration. In *Anthropology and Migration: Essays on Transnationalism, Ethnicity, and Identity*, ed. C. Brettel, 23–45. Walnut Creek: AltaMira Press.

Brunson, Jan. 2011. Moving away from Marital Violence: Nepali Mothers Who Refuse to Stay. *Practicing Anthropology* 33(3): 17–21.

Brunson, Jan. 2016. *Planning Families in Nepal: Global and Local Projects of Reproduction*. New Brunswick: Rutgers University Press.

Burghart, Richard. 1994. The Political Culture of Panchayat Democracy. In *Nepal in the Nineties*, ed. M. Hutt, 1–13. Delhi: Oxford University Press.

Cabezón, José. 1996. Firm Feet and Long Lives: The *zhabs brtan* Literature of Tibetan Buddhism. In *Tibetan Literature: Studies in Genre*, ed. J. Cabezón and R. Jackson, 344–57. Ithaca: Snow Lion.

Caldwell, John C. 1976. Toward a Restatement of Demographic Transition Theory. *Population and Development Review* 2(3–4): 321–66.

Caldwell, John C. 1980. Mass Education as a Determinant of the Timing of Fertility Decline. *Population and Development Review* 6(2): 225–55.

Caldwell, John C. 1998. The Global Fertility Transition and Nepal. *Contributions to Nepalese Studies* 25 (Special Issue): 1–7.

Caldwell, John C., and Pat Caldwell. 1987. The Cultural Context of High Fertility in Sub-Saharan Africa. *Population and Development Review* 13(3): 409–37.

Caltabiano, Marcontonio, and Maria Castiglioni. 2008. Changing Family Formation in Nepal: Marriage, Cohabitation and First Sexual Intercourse. *International Family Planning Perspectives* 34(1): 30–39.

Castle, Sarah E. 1995. Child Fostering and Children's Nutritional Outcomes in Rural Mali: The Role of Female Status in Directing Child Transfers. *Social Science and Medicine* 40(5): 679–93.

Castles, Stephen, Hein de Haas, and Mark Miller. 2014. *The Age of Migration: International Population Movements in the Modern World.* New York: Guilford.

Chagnon, Napoleon A., Mark V. Flinn, and Thomas F. Melancon. 1979. Sex-Ratio Variation among the Yanomamö Indians. In *Evolutionary Biology and Human Social Behavior: An Anthropological Perspective*, ed. N. Chagnon and W. Irons, 290–320. North Scituate: Duxbury.

Chibnik, Michael. 2011. *Anthropology, Economics, and Choice.* Austin: University of Texas Press.

Childs, Geoff. 1999. Refuge and Revitalization: Hidden Himalayan Sanctuaries (Sbas-yul) and the Preservation of Tibet's Imperial Lineage. *Acta Orientalia* 60: 126–58.

Childs, Geoff. 2001a. A Brief History of Nub-ri: Ethnic Interface, Sacred Geography, and Historical Migrations in a Himalayan Locality. *Zentralasiatische Studien* 31: 7–29.

Childs, Geoff. 2001b. Old-Age Security, Religious Celibacy, and Aggregate Fertility in a Tibetan Population. *Journal of Population Research* 18(1): 52–66.

Childs, Geoff. 2003. Polyandry and Population Growth in a Historical Tibetan Society. *The History of the Family* 8(3): 423–44.

Childs, Geoff. 2004. *Tibetan Diary: From Birth to Death and Beyond in a Himalayan Valley of Nepal.* Berkeley: University of California Press.

Childs, Geoff. 2008. *Tibetan Transitions: Historical and Contemporary Perspectives on Fertility, Family Planning, and Demographic Change.* Leiden: Brill.

Childs, Geoff. 2015. Renouncing the World, Renouncing the Family: The Social Consequences of Spiritual Aspirations. In *The Buddhist World*, ed. John Powers, 453–69. New York: Routledge.

Childs, Geoff, and Gareth Barkin. 2006. Reproducing Identity: Using Images to Promote Pronatalism and Sexual Endogamy among Tibetan Exiles in South Asia. *Visual Anthropology Review* 22(2): 34–52.

Childs, Geoff, and Namgyal Choedup. 2014. Indigenous Management Strategies and Socioeconomic Impacts of Yartsa Gunbu (Ophiocordyceps sinensis) Harvesting in Nubri and Tsum, Nepal. *Himalaya* 34(1): 8–22.

Childs, Geoff, and Namgyal Choedup. 2015. From Servant (g.yog mo) to Disciple (slob ma): Modernity, Migration, and Evolving Life Course Options for Buddhist Nuns. In *From Bhakti to Bon: Festschrift for Per Kvaerne*, ed. H. Havnevik and C. Ramble, 171–84. Oslo: Novus.

Childs, Geoff, Melvyn C. Goldstein, Ben Jiao, and Cynthia M. Beall. 2005. Tibetan Fertility Transitions in China and South Asia. *Population and Development Review* 31(2): 337–49.

Childs, Geoff, Sienna Craig, Cynthia M. Beall, and Buddha Basnyat. 2014. Depopulating the Himalayan Highlands: Education and Outmigration from Ethnically Tibetan Communities of Nepal. *Mountain Research and Development* 34(2): 85–94.

Childs, Geoff, and Michael Walter. 2000. Tibetan Natal Horoscopes. *Tibet Journal* 25(1): 51–62.

Cho, Lee-Jay, Robert D. Retherford, and Minja Kim Choe. 1986. *The Own-Children Method of Fertility Estimation.* Honolulu: East-West Center.

Choe, Minja Kim, Shyam Thapa, and Vinod Mishra. 2005. Early Marriage and Early Motherhood in Nepal. *Journal of Biosocial Science* 37: 143–62.

Choedup, Namgyal. 2015. From Tibetan Refugees to Transmigrants: Negotiating Cultural Continuity and Economic Mobility through Migration. PhD dissertation, Dept. of Anthropology, Washington University in St. Louis.

Chogtrul Karma Migyur Dorje. 2017. *Nub ri sbas yul skyid mo lung gi gnas bshad. Guide to the Nubri Hidden Land Kyimolung.* Kathmandu: Swayambhu Press.

Choy, Catherine Ceniza. 2010. Nurses across Borders: Foregrounding International Migration in Nursing History. *Nursing History Review* 18(1): 12–28.

Clark, Gracia. 1989. Separation between Trading and Home for Asante Women in Kumasi Central Market, Ghana. In *The Household Economy: Reconsidering the Domestic Mode of Production*, ed. R. Wilk, 91–118. Boulder: Westview Press.

Clarke, Graham. 1980. A Helambu History. *Journal of the Nepal Research Centre* 4: 1–38.

Clarke, Graham. 1990. Ideas of Merit (Bsod-nams), Virtue (Dge-ba), Blessing (byin-rlabs) and Material Prosperity (rten-'brel) in Highland Nepal. *Journal of the Anthropological Society of Oxford* 21(2): 165–84.

Cleland, John, and Christopher Wilson. 1987. Demand Theories of the Fertility Transition: An Iconoclastic View. *Population Studies* 41: 5–30.

Coburn, Brot. 2017. Preaching on High: A Christian Evangelical Group Is Converting Buddhists in Holy Himalayan Valleys. *Nepali Times* 23–25 August #873.

Cohen, Jeffrey H. 2004. *The Culture of Migration in Southern Mexico.* Austin: University of Texas Press.

Cohen, Jeffrey H., and Ibrahim Sirkeci. 2011. *Cultures of Migration: The Global Nature of Contemporary Mobility.* Austin: University of Texas Press.

Conway, George A., and John C. Slocum. 1979. Plants Used as Abortifacients and Emmenagogues by Spanish New Mexicans. *Journal of Ethnopharmacology* 1(3): 241–61.

Corbett, Michael. 2007. *Learning to Leave: The Irony of Schooling in a Coastal Community.* Winnipeg: Fernwood Publishing.

Craig, Sienna R. 2011. Migration, Social Change, Health, and the Realm of the Possible: Women's Stories between Nepal and New York. *Anthropology and Humanism* 36(2): 193–214.

Craig, Sienna R., Geoff Childs, and Cynthia M. Beall. 2016. Closing the Womb Door: Contraception Use and Fertility Transition among Culturally Tibetan Women in Highland Nepal. *Maternal and Child Health Journal* 20(12): 2437–50.

Curren, Sara R., and Estela Rivero-Fuentes. 2003. Engendering Migrant Networks: The Case of Mexican Migration. *Demography* 40(2): 289–307.

Dahal, Dilli R., Tom Fricke, and Arland Thornton. 1993. The Family Contexts of Marriage Timing in Nepal. *Ethnology* 32(4): 305–23.

Dargyay, Eva M. 1982. *Tibetan Village Communities.* New Delhi: Vikas.

Das Gupta, Monica. 1987. Selective Discrimination against Female Children in Rural Punjab, India. *Population and Development Review* 13(1): 77–100.

de Haas, Hein. 2010. The Internal Dynamics of Migration Processes: A Theoretical Inquiry. *Journal of Ethnic and Migration Studies* 36(10): 1587–1617.

de Lange, Albertine. 2007. Child Labour Migration and Trafficking in Rural Burkina Faso. *International Migration* 45(2): 147–67.

Depp, Colin A., and Dilip V. Jeste. 2006. Definitions and Predictors of Successful Aging: A Comprehensive Review of Larger Quantitative Studies. *American Journal of Geriatric Psychiatry* 14(1): 6–20.

Diemberger, Hildegard. 2007. *When a Woman Becomes a Religious Dynasty: The Samding Dorje Phagmo of Tibet.* New York: Columbia University Press.

Dobson, Madeleine E. 2009. Unpacking Children in Migration Research. *Children's Geographies* 7(3): 355–60.

Dodin, Thierry, and Heinz Räther, eds. 2001. *Imagining Tibet: Perceptions, Projections, and Fantasies.* Boston: Wisdom.

Donner, William W. 1999. Sharing and Compassion: Fosterage in a Polynesian Society. *Journal of Comparative Family Studies* 30(4): 703–22.

Dreyfus, George B. 2003. *The Sounds of Two Hands Clapping: The Education of a Tibetan Buddhist Monk.* Berkeley: University of California Press.

Dustmann, Christian, and Albrecht Glitz. 2011. Education and Migration. In *Handbooks in Economics Vol. 4: Economics of Education,* ed. E. Hanushek, S. Machin and L. Woessmann, 337–440. Amsterdam: North-Holland.

Ehrhard, Franz-Karl. 1997. A "Hidden Land" in the Tibetan-Nepalese Borderlands. In *Mandala and Landscape,* ed. A.W. Macdonald, 335–64. New Delhi: D.K. Printworld.

Eloundou-Enyegue, Parfait M., and C. Shannon Stokes. 2002. Will Economic Crises in Africa Weaken Rural-Urban Ties? Insights from Child Fosterage Trends in Cameroon. *Rural Sociology* 67(2): 278–98.

Emran, M. Shahe, Fenohasina Maret-Rakotondrazakab, and Stephen C. Smith. 2014. Education and Freedom of Choice: Evidence from Arranged Marriages in Vietnam. *Journal of Development Studies* 50(4): 481–501.

England, Paula. 1993. The Separative Self: Androcentric Bias in Neoclassical Assumptions. In *Beyond Economic Man: Feminist Theory and Economics,* ed. M. Ferber and J. Nelson, 37–53. Chicago: University of Chicago Press.

Engle, Artemus B. 2009. *The Inner Science of Buddhist Practice: Vasubhandu's Summary of the Five Heaps with Commentary by Sthirimati.* Ithaca: Snow Lion.

Fawcett, James T. 1989. Networks, Linkages, and Migration Systems. *International Migration Review* 23(3): 671–80.

Feeney, Griffith, Shyam Thapa, and Keshav R. Sharma. 2001. One and a Half Centuries of Demographic Transition in Nepal. *Journal of Health, Population and Nutrition* 19(3): 160–66.

Fisher, James F. 1986. *Trans-Himalayan Traders.* Delhi: Motilal Banarsidass.

Fisher, William F. 2001. *Fluid Boundaries: Forming and Transforming Identity in Nepal.* New York: Columbia University Press.

Folbre, Nancy. 1986. Hearts and Spades: Paradigms of Household Economics. *World Development* 14(2): 245–55.

Fox, Greer Litton. 1975. Love Match and Arranged Marriage in a Modernizing Nation: Mate Selection in Ankara, Turkey. *Journal of Marriage and Family* 37(1): 180–93.

Frechette, Ann. 2004. *Tibetans in Nepal: The Dynamics of International Assistance among a Community in Exile.* New York: Berghahn.

Fricke, Tom. 1994. *Himalayan Households.* New York: Columbia University.

Fricke, Tom. 1997. Culture Theory and Demographic Process. Toward a Thicker Demography. In *Anthropological Demography*, ed. David Kertzer and Tom Fricke, 248–78. Chicago: University of Chicago Press.

Fricke, Tom, and Jay D. Teachman. 1993. Writing the Names: Marriage Style, Living Arrangements, and First Birth Interval in a Nepali Society. *Demography* 30(2): 175–88.

Fricke, Tom, Arland Thornton, and Dilli R. Dahal. 1998. Netting in Nepal: Social Change, the Life Course, and Brideservice in Sangila. *Human Ecology* 26(2): 213–37.

Fürer-Haimendorf, Christoph von. 1975. *Himalayan Traders: Life in Highland Nepal.* London: John Murray.

Fürer-Haimendorf, Christoph von. 1981. Social Structure and Spatial Mobility among the Thakalis of Western Nepal. In *Asian Highland Societies in Anthropological Perspective*, ed. C. von Fürer-Haimendorf, 1–9. New Delhi: Sterling.

Gentry, James Duncan. 2014. Substance and Sense: Objects of Power in the Life, Writings, and Legacy of the Tibetan Ritual Master Sog bzlog pa Blo gros rgyal mtshan. PhD dissertation, Harvard University.

Ghana Statistical Service (GSS), Ghana Health Service (GHS), and ICF International. 2015. *Ghana Demographic and Health Survey 2014.* Rockville: GSS, GHS, and ICF International.

Ghimire, Anita, and Fiona Samuels. 2014. *Change and Continuity in Social Norms and Practices around Marriage and Education in Nepal.* London: Overseas Development Institute.

Ghimire, Dirgha J., William G. Axinn, Scott T. Yabiku, and Arland Thornton. 2006. Social Change, Premarital Nonfamily Experience, and Spouse Choice in an Arranged Marriage Society. *American Journal of Sociology* 111(4): 1181–1218.

Giani, Laura. 2006. Migration and Education: Child Migrants in Bangladesh. Sussex Migration Working Paper no. 33. Sussex Centre for Migration Research, University of Sussex.

Gillis, John R., Louise A. Tilly, and David Levine. 1992. Introduction: The Quiet Revolution. In *The European Experience of Declining Fertility, 1850–1970: The Quiet Revolution*, ed. J. Gillis, L. Tilly, and D. Levine, 1–9. Cambridge: Blackwell.

Goldstein, Melvyn C. 1971. Stratification, Polyandry, and Family Structure in Central Tibet. *Southwest Journal of Anthropology* 27: 64–74.

Goldstein, Melvyn C. 1976. Fraternal Polyandry and Fertility in a High Himalayan Valley in Northwest Nepal. *Human Ecology* 4(2): 223–33.

Goldstein, Melvyn C. 1978. Ethnogenesis and Resource Competition among Tibetan Refugees in South India: A New Face to the Indo-Tibetan Interface.

In *Himalayan Anthropology: The Indo-Tibetan Interface*, ed. J. Fisher, 395–420. The Hague: Mouton.

Goldstein, Melvyn C. 1981. New Perspectives on Tibetan Fertility and Population Decline. *American Ethnologist* 8(4): 721–38.

Goldstein, Melvyn C. 1986. Reexamining Choice, Dependency and Command in the Tibetan Social System: "Tax Appendages" and Other Landless Serfs. *Tibet Journal* 11(4): 79–112.

Goldstein, Melvyn C. 1989. *A History of Modern Tibet, 1913–1951: The Demise of the Lamaist State*. Berkeley: University of California Press.

Goldstein, Melvyn C. 1998. The Revival of Monastic Life in Drepung Monastery. In *Buddhism in Contemporary Tibet: Religious Revival and Cultural Identity*, ed. M. Goldstein and M. Kapstein, 15–52. Berkeley: University of California Press.

Goldstein, Melvyn C. 2009. Bouddhisme Tibétain et Monachisme de Masse. In *Moines et Moniales par le Monde: La Vie Monastique au Miroir de la Parenté*, ed. A. Herrou and G. Krauskopff. Paris: L'Harmattan. English version available on the Center for Research on Tibet website http://www.case .edu/affil/tibet/

Gonzalez, Nancie L. Solien de. 1961. Family Organization in Five Types of Migratory Wage Labor. *American Anthroplogist* 63(6): 1264–80.

Goodall, Sarah K. 2004. Rural-to-Urban Migration and Urbanization in Leh, Ladakh: A Case Study of Three Nomadic Pastoral Communities. *Mountain Research and Development* 24(3): 220–27.

Goody, Esther. 1975. Delegation of Parental Roles in West Africa and the West Indies. In *Changing Social Structure in Ghana: Essays in the Comparative Sociology of a New State and an Old Tradition*, ed. J. Goody, 137–65. London: International African Institute.

Goody, Esther. 1982. *Parenthood and Social Reproduction: Fostering and Occupational Roles in West Africa*. London: Cambridge University Press.

Grandin, Barbara. 1988. *Wealth Ranking in Smallholder Communities: A Field Manual*. Rugby: Intermediate Technology Publications.

Granovetter, Mark. 1973. The Strength of Weak Ties. *American Journal of Sociology* 78: 1360–80.

Granovetter, Mark. 1982. The Strength of Weak Ties: A Network Theory Revisited. In *Social Structure and Network Analysis*, ed. P. Marsden and N. Lin, 105–30. Beverly Hills: Sage.

Greenhalgh, Susan, ed. 1995. *Situating Fertility: Anthropology and the Demographic Inquiry*. Cambridge: Cambridge University Press.

Grey, Mark A., and Anne C. Woodrick. 2002. Unofficial Sister Cities: Meatpacking Labor Migration between Villachuoto, Mexico and Marshalltown, Iowa. *Human Organization* 61(4): 364–76.

Guilmoto, Christophe Z. 2009. The Sex Ratio Transition in Asia. *Population and Development Review* 35(3): 519–49.

Gutschow, Kim. 2004. *Being a Buddhist Nun: The Struggle for Enlightenment in the Himalayas*. Cambridge: Harvard University Press.

Gyatso, Janet, and Hanna Havnevik, eds. 2005. *Women in Tibet: Past and Present*. New York: Columbia University Press.

Gyatso, Sherab. 2003. Of Monks and Monasteries. In *Exile as Challenge: The Tibetan Diaspora*, ed. D. Bernstorff and H. von Welck, 213–44. New Delhi: Orient Longman.

Haddix, Kimber. 2001. Leaving Your Wife and Your Brothers: When Polyandrous Marriages Fall Apart. *Evolution and Human Behavior* 22: 47–60.

Haines, M.R. 1989. American Fertility in Transition: New Estimates of Birth Rates in the United States, 1900–1910. *Demography* 26(1): 137–48.

Hammel, E.A. 1984. On the *** of Studying Household Form and Function. In *Households: Comparative and Historical Studies of the Domestic Group*, ed. R. Netting et al., 29–43. Berkeley: University of California Press.

Harris, Marvin, and Eric B. Ross. 1987. *Death, Sex, and Fertility: Population Regulation in Preindustrial and Developing Societies*. New York: Columbia University Press.

Hashim, Iman. 2007. Independent Child Migration and Education in Ghana. *Development and Change* 38(5): 911–31

Hashim, Iman, and Dorte Thorsen. 2011. *Child Migrants in Africa*. Uppsala: Nordic Africa Institute.

Havnevik, Hanna. 1989. *Tibetan Buddhist Nuns: History, Cultural Norms and Social Reality*. Oslo: Norwegian University Press.

Heirman, Ann. 2011. Buddhist Nuns: Between Past and Present. *Numen* 58: 603–31.

Hern, Warren. 1976. Knowledge and Use of Herbal Contraceptives in a Peruvian Amazon Village. *Human Organization* Spring 35(1): 9–19.

Herzfeld, Michael. 2015. The Village in the World and the World in the Village: Reflections on Ethnographic Epistemology. *Critique of Anthropology* 35(3): 338–43.

Hirsch, Jennifer S. 2007. "Love Makes a Family": Globalization, Companionate Marriage, and the Modernization of Gender Inequality. In *Love and Globalization: Transformations of Intimacy in the Contemporary World*, ed. M. Padilla et al., 93–106. Nashville: Vanderbilt University Press.

Hirsch, Jennifer S., and Holly Wardlow, eds. 2006. *Modern Loves: The Anthropology of Romantic Courtship and Companionate Marriage*. Ann Arbor: University of Michigan Press.

Hirsch, Jennifer S., Holly Wardlow, Daniel Jordan Smith, Harriet M. Phinney, Shanti Parikh, and Constance A. Nathanson, eds. 2010. *The Secret: Love, Marriage, and HIV*. Nashville: Vanderbilt University Press.

Hoelter, Lynette F., William G. Axinn, and Dhirga J. Ghimire. 2004. Social Change, Premarital Nonfamily Experiences, and Marital Dynamics. *Journal of Marriage and the Family* 66(5): 1131–51.

Höfer, Andras. 1979. *The Caste Hierarchy and the State in Nepal*. Innsbruck: Universitätsverlag Wagner.

Holmberg, David H. 1989. *Order in Paradox: Myth, Ritual and Exchange among Nepal's Tamang*. Ithaca: Cornell University Press.

Holmberg, David. 2007. Outcastes in an "Egalitarian" Society: Tamang/Blacksmith Relations from a Tamang Perspective. *Occasional Papers in Sociology and Anthropology* 10: 124–40.

Horváth, István. 2008. The Culture of Migration of Rural Romanian Youth. *Journal of Ethnic and Migration Studies* 34(5): 771–86.

Howell, Nancy. 1979. *Demography of the Dobe !Kung.* New York: Academic.

Huber, Toni. 2001. Shangri-la in Exile: Representations of Tibetan Identity and Transnational Culture. In *Imagining Tibet: Perceptions, Projections, and Fantasies,* ed. T. Dodin and H. Räther, 357–71. Boston: Wisdom Publications.

Huber, Toni. 2004a. The Chase and the Dharma: The Legal Protection of Wild Animals in Pre-modern Tibet. In *Wildlife in Asia: Cultural Perspectives,* ed. J. Knight, 36–55. London: RoutledgeCurzon.

Huber, Toni. 2004b. Territorial Control by "Sealing" (rgya sdom-pa): A Religio-Political Practice in Tibet. *Zentralasiatische Studien* 33: 127–52.

Huber, Toni. 2008. *The Holy Land Reborn: Pilgrimage and the Tibetan Reinvention of Buddhist India.* Chicago: University of Chicago Press.

Hutt, Michael. 2004. *Himalayan People's War: Nepal's Maoist Rebellion.* Bloomington: Indiana University Press.

Institut National de la Statistique (INS) et ICF International, 2013. *Enquête Démographique et de Santé et à Indicateurs Multiples du Niger 2012.* Calverton: INS et ICF International.

Isiugo-Abanihe, Uche C. 1985. Child Fosterage in West Africa. *Population and Development Review* 11(1): 53–73.

Jensen, Eric R., and Dennis A. Ahlburg. 2004. Why Does Migration Decrease Fertility? Evidence from the Philippines. *Population Studies* 58(2): 219–31.

Kandel, William, and Douglas S. Massey. 2002. The Culture of Mexican Migration: A Theoretical and Empirical Analysis. *Social Forces* 80(3): 981–1004.

Karki, Arjun, and David Seddon, eds. 2003. *The People's War in Nepal: Left Perspectives.* Delhi: Adroit Publishing.

Karmay, Samten. 1993. The Wind-Horse and the Well-Being of Man. In *Anthropology of Tibet and the Himalaya,* ed. C. Ramble and M. Braun, 150–57. Zurich: Ethnological Museum of the University of Zurich.

Karmay, Samten. 1998. The Local Deities and the Juniper Tree: A Ritual for Purification (bsang). In *The Arrow and the Spindle: Studies in History, Myths, Rituals, and Beliefs in Tibet,* ed. S. Karmay, 380–412. Kathmandu: Mandala Book Point.

Kertzer, David. 1993. *Sacrificed for Honor: Italian Infant Abandonment and the Politics of Reproductive Control.* Boston: Beacon Press.

Kertzer, David I., and Tom Fricke. 1997. Toward an Anthropological Demography. In *Anthropological Demography,* ed. David Kertzer and Tom Fricke, 1–35. Chicago: University of Chicago Press.

Kielland, A., and I. Sanogo. 2002. *Burkina Faso: Child Labour Migration from Rural Areas.* Washington DC: The World Bank.

Klieger, P. Christiaan. 1992. *Tibetan Nationalism: The Role of Patronage in the Accomplishment of a National Identity.* Berkeley: Folklore Institute.

Knight, John, and John W. Traphagan. 2003. The Study of the Family in Japan: Integrating Anthropological and Demographic Approaches. In *Demographic Change and the Family in Japan's Aging Society,* ed. J. Traphagan and J. Knight, 3–24. Albany: SUNY Press.

Kulu, Hill. 2005. Migration and Fertility: Competing Hypotheses Re-examined. *European Journal of Population* 21: 51–87.

Kyimolung Lamyig. 1983 [14th CE?]. Sbas yul sKyid mo lung gi lam yig gags sel. Guide to the Hidden Land Kyimolung, Discovered in 1366 at Zangzang Lhadrag by Rigzen Gödemchen. In *Collected Biographies and Prophesies of the Byang gter Tradition*, 557–98. Gangtok: Sherab Gyaltsen and Lama Dawa.

Lamb, Sarah, ed. 2017. *Successful Aging as a Contemporary Obsession: Global Perspectives*. New Brunswick: Rutgers University Press.

Lee, James Z., and Wang Feng. 1999. *One Quarter of Humanity: Malthusian Mythologies and Chinese Realities*. Cambridge: Harvard University Press.

Lee, Ronald D., and David S. Reher. 2011. Introduction: The Landscape of Demographic Transition and Its Aftermath. *Population and Development Review* 37 (Supplement): 1–7.

Leinaweaver, Jessaca B. 2008. *The Circulation of Children: Kinship, Adoption, and Morality in Andean Peru*. Durham: Duke University Press.

Lempert, Michael. 2012. *Discipline and Debate: The Language of Violence in a Tibetan Buddhist Monastery*. Berkeley: University of California Press.

Lesthaeghe, Ron. 1989. Social Organization, Economic Crises, and the Future of Fertility Control in Africa. In *Reproduction and Social Organization in Sub-Saharan Africa*, ed. R. Lesthaeghe, 475–505. Berkeley: University of California Press.

Levine, Nancy E. 1987. Differential Child Care in Three Tibetan Communities: Beyond Son Preference. *Population and Development Review* 13(2): 281–304.

Levine, Nancy. 1988. *The Dynamics of Polyandry: Kinship, Domesticity and Population on the Tibetan Border*. Chicago: University of Chicago Press.

Liberia Institute of Statistics and Geo-Information Services (LISGIS), Ministry of Health and Social Welfare [Liberia], National AIDS Control Program [Liberia], and ICF International. 2014. *Liberia Demographic and Health Survey 2013*. Monrovia: Liberia Institute of Statistics and Geo-Information Services (LISGIS) and ICF International.

Lim, Francis K. G. 2008. *Imagining the Good Life: Negotiating Culture and Development in Nepal Himalaya*. Leiden: Brill.

Lin, Nan. 1999. Social Networks and Status Attainment. *Annual Review of Sociology* 25: 467–87.

Lin, Nan, Walter M. Ensel, and John C. Vaughn. 1981. Social Resources and Strength of Ties: Structural Factors in Occupational Status Attainment. *American Sociological Review* 46(4): 393–405.

Livi-Bacci, Massimo. 1997. *A Concise History of World Population* (2nd edition). Malden: Blackwell.

Lo Bue, Erberto. 2015. A Zhabs-brtan Ceremony Performed in a Rnying-ma Household at Jawalakhel, Lalitpur, Nepal (1986). In *From Bhakti to Bon: Festschrift for Per Kvœrne*, ed. H. Havnevik and C. Ramble, 325–36. Olso: Novus Press.

Lockwood, Victoria. 1989. Tubuai Women Potato Planters and the Political Economy of Intra-Household Gender Relations. In *The Household Economy:*

Reconsidering the Domestic Mode of Production, ed. R. Wilk, 197–220. Boulder: Westview Press.

Lodro Gyaltsen. 1975 [17th CE]. sLan chad kyang sog bzlog mdzad pa po rnams la phan pa'i phyir du rang nyid kyi bzlog bgyis tshul. In *Collected Writings of Sogdogpa Lodro Gyaltsen*, vol. I, 203–59. New Delhi: Sanje Dorji.

Lokshin, Michael, Mikhail Bontch-Osmolovski, and Elena Glinskaya. 2010. Work-Related Migration and Poverty Reduction in Nepal. *Review of Development Economics* 14(2): 323–32.

Long, Karen J. 2004. Units of Analysis. In *The Sage Encyclopedia of Social Science Research Methods*, ed. M. Lewis-Beck, A. Bryman, and T. Liao, 1157–58. Thousand Oaks: Sage.

Lopez, Donald S. 1997. Introduction. In *Religions of Tibet in Practice*, ed. D. Lopez, 1–36. Princeton: Princeton University Press.

Lopez, Donald S. 1998. *Prisoners of Shangri-La: Tibetan Buddhism and the West*. Chicago: University of Chicago Press.

Macfarlane, Alan. 1976. *Resources and Population: A Study of the Gurungs of Nepal*. Cambridge: Cambridge University Press.

Maitra, Pushkar. 2004. Effect of Socioeconomic Characteristics on Age at Marriage and Total Fertility in Nepal. *Journal of Health, Population and Nutrition* 22(1): 84–96.

March, Kathryn S. 2002. *"If Each Comes Halfway": Meeting Tamang Women in Nepal*. Ithaca: Cornell University Press.

Marston, Cicely, and John Cleland. 2003. Relationship between Contraception and Abortion: A Review of the Evidence. *International Family Planning Perspectives* 29(1): 6–13.

Massey, Douglas S. 1990. Social Structure, Household Strategies, and the Cumulative Causation of Migration. *Population Index* 56(1): 3–26.

Massey, Douglas S., J. Arango, G. Hugo, A. Kouaouci, A. Pellegrino, and J.E. Taylor. 1993. Theories of International Migration: A Review and Appraisal. *Population and Development Review* 19(3): 431–66.

Massey, Douglas S., and Kristin E. Espinosa. 1997. What's Driving Mexico-U.S. Migration? A Theoretical, Empirical, and Policy Analysis. *American Journal of Sociology* 102(4): 939–99.

Massey, Douglas S., J. Arango, G. Hugo, A Kouaouci, A. Pellegrino, and J.E. Taylor. 1998. *Worlds in Motion: Understanding International Migration at the End of the Millennium*. Oxford: Clarendon.

Milarepa. 1985. *rdo rje'i mgur drug gsung rgyun thor bu*. Collected Songs of Esoteric Realization Attributed to Milarepa (1052–1135). Delhi: Sonam Rabten.

Mills, Martin. 2000. Vajra Brother, Vajra Sister: Renunciation, Individualism and the Household in Tibetan Buddhist Monasticism. *Journal of the Royal Anthropological Institute* 6(1): 17–34.

Mills, Martin. 2003. *Identity, Ritual, and State in Tibetan Buddhism: The Foundations of Authority in Gelukpa Monasticism*. London: RoutledgeCurzon.

Mills, Martin. 2009. La Double Figure du Moine Monachisme et Maisons dans le Bouddhisme Tibétain. In *Moines et Moniales par le Monde: La Vie*

Monastique au Miroir de la Parenté, ed. A. Herrou and G. Krauskopff, 161–73. Paris: L'Harmattan. (English translation provided by the author.)

Ministry of Health and Population (MOHP) [Nepal], New ERA, and ICF International Inc. 2012. *Nepal Demographic and Health Survey 2011*. Kathmandu: Ministry of Health and Population, New ERA, and ICF International, Calverton, Maryland.

Mishra, Pratikshya. 2011. Nepalese Migrants in the United States of America: Perspectives on Their Exodus, Assimilation Pattern and Commitment to Nepal. *Journal of Ethnic and Migration Studies* 37(9): 1527–37.

Mohr, Thea, and Jampa Tsedroen, eds. 2010. *Dignity and Discipline: Reviving Full Ordination for Buddhist Nuns*. Somerville: Wisdom.

Moran, Peter. 2004. *Buddhism Observed: Travelers, Exiles and Tibetan Dharma in Kathmandu*. London: RoutledgeCurzon.

Morgan, Lewis Henry. 1871. *Systems of Consanguinity and Affinity of the Human Family*. Washington: Smithsonian.

Mrozik, Susanne. 2009. A Robed Revolution: The Contemporary Buddhist Nun's (Bhikṣuṇī) Movement. *Religious Compass* 3(3): 360–78.

Mullard, Saul. 2011. *Opening the Hidden Land: State Formation and the Construction of Sikkimese History*. Leiden: Brill.

Mullin, Glenn H., trans. 1998. Death and the Bodhisattva Training, by Gyalwa Tubten Gyatso, the Thirteenth Dalai Lama. In *Living in the Face of Death: The Tibetan Tradition*, ed. G. Mullin, 45–68. Ithaca: Snow Lion.

Nagarjuna. 2013. *Nagarjuna's Letter to a Friend*. Ithaca: Snow Lion.

Nālandā Translation Committee. 1997. A Smoke Purification Song. In *Religions of Tibet in Practice*, ed. D. Lopez, 401–405. Princeton: Princeton University Press.

Niraula, Bhanu B. 1994. Marriage Changes in the Central Nepali Hills. *Journal of Asian and African Studies* 29(1–2): 91–109.

Notestein, Frank W. 1953. Economic Problems of Population Change. In *Proceedings of the Eighth International Conference of Agricultural Economists*. London: Oxford University Press.

Nowak, Margaret. 1984. *Tibetan Refugees: Youth and the New Generation of Meaning*. New Brunswick: Rutgers University Press.

Oppitz, Michael. 1968. *Geschichte und Sozialordnung der Sherpa*. Innsbruck: Universitätsverlag Wagner.

Ortner, Sherry B. 1989. *High Religion: A Cultural and Political History of Sherpa Buddhism*. Princeton: Princeton University Press.

Ortner, Sherry B. 1999. *Life and Death on Mt. Everest: Sherpas and Himalayan Mountaineering*. Princeton: Princeton University Press.

Padilla, Mark, Jennifer S. Hirsch, Miguel Muñoz-Laboy, Robert E. Sember, and Richard G. Parker, eds. 2007a. *Love and Globalization: Transformations of Intimacy in the Contemporary World*. Nashville: Vanderbilt University Press.

Padilla, Mark, Jennifer S. Hirsch, Miguel Muñoz-Laboy, Robert E. Sember, and Richard G. Parker. 2007b. Introduction: Cross-Cultural Reflections on an Intimate Intersection. In *Love and Globalization: Transformations of Intimacy in the Contemporary World*, ed. M. Padilla et al., ix–xxxi. Nashville: Vanderbilt University Press.

Parreñas, Rhacel Salazar. 2005. *Children of Global Migration: Transnational Families and Gendered Woes.* Palo Alto: Stanford University Press.

Patterson, Cynthia. 1985. "Not Worth the Rearing": The Causes of Infant Exposure in Ancient Greece. *Transactions of the American Philological Association* 115: 103–23.

Paudel, Krishna. 2008. Ghale Language: A Brief Introduction. *Nepalese Linguistics* 23: 168–87.

Pema, Jetsun. 2003. Caring for the Weakest: The Children's Villages. In *Exile as Challenge: The Tibetan Diaspora*, ed. D. Bernstorff and H. von Welck, 279–94. New Delhi: Orient Longman.

Pema Döndrup. 1979 [18th CE]. bDag bya btang ras pa Padma Don-grub kyi chos byas 'tshul dang bka' ba spyad 'tshul rnams. Autobiography of Pema Döndrup. In *Autobiographies of Three Spiritual Masters of Kutang*, 1–143. Thimphu: Kunsang Topgay and Mani Dorji.

Pema Lhundrup. 1979 [18th CE]. rNam 'byor ras pa Padma Lhun grub bsTan 'dzin rGya mtsho'I gsung pa'I rnam mthar kun gsal me long. The Autobiography of Pema Lhundrup. In *Autobiographies of Three Spiritual Masters of Kutang*, 591–757. Thimphu: Kunsang Topgay and Mani Dorji.

Pema Wangdu. 1979 [18th CE]. mKha' mnyams 'gro ba'i rtsug brgyan Padma dBang 'dus kyi rnam par thar pa gsal bar bkod pa la rmongs mun thib po las ba'i sgron me. Autobiography of Pema Wangdu. In *Autobiographies of Three Spiritual Masters of Kutang*, 145–495. Thimphu: Kunsang Topgay and Mani Dorji.

Petech, Luciano. 1980. Ya-ts'e, Gu-ge, Pu-rang: A New Study. *Central Asiatic Journal* 24(1): 85–111.

Petech, Luciano. 1994. The Disintegration of the Tibetan Empire. In *Tibetan Studies*, ed. P. Kvaerne, 649–59. Oslo: Institute for Comparative Research in Human Culture.

Pettigrew, Judith. 2013. *Maoists at the Hearth: Everyday Life in Nepal's Civil War.* Philadelphia: University of Pennsylvania Press.

Pignède, Bernard. 1993 [1966]. *The Gurungs.* Kathmandu: Ratna Pustak Bhandar.

Pokhrel, Badri. 2014. Household and Household Structure in Nepal. In *Population Monograph of Nepal, Volume 3 (Economic Demography)*, 223–42. Kathmandu: Central Bureau of Statistics.

Pradhan, A., et al. 1997. *Nepal Family Health Survey 1996.* Kathmandu and Calverton: Ministry of Health [Nepal], New ERA, and Macro International.

Pradhan, Kumar. 1991. *Gorkha Conquest: The Process and Consequences of the Unification of Nepal, with Particular Reference to Eastern Nepal.* Calcutta: Oxford University Press.

Quintman, Andrew. 2014. *The Yogin and the Madman: Reading the Biographical Corpus of Tibet's Great Saint Milarepa.* New York: Columbia University Press.

Radcliffe-Brown, A. R. 1940. On Joking Relationships. *Journal of the International African Institute* 13(3): 195–210.

Ramble, Charles. 1993. The Name Bhotey. *Himal* 6(5): 17.

Ramble, Charles. 2008. *The Navel of the Demoness: Tibetan Buddhism and Civil Religion in Highland Nepal.* New York: Oxford University Press.

Ramble, Charles. 2009. A Nineteenth-Century Pilgrim in Western Tibet and Nepal: Episodes from the Life of dKar ru Grub dbang bsTan 'dzin Rin chen. In *Tibetan Studies in Honor of Samten Karmay*, ed. F. Pommaret and J. Achard, 481–502. Dharamsala: Amnye Machen Institute.

Ramble, Charles, and Nyima Drandul. 2017. Reason against Tradition: An Attempt at Cultural Reform in a Tibetan-Speaking Community in Panchayat-Era Nepal. In *Social Regulation: Case Studies from Tibetan History*, ed. Jeannine Bischoff and Saul Mullard, 49–63. Leiden: Brill.

Ransel, David. 1988. *Mothers of Misery: Child Abandonment in Russia*. Princeton: Princeton University Press.

Reher, David S. 2011. Economic and Social Implications of the Demographic Transition. *Population and Development Review* 37 (Supplement): 11–33.

Retherford, Robert D., Lee-Jay Cho, and Nam-Il Kim. 1984. Census-Derived Estimates of Fertility by Duration of First Marriage in the Republic of Korea. *Demography* 21(4): 537–58.

Retherford, Robert D., and Shyam Thapa. 1998. Fertility Trends in Nepal, 1977–1995. *Contributions to Nepalese Studies* 25 (Special Issue): 9–58.

Ricard, Matthieu. 1994. *The Life of Shabkar: The Autobiography of a Tibetan Yogin*. Albany: State University of New York Press.

Riddle, John M. 1991. Oral Contraceptives and Early-Term Abortifacients during Classical Antiquity and the Middle Ages. *Past and Present* 132: 3–32.

Riddle, John M. 1994. *Contraception and Abortion from the Ancient World to the Renaissance*. Cambridge: Harvard University Press.

Riddle, John M. 1999. *Eve's Herbs: A History of Contraception and Abortion in the West*. Cambridge: Harvard University Press.

Rigzen, Tsepak. 2003. The Tibetan Schools in the Diaspora. In *Exile as Challenge: The Tibetan Diaspora*, ed. D. Bernstorff and H. von Welck, 266–78. New Delhi: Orient Longman.

Rigzen Tsewang Norbu. 1974 [1745]. Bod rje lha btsan po'i gdung rabs tshigs nyung don gsal yid kyi me long. History of the Descendants of the Tibetan Emperors. In *Rare Tibetan Historical and Literary Texts from the Library of Tsepon W. D. Shakabpa*. New Delhi: T.Tsepal Taikhang.

Rigzen Tsewang Norbu. 1977 [18th CE]. Chab shog khag. Collection of Letters and Small Instructions. In *Collected Works of Katog Rigzin Tsewang Norbu*, Vol.III, 403–748. Dalhousie: Damcho Sangpo.

Rigzen Tsewang Norbu. 1990 [1749]. Bod rje lha btsad po'i gdung rabs mNga' ris smad Gung thang du ji ltar byung ba'i tshul deb ther dwangs shel 'phrug gyi me long. History of the Gungtang Kings. In *Bod kyi lo rgyus deb ther khag lnga*, ed. Jampel Tsetan Puntsok. Lhasa: Tibetan Manuscript Publishing House of Tibet.

Rindfuss, Ronald R., and S. Philip Morgan. 1983. Marriage, Sex, and the First Birth Interval: The Quiet Revolution in Asia. *Population and Development Review* 9(2): 259–78.

Rogers, Clint. 2009. *Where Rivers Meet: A Tibetan Refugee Community's Struggle to Survive in the High Mountains of Nepal*. Kathmandu: Mandala Book Point.

Rose, L. 1971. *Nepal: Strategy for Survival.* Berkeley: University of California Press.

Rowe, John W., and Robert L. Kahn. 1997. Successful Aging. *The Gerontologist* 37(4): 433–40.

Ruegg, D. Seyfort. 1991. Mchod yon, yon mchod and rnchod gnas/yon gnas: On the Historiography and Semantics of a Tibetan Religio-Social and Religio-Political Concept. In *Tibetan History and Language: Studies Dedicated to Uray Geza on His Seventieth Birthday,* ed. E. Steinkellner, 441–53. Vienna: Vienna University.

Sanjek, Roger. 1996. Households. In *Encyclopedia of Social and Cultural Anthropology,* ed. Alan Barnard and Jonathan Spencer, 357–61. London: Routledge.

Santow, Gigi. 1995. Coitus Interruptus and the Control of Natural Fertility. *Population Studies* 49(1): 19–43.

Scelza, Brook A., and Joan B. Silk. 2014. Fosterage as a System of Dispersed Cooperative Breeding: Evidence from the Himba. *Human Nature* 25(4): 448–64.

Schaeffer, Kurtis R. 2004. *Himalayan Hermitess: The Life of a Tibetan Buddhist Nun.* Oxford: Oxford University Press.

Scheper-Hughes, Nancy. 1997. Demography without Numbers. In *Anthropological Demography,* ed. David Kertzer and Tom Fricke, 201–22. Chicago: University of Chicago Press.

Schneider, Hanna. 2002. Tibetan Legal Documents of South-Western Tibet: Structure and Style. In *Tibet, Past and Present,* ed. Henk Blezer, 415–27. Leiden: Brill.

Schneider, Peter, and Jane Schneider. 1995. High Fertility and Poverty in Sicily: Beyond the Culture versus Rationality Debate. In *Situating Fertility: Anthropology and Demographic Inquiry,* ed. S. Greenhalgh, 179–201. Cambridge: Cambridge University Press.

Schrempf, Mona. 2008. Planning the Modern Tibetan Family. In *Figurations of Modernity: Global and Local Representations in Comparative Perspective,* ed. V. Houben and M. Schrempf, 121–52. Frankfurt: Campus Verlag.

Schroeder, Robert, and Robert D. Retherford. 1979. Application of the Own-Children Method of Fertility Estimation to an Anthropological Census of a Nepalese Village. *Demography India* 8(1–2): 247–56.

Schuler, Sidney R. 1987. *The Other Side of Polyandry.* Boulder: Westview.

Schulz, Richard, and Jutta Heckhausen. 1996. A Life Span Model of Successful Aging. *American Psychologist* 51(7): 702–14.

Scrimshaw, Susan C. 1978. Infant Mortality and Behavior in the Regulation of Family Size. *Population and Development Review* 4: 383–403.

Scrimshaw, Susan C. 1983. Infanticide as Deliberate Fertility Regulation. In *Determinants of Fertility in Developing Countries. Volume 2. Fertility Regulation and Institutional Influences,* ed. R. Bulatao and R. Lee, 245–66. New York: Academic Press.

Seddon, David, Jagannath Adhikari, and Ganesh Gurung. 2002. Foreign Labor Migration and the Remittance Economy of Nepal. *Critical Asian Studies* 34(1): 19–40.

Sever, Adrian. 1993. *Nepal under the Ranas*. Sittingbourne: Asia Publishing House.

Shakabpa, T. 1984 [1967]. *Tibet: A Political History*. New York: Potala.

Shakya, Tsering. 1999. *The Dragon in the Lank of Snow: A History of Modern Tibet since 1947*. New York: Columbia University Press.

Sharma, P. R. 1978. Nepal: Hindu-Tribal Interface. *Contributions to Nepalese Studies* 6(1): 1–14.

Shneiderman, Sara. 2015a. *Rituals of Ethnicity: Thangmi Identities between Nepal and India*. Philadelphia: University of Pennsylvania Press.

Shneiderman, Sara. 2015b. Regionalism, Mobility, and "the Village" as a Set of Social Relations: Himalayan Reflections on a South Asian Theme. *Critique of Anthropology* 35(3): 318–37.

Skinner, G. William. 1997. Family Systems and Demographic Processes. In *Anthropological Demography*, ed. David Kertzer and Tom Fricke, 53–95. Chicago: University of Chicago Press.

Smith, E. Gene. 2001. *Among Tibetan Texts: History and Literature of the Himalayan Plateau*. Somerville: Wisdom Publications.

Smith, Sara H., and Mabel Gergan. 2015. The Diaspora Within: Himalayan Youth, Education-Driven Migration, and Future Aspirations in India. *Environment and Planning D: Society and Space* 33(1): 119–35.

Snellgrove, David. 1967. *Four Lamas of Dolpo: Autobiographies of Four Tibetan Lamas (15th-18th Centuries)*. Oxford: Bruno Cassirer.

Snellgrove, David L. 1989 [1958]. *Himalayan Pilgrimage*. Boston: Shambhala.

Solmsdorf, Nikolai. 2013. Sojourning in the "Valley of Happiness": Shedding New Light on the *sbas yul* sKyid mo lung. *Bulletin of Tibetology* 49(1): 113–36.

Sörensen, Per. 1994. *The Mirror Illuminating the Royal Genealogies: Tibetan Buddhist Historiography*. Wiesbaden: Harrassowitz.

Srinivasan, Sharada, and Arjun Singh Bedi. 2008. Daughter Elimination in Tamil Nadu, India: A Tale of Two Ratios. *Journal of Development Studies* 44(7): 961–90.

Stark, Oded, and David E. Bloom. 1985. The New Economics of Labor Migration. *American Economic Review* 75(2): 173–78.

Stark, Oded, and J. Edward Taylor. 1991. Migration Incentives, Migration Types: The Role of Relative Deprivation. *The Economic Journal* 101(408): 1163–78.

Statistics Sierra Leone (SSL) and ICF International. 2014. *Sierra Leone Demographic and Health Survey 2013*. Freetownand Rockville: SSL and ICF International.

Stearns, Cyrus. 2000. *Hermit of Go Cliffs: Timeless Instructions from a Tibetan Mystic*. Boston: Wisdom Publications.

Stein, Rolf A. 1959. *Les Tribus Anciennes des Marches Sino-Tibétans*. Paris: Bibliothèque de l'Institute des Hautes Études Chinoises.

Stein, Rolf A. 1972. *Tibetan Civilization*. Palo Alto: Stanford University Press.

Steinmann, Brigitte. 1991. The Political and Diplomatic Role of a Tibetan Village Chieftain ('go ba) on the Nepalese Frontier. In *Tibetan History and Language: Studies Dedicated to Uray Geza on His Seventieth Birthday*, ed. E. Steinkellner, 43–62. Vienna: Universität Wien.

Stiller, Ludwig F. 1975. *The Rise of the House of Gorkha*.

Stokes, C. Shannon. 1995. Explaining the Demographic Transition: Institutional Factors in Fertility Decline. *Rural Sociology* 60(1): 1–22.

Surkhang, W. 1966. Tax Measurement and Lag 'Don Tax. *Bulletin of Tibetology* 3(1): 15–28.

Surkhang, W. 1986. Government, Monastic and Private Taxation in Tibet. *Tibet Journal* 11(1): 31–39.

Sussman, Robert W. 2014. *The Myth of Race: The Troubling Persistence of an Unscientific Idea*. Cambridge: Harvard University Press.

Tan, Lin, and Susan E. Short. 2004. Living as Double Outsiders: Migrant Women's Experiences of Marriage in a County-Level City. In *On the Move: Women and Rural-to-urban Migration in Contemporary China*, ed. A. M. Gaetano and T. Jacka, 151–74. New York: Columbia University Press.

Tashi Dorje. 2010. *mNga' bdag lo rgyus dung gi phreng ba*. Kathmandu: Tashi Dorje.

Tashi Khedrup. 1998. *Adventures of a Tibetan Fighting Monk*. Bangkok: Orchid Press.

Taylor, E. J. 1999. The New Economics of Labour Migration and the Role of Remittances in the Migration Process. *International Migration* 371: 63–88.

The Gambia Bureau of Statistics (GBOS) and ICF International. 2014. *The Gambia Demographic and Health Survey 2013*. Banjul and Rockville: GBOS and ICF International.

Thieme, Susan, and Simone Wyss. 2005. Migration Patterns and Remittance Transfer in Nepal: A Case Study of Sainik Basti in Western Nepal. *International Migration* 43(5): 59–98.

Thornton, Arland. 2001. The Developmental Paradigm, Reading History Sideways, and Family Change. *Demography* 38(4): 449–65.

Thornton, Arland. 2005. *Reading History Sideways: The Fallacy and Enduring Impact of the Development Paradigm on Family Life*. Chicago: University of Chicago Press.

Tilly, Charles. 1978. The Historical Study of Vital Processes. In *Historical Studies of Changing Fertility*, ed. C. Tilly, 3–56. Princeton: Princeton University Press.

Tobler, Judy. 2006. Tibetan Buddhist Nuns in Exile: Creating a Sacred Space to Be at Home. *Journal for the Study of Religion* 19(1): 41–62.

Tourangeau, Roger, and Tin Yan. 2007. Sensitive Questions in Surveys. *Psychological Bulletin* 133(5): 859–83.

Trennert, Robert A. 1988. *The Phoenix Indian School: Forced Assimilation in Arizona, 1891–1935*. Norman: University of Oklahoma Press.

Tsomo, Karma Lekshe. 2004. Tibetan Nuns: New Roles and Possibilities. In *Exile as Challenge: The Tibetan Diaspora*, ed. Dagmar Bernstorff and Hubertus von Welck, 342–66. Hyderabad: Longman.

Tsultrim, Yeshi, Ngawang Chödar, Lobsang Gyaltsen, and Kelsang Drolkar, eds. 1989 [1830]. *lCags stag zhib gzhung*. Lhasa: China Tibetan Wisdom Publishing House.

Tulku Urgyen Rinpoche. 2005. *Blazing Splendor: The Memoirs of Tulku Urgyen Rinpoche as told to Erik Pema Kunsang and Marcia Binder Schmidt*. Boudhanath: Rangjung Yeshe Publications.

Tylor, Edward Burnett. 1871. *Primitive Culture*. London: John Murray.

van de Walle, Etienne, and Elisha P. Renne, eds. 2001. *Regulating Menstruation: Beliefs, Practices, Interpretations*. Chicago: University of Chicago Press.

van Krieken, Robert. 1999. The "Stolen Generation" and Cultural Genocide: The Forced Removal of Australian Indigenous Children from their Families and its Implications for the Sociology of Childhood. *Childhood* 6(3): 297–311.

van Spengen, Wim. 2000. *Tibetan Border Worlds: A Geohistorical Analysis of Trade and Traders*. London: Kegan Paul International.

Vinding, M. 1978. The Local Oral Tradition about the Kingdom of Thin Garal Dzong. *Kailash* 6(3): 181–93.

Vitali, Roberto. 1996. *The Kingdoms of Gu.ge and Pu.hrang*. Dharamsala: Tho ling gtsug lag khang lo gcig stong 'khor ba'i rjes dran mdzad sgo'i go sgrig tshogs chung.

Weller, Susan C., and A. Kimball Romney. 1988. *Systematic Data Collection*. Newbury Park: Sage.

Whelpton, John. 2005. *A History of Nepal*. Cambridge: Cambridge University Press.

Wilk, Richard R. 1989. Decision Making and Resource Flows within the Household: Beyond the Black Box. In *The Household Economy: Reconsidering the Domestic Mode of Production*, ed. R. Wilk, 24–52. Boulder: Westview Press.

Wilk, Richard R., and Stephen Miller. 1997. Some Methodological Issues in Counting Communities and Households. *Human Organization* 56(1): 64–70.

Williams, Nathalie. 2009. Education, Gender, and Migration in the Context of Social Change. *Social Science Research* 38(4): 883–96.

Williams-Oerberg, Elizabeth. 2016. Educational Migration among Ladakhi Youth. In *Internal Migration in Contemporary India*, ed. Deepak K. Mishra, 154–79. New Delhi: Sage.

Wrigley, Julia, ed. 2005. *Education and Gender Equality*. London: The Falmer Press.

Xu Xiaohe, and Martin King Whyte. 1990. Love Matches and Arranged Marriages: A Chinese Replication. *Journal of Marriage and Family* 52(3): 709–22.

Yabiku, Scott T. 2004. Marriage Timing in Nepal: Organizational Effects and Individual Mechanisms. *Social Forces* 83(2): 559–86.

Yabiku, Scott T. 2005. The Effect of Non-Family Experiences on Age of Marriage in a Setting of Rapid Social Change. *Population Studies* 59(3): 339–54.

Yarmohammadi, Hassan, Behnam Dalfardi, Alireza Mehdizadeh, and Sina Haghighat. 2013. Al-Akhawayni, a Contributor to Medieval Persian Knowledge on Contraception. *The European Journal of Contraception and Reproductive Health Care* 18(6): 435–40.

Zablocki, Abraham. 2009. "The Taiwanese Connection: Politics, Piety, and Patronage in Transnational Tibetan Buddhism." In *Buddhism between Tibet and China*, ed. Matthew T. Kapstein, 379–414. Somerville: Wisdom.

Zablocki, Abraham. 2016. Contemporary Tibetan Buddhism. In *The Oxford Handbook of Contemporary Buddhism*, ed. M. Jerryson, 143–60. Oxford: Oxford University Press.

Index